6L
(EJ)

10317420

790.10684
DRU

590.10PS
060

Quality Issues in Heritage Visitor Attractions

To Ciara and Hugo
and
to Helen, Catherine, Hugh, Eve, Ella and Harry

Quality Issues in Heritage Visitor Attractions

Edited by
Siobhan Drummond and Ian Yeoman

BUTTERWORTH
HEINEMANN

OXFORD   AUCKLAND   BOSTON   JOHANNESBURG   MELBOURNE   NEW DELHI

Butterworth-Heinemann
Linacre House, Jordan Hill, Oxford OX2 8DP
225 Wildwood Avenue, Woburn, MA 01801-2041
A division of Reed Educational and Professional Publishing Ltd

℞ A member of the Reed Elsevier plc group

First published 2001

© Siobhan Drummond and Ian Yeoman 2001

All rights reserved. No part of this publication may be reproduced in
any material form (including photocopying or storing in any medium by
electronic means and whether or not transiently or incidentally to some
other use of this publication) without the written permission of the
copyright holder except in accordance with the provisions of the Copyright,
Designs and Patents Act 1988 or under the terms of a licence issued by the
Copyright Licensing Agency Ltd, 90 Tottenham Court Road, London,
England W1P 0LP. Applications for the copyright holder's written
permission to reproduce any part of this publication should be addressed
to the publishers

British Library Cataloguing in Publication Data
A catalogue record for this book is available from the British Library

ISBN 0 7506 4675 6

Printed and bound in Great Britain by
Biddles Ltd, Guildford and King's Lynn

FOR EVERY TITLE THAT WE PUBLISH, BUTTERWORTH-HEINEMANN
WILL PAY FOR BTCV TO PLANT AND CARE FOR A TREE.

Library and Information Services
University of Wales Institute, Cardiff
Colchester Avenue
Cardiff
CF23 7XR

Contents

Contents

Figures

Tables

Contributors

Editors

Siobhan Drummond is a Senior Lecturer in Tourism at the University of Paisley, Scotland. She has been working in a managerial capacity in a range of tourism posts from national tourist organizations to international hotel companies. Her research interests are centred on the management of service quality in tourism operations, development of small businesses and the impact of cultural variations on tourism service.

Ian Yeoman is a Lecturer in Operations Management at Napier University, Edinburgh. Ian has authored and edited a range of articles and texts on yield management and heritage management.

Contributors

Graham Black is a heritage interpreter specializing in the creation of major museum displays. He has contributed to other texts on Operations Management in the heritage sector. Graham is also subject leader in Heritage Studies at the Nottingham Trent University.

Kathryn A. Burnett is a Lecturer in Applied Social Studies at the University of Paisley, Scotland. Her doctorate research centred on Heritage and Culture. She has published in these and other related areas. Kathryn has recently been involved in an international study investigating the links between propensity to travel and ethnic origins.

Margaret A. Deery is a Lecturer in Human Resource Management in the School of Management at Victoria University, Melbourne. Her doctoral thesis investigated the role of turnover culture and turnover culture in the hotel industry. Margaret has published in the role and management of volunteers in heritage visitor attractions.

Isabelle Frochot is a Lecturer in Tourism at the Universite de Savoie, France. Her doctorate research centred on the use of SERVQUAL dimensions in heritage visitor attractions. Isabelle formerly lectured at the University of Strathclyde, Glasgow.

Szilvia Gyimóthy is a postgraduate researcher at the Research Centre of Bornholm, Denmark. Her main interest is in measuring experiential aspects of quality in tourism-related services.

Julian Hoseason is a Lecturer of Anglia Polytechnic University, based at City College, Norwich, where he leads degree and diploma programmes in Travel and Tourism Management. Julian originally worked in tour operations for the former family business based at Lowestoft and has run his own specialist activity travel company.

Leo K. Jago is Associate Professor in the School of Hospitality, Tourism and Marketing at Victoria University, Melbourne. His doctorate and research interests are in the area of events and heritage attractions. Leo has published in this field and has a special interest in the management and role of volunteers in heritage visitor attractions.

Nick Johns currently holds Senior Research Fellowships at Hong Kong Polytechnic University and at the Research Centre of Bornholm, Denmark. His extensive research interests include operational and marketing aspects of service quality. Nick has written and contributed to many textbooks and journals.

Eric Laws is the author of four books on tourism management, and has co-edited three others. His research is centred on the meaning and management of service quality in tourism, and this interest has led him to study tourism in destinations throughout Europe, Asia, the Pacific and North America. After teaching in British and Australian universities he is now an independent tourism researcher.

Preface

The tourist industry at large is grappling with the issue of quality and recognizes that it is the key to long-term success. This book provides readers with a framework to look at quality issues in the specialist sector of heritage visitor attractions. Each section enables them to discover methods and approaches to build quality into the very fabric of the organizations to help them improve their performance for the customers and the tourism industry at large. This book has been designed to enable the reader to dip in and out of the quality issues that are relevant and of interest to them. Each section presents a different flavour of quality to represent the individual authors' interests and experience. It therefore does not follow any particular sequence and allows a range of starting and finishing points.

The first part presents an overview of quality; edited by Siobhan Drummond and Kathryn Burnett. It provides a valuable insight into the evolution and development of quality and explores what is meant by heritage visitor attractions. The contemporary quality issues are addressed including preservation, conservation and funding. The critical success factors for heritage organizations are identified and discussed in detail – from image to motivation and accessibility to amenities. Methods for quality improvement are suggested and outlined. These range from quality systems to standards like Investors in People, and from techniques like benchmarking to continuous improvement programmes. Part One concludes with a focus on authenticity.

Part Two introduces the reader to the reasons why tourists go to heritage sites and proceeds to examine the way in which the industry has been commercialized. Eric Laws discusses the difficulties in reconciling the management of heritage attractions with customer satisfaction. The interaction between tourism and heritage is illustrated through two major case studies – Canterbury and nearby Leeds Castle in England.

The third part explores the specific issues involved in developing a concept for a heritage attraction. Graham Black reflects the needs of the heritage professional and considers the dominant concerns for conservation and the retention of the integrity of the heritage site. The chief exclusions from these chapters are locations whose primary function is to make a profit. It emphasizes that the development of the concept is first a management issue but requires team effort and long-term strategic planning. It provides the answers to the quality issues such as 'what do you wish to present?' 'Why do you wish to change or develop the heritage visitor attraction?' 'Who are you targeting the presentation at ?' and 'how do you intend to present the concept?'

In Part Four, Isabelle Frochot discusses the nature of services with a focus on heritage and examines the reasons for delivering a quality service. These quality issues are vital in providing management with a blueprint for improving operations in the heritage sector. It provides detailed analysis of the SERVQUAL model for measuring the quality of service offered and adapts this for the heritage industry through the development of HISTO-QUAL. This scale can be used by operational managers as a 'ready-made' tool to evaluate the quality of service they are providing and can be combined with general measures of customer satisfaction. The model can also be used to identify potential areas for quality improvement, monitoring of changes and evaluation of quality dimensions.

Margaret Deery and Leo Jago start Part Five by emphasizing the importance of managing a quality workforce in the heritage sector. It looks at the changing requirements of employees and the need for improved customer service skills and flexibility. It details the human resource practices in heritage visitor attractions from selection through induction, training, development and appraisal.Chapter 12 examines the role of the volunteers in heritage attractions. For too long they have been undervalued and as major players in this sector the authors highlight the quality issues emanating from their relationship with paid employees and customers.

In the final part of the book, Nick Johns and colleagues suggest what the future will be like for those in heritage visitor attractions. It discusses quality in terms of both visitor demand and the way in which the demand is met. It recognizes that customers will demand higher quality but any predictions are at best a gamble. It stimulates thought through its vision of changing markets and the patterns of work. It also identifies tension between authenticity and entertainment in the heritage visitor attraction sector. It concludes by stating that the heritage experience only exists as a whole in visitors' minds.

We must therefore recognize that, like the visitor experience, the individual quality issues for the customer may be locked in their minds too and operational managers and designers can make use of quality methods and techniques to unlock them and continuously improve quality to sustain our global heritage for future generations.

Further, a comprehensive tutor's guide is available to support this reader. For details about registration please email bhmarketing@repp.co.uk or find details from the Butterworth-Heinemann web site http://www.bh.com/hospitality

Siobhan Drummond and Ian Yeoman

Abbreviations

AASLH	American Association for State and Local History
ABS	Australian Bureau of Statistics
AONB	area of outstanding natural beauty
ASVA	Association of Scottish Visitor Attractions
BTR	Bureau of Tourism Research
CCCI	Canterbury City Centre Initiative
DNH	Department of National Heritage
DoE	Department of the Environment
EIU	Economist Intelligence Unit
ETB	English Tourist Board
HR	human resource
HRM	human resource management
HVA	heritage visitor attraction
ICOMOS	International Council of Monuments and Sites
IIP	Investors in People
ISO	International Standards Organization
MGC	Museums and Galleries Commission
NADFAS	National Association of Decorative and Fine Art Societies
NGMW	National Galleries and Museums of Wales
NSA	national scenic area
NNR	natural nature reserve
PAT	profile accumulation technique
RGT	repertory grid technique
SAC	Special Area of Conservation
SNH	Scottish Natural Heritage
SRH	sport/recreation/hobby
SSSI	site of special scientific interest
TQM	total quality management
UNESCO	United Nations Educational, Scientific, and Cultural Organization
WASP	white Anglo-Saxon Protestant
WTO	World Tourism Organization

Part One

Overview of Quality Issues

Siobhan Drummond

Introduction

The four chapters in this part begin by examining the origins and the development of quality and what is meant by the heritage visitor attraction. Chapter 2 reviews the major quality issues that face this sector of the tourism industry in the twenty-first century and identifies the key success factors for organizations involved in heritage. Chapter 3 provides a tool kit for continuously improving quality, and some of the themes addressed at this stage are picked up later in the text by other authors while in other instances they are discussed more fully. Chapter 4 considers the relationship between heritage, history and authenticity.

Quality

Quality is now viewed as a major factor associated with the competitiveness and development of tourism as we move into the twenty-first century. The continued expansion of international tourism beyond 2000 and easy access (real and virtual) to previously remote areas enhance the heritage issues. Awareness of 'heritage' is more acute as the world becomes increasingly concerned with finite resources and the irreplaceable nature of some of the global heritage visitor attractions. This is coupled with the growth of the service sector as manufacturing declines in tourism-generating economies. The subject matter of quality in the tourism industry is growing annually, as there are many issues and interfaces to consider as well as a number of techniques which tourism organizations can use to improve their performance and achieve competitive advantage.

What has prompted so many businesses in all sectors of the economy to consider quality as a management tool? According to Dale, Lascelles and Plunkett the most important factors are:

- the imposition of quality requirements by customers – external and internal, at every link of the customer–supplier chain
- loss of market share to competitors
- the teachings of internationally respected quality experts who have helped turn organizations and economies around – notable experts like W. Edwards Deming and J. M. Juran as well as Crosby, Feigenbaum, Ishikawa, Shingeo and Taguchi
- published case studies that focus on how organizations have set about introducing and developing quality in their philosophy.

We can add to that the drive by governments to promote quality through quality programmes such as national quality awards, in the USA the Malcolm Baldrige Award, and its counterpart in Europe, the European Foundation Quality Award – a Model of Excellence.

In tourism economies throughout the world there are examples of quality awards as well as quality assurance schemes. Some of these have been put in place by the national tourism agencies, such as the Thistle Awards in Scotland and the Quality Assurance scheme for Visitor Attractions operated by the Scottish Tourist Board while others have been developed by the heritage visitor attractions sector – for example, the American Association of Museums' quality appraisal system which offers accreditation of museums including the criteria of interpretation.

Tourism awards have been introduced for a variety of reasons but they are a useful way in which to pull the different sectors of the industry together, to highlight examples of 'best practice' at small and large operator level, to encourage businesses to continuously improve and to attract media coverage for publicity and promotion.

The awards ceremonies themselves attract attention from a variety of media sources and as a result the public awareness of quality is greater than ever. In some countries, including the USA, Canada and Ireland, public funding criteria and peer review processes assure that only heritage projects which meet a minimum set of criteria for quality receive project funding. This varies from sector to sector and country to country.

Consumers, particularly tourism consumers, have become more sophisticated over the years with their range of experiences of a variety of products and services around the world and their current expectations, which are not always readily visible, place new demands on the suppliers. This 'quality revolution' has placed more power in the hands of the customers, who have a greater choice of services and products than ever before. As a consequence, continuous quality improvement has become a matter of survival for all organizations.

Globalization increases the complexity of doing business in the tourism sector, as there is a need to cater for the tastes of foreign visitors and employ people from different cultures. Awareness, understanding and implementation of quality are therefore fundamental for any business. In a booklet, *How to Take Part in the Quality Revolution: A Management Guide*, Smith argues that the chief executive will draw little comfort from the writings of the quality gurus in the task of leading quality improvement in his organization. He says that 'just deciding where to begin is so difficult that many never get off the starting block' (Smith, 1986). There is little doubt that many tourism businesses, small and large, are confused by the sheer volume and variety of advice that is available – even the title of this text, *Quality Issues in Heritage Visitor Attractions*, needs some discussion before looking at some of the key factors that will affect tourism organizations in the twenty-first century. Some fundamental questions need to be answered before we look at quality issues.

How do we define heritage visitor attractions? What are the quality issues that are so important for this sector of the tourist industry? How can we use quality as a means of gaining competitive advantage in a global economy? The four introductory chapters help us answer these questions by providing an overview of the tourist attractions included under the 'heritage' banner, discussing authenticity, exploring the nature of the quality factor and illustrating how a number of heritage visitor attractions have effectively managed quality issues to contribute to their success.

References and further reading

Dale, B. G. and Plunkett, J. J. (1990). *Managing Quality*. Philip Allan.
Smith, S. (1986). *How to Take Part in the Quality Revolution: A Management Guide*. PA Management Consultants.

1

Introduction to quality

Siobhan Drummond

Introduction

The growth in the heritage sector and the development in the quality phenomenon has left everyone involved eager to find out ways in which business performance can be enhanced. This chapter summarizes some of the many definitions of quality and seeks to find out what is meant by the HVA. It looks at the growth in the heritage business and suggests a structure for this sector of the tourism industry. The levels in quality development are illustrated and the growth of service quality is explored together with the relationship with tourism.

Definition and evolution of heritage visitor attractions

A range of texts from a number of countries has provided definitions of the visitor attraction sector of the tourism industry – Yale (1992), Holloway (1998), Pearce (1995), Boniface and Fowler (1993) among them. Heritage visitor attractions may be grouped into those that have naturally evolved and those that have been created by humans. The former, natural heritage includes land and seascapes, vegetation, forests and wildlife. The artificial or human-made heritage attractions comprise the products of history, culture and tradition such as historic houses, ancient and archaeological sites, museums and events. This simple categorization of part of the tourism industry tends to hide the complexity of the industry's composition and it is important to view it in context.

Tourism attractions, including HVAs, form the nucleus of the tourist industry in many destinations. Transport and accommodation may be essential components of tourism but without an 'attraction' there would not be the same demand for these other elements.

The word 'heritage' began to creep into tourism during the 1970s, although it has been around from the early days of the Babylonian and Egyptian empires when religious festivals attracted many to view the famous buildings and works of art in cities as well as attracting the ardent worshipper. 'Heritage' is now a widely used word associated with a range of different tourism products and services – examples include national heritage, heritage coasts, heritage trails, heritage hotels, heritage productions and heritage centres such as those in Edinburgh (Whisky), Wigan (Pier) and York (Jorvik). The National Heritage Act helped to focus attention on the term and it has been used very successfully as a marketing tool by a plethora of visitor attractions. The trend in increased usage has not been restricted to the UK – 1980 was Heritage Year in France, the United Nations Educational, Scientific, and Cultural Organization (UNESCO) has designated an increasing number of World Heritage Sites and during the last decade America opened a Heritage USA theme park in North Carolina.

A simple definition of heritage is 'what is or may be inherited' – this can include traditions, values, historical events, industrial machinery from a bygone era, historic houses, art collections, cultural activities and natural riches such as beaches, mountains, flora and fauna. This definition encompasses a myriad of attractions and activities upon which to build a lucrative tourist industry and it is therefore not surprising that many destinations are discovering or rediscovering their 'heritage'.

According to Boniface and Fowler (1993), however, heritage has no existence because it has no intrinsic meaning. It is there as bits of stone and mud, metal and wood 'but it only becomes "heritage" when we give it a value-laden significance in anthropogenic terms'. In other words, tourists go not just to see artefacts but also to 'feel' what happened at a given time and each individual will come away with a different experience, having probably arrived at the 'attraction' with different expectations in the first place.

Heritage visitor attractions are therefore multipurpose – they can provide a range of enjoyable leisure experiences, a focus for community identity, sources for education and a means of economic generation. Ironbridge Gorge Museum in Shropshire, England, provides an example of these different facets. It was formed as an educational charity to seek and foster understanding of the Industrial Revolution in the context of economic regeneration. It is one of over 500 UNESCO World Heritage Sites.

Growth in the heritage business

The growth in the heritage attraction sector has been phenomenal during the 1980s and 1990s. In the UK alone in terms of volume and value it is roughly estimated that it has increased 5 per cent and 10 per cent respectively on an annual basis. This amounts to a 50 per cent increase in the number of visitors to HVAs since 1980 and today these attractions generate in excess of £3 billion. The ways in which the different organizations involved in this sector gather information and define 'visitor', 'tourist' and 'trip' makes it difficult to determine the accuracy of this information but the growth rate highlights the significance of HVAs to the tourism industry.

Since the early 1960s, public interest in 'heritage' has been resurrected for many reasons including:

- interest in bygone days when the world was a different place to live in
- more disposable income and 'free' time for leisure activity
- increased public awareness as new developments replace old 'heritage' sites
- government and private organizations realizing the benefits and value of heritage
- improved technology providing easy access to information on and location of HVAs.

In terms of rural and urban regeneration the interest in heritage, especially industrial heritage, has helped resurrect and convert many redundant buildings and obsolete machinery. The variety within the industrial sector of HVAs is remarkable – early mining sites (coal, slate, copper), former steam railways, docks and transport, as well ships, aircraft and automotive vehicles. Interest in industrial heritage has now spread to an interest in modern industry – also part of a nation's heritage. Many companies have realized the marketing and commercial value of opening their doors to tourists – to view work in progress, how work was undertaken in the past and even an opportunity to produce a product! Many smaller businesses in the craft sector depend upon tourists visiting their studios to keep them in production.

It is clear that as the tourism industry becomes more crucial to many national and local economies it increasingly feeds off a wide range of heritage attractions to provide a unique selling point – national monuments (e.g. Scottish castles and Indian palaces), indigenous cultures and traditions (e.g. Australia and the Aborigines, South America and the Incas), art treasures (e.g. the British Crown Jewels, the Spanish Armada spoils), ideas and images (e.g. Milan for fashion, the Loire Valley for chateaux and heritage wine).

The role of heritage attractions can change depending on the type of attraction and the consumer markets that the providers wish to develop. Heritage attractions can entertain, educate, help maintain or reintroduce culture and traditions, promote pride in a nation and conserve our environment, among other things. The attractions can do these things collectively or exclusively to a variety of market segments and the opportunities for heritage growth are enormous. Where growth is rapid there may be concerns about authenticity and exploitation of heritage but, where *quality* is a major consideration in the development and operation of the attractions, many of these concerns will be addressed.

The structure of heritage visitor attractions

We can see from the discussion on growth that HVAs can play an increasingly important part in the economy of any tourist destination. However, the structure of this tourism sector highlights some of the difficulties that prevent it from presenting a co-ordinated image under the heritage banner. There are variations in the location, size, nature and role of attractions as well as the funding, ownership and management structures. Heritage visitor attractions can be located in both rural and urban areas as well as underwater and on dry land. They can range from a small, indoor fixed site such as a community-owned and managed museum to a cultural event like the Edinburgh Festival with both public and private funding and varying degrees and forms of management.

The categories of tourist attractions outlined by Pat Yale (1991) in *From Tourist Attractions to Heritage Tourism* can be equally applied to the heritage sector. These include:

- *Indoor and outdoor heritage attractions* – historic buildings (palaces, stately homes), museums, art galleries and theatres. Outdoor attractions include historic gardens, archaeological sites and heritage trails.

- *Differentiation between 'human-made' and 'natural'* helps to further distinguish heritage attractions. The former category would include attractions such as the great pyramids and the Tower of London, whereas many attractions in the latter category rarely remain completely natural – e.g. the Grand Canyon in America and Ayres Rock in Australia – the accommodation, camps, restaurants, parking areas and retail outlets that enable these attractions to be accessible and visitor-friendly are human-made. However, throughout the world areas have been designated as unique to preserve each area's natural heritage.

  Global examples include national parks, sites of special scientific interest (SSSIs), areas of outstanding natural beauty (AONBs) and, in the UK, a charitable trust, the National Trust, purchasing Snowdonia in Wales in an attempt to preserve it.

- *Site and event heritage attractions* cover fixed, permanent attractions under the first of these such as the sculpted presidential faces at Mount Rushmore in the USA or the Prado museum in Madrid and temporary attractions under the latter such as the Mardi Gras Festival in New Orleans and the Oxford and Cambridge Boat Race. The National Tourist Boards in the UK categorize those attractions with an admissions charge and those that are free. Heritage attractions included by the Scottish Tourist Board in these categories are listed in Figure 1.1.
- *Nodal and linear heritage attractions* may also be included as a category – the former attractions forming the focus of a visit, e.g. Gaudi's architecture in Barcelona, whereas the latter may be visited in a series of touring stops, e.g. the Whisky Heritage Trail in Speyside, Scotland.

These categories indicate the difficulty of pulling different HVAs into a defined structure. However, it is clear that as this sector grows in importance the image projected is affected by the quality of service offered by any organization within it. It is therefore in everyone's interest, whether a small, large, private or public heritage attraction, to work together and strive for continuous quality improvement which will strengthen the structure of the sector.

An initial understanding of how quality tools, techniques and management can assist in this process is the first step – the second is the adoption of quality to rise to challenge of the issues facing heritage organizations in the future.

Attractions with free admission	Visitors 1996	Visitors 1997	% change 1996–97
Kelvingrove Art Gallery and Museum Glasgow	1 059 625	1 053 745	−1%
Royal Botanic Gardens, Edinburgh	775 133	899 316	+16%
Royal Museum of Scotland, Edinburgh	593 728	591 512	0%
Scottish United Services Museum, Edinburgh	436 384	455 738	+4%
Museum of Transport, Glasgow	430 064	438 429	+2%
Gallery of Modern Art, Glasgow	560 717	410 332	−27%
National Gallery of Scotland, Edinburgh	542 662	404 841	−25%
New Lanark Village, New Lanark	410 000*	400 000*	−2%
Glasgow Botanical Gardens, Glasgow	450 000*	400 000*	−11%
Antartex Village Visitor Centre, Alexandria	346 000*	365 544	+6%

Attractions with paid admission	Visitors 1996	Visitors 1997	% change 1996–97
Edinburgh Castle, Edinburgh	1 165 132	1 238 140	+6%
Edinburgh Zoo, Edinburgh	537 384	548 426	+2%
Blacksmith Shop Visitor Centre, Gretna Green	500 000*	500 000*	0%
Deep Sea World, North Queensferry	403 319	428 011	+6%
Stirling Castle, Stirling	414 187	422 615	+2%
Burns National Heritage Park, Alloway	344 074*	300 000*	−13%
Palace of Holyroodhouse, Edinburgh	277 136	272 429	−2%
Urquhart Castle, nr Drumnadrochit	242 786	244 786	+1%
Loudon Castle Park, Ayr	171 943	233 253	+36%
Glenturret Distillery, Crieff	228 417	215 263	−6%
Total (all attractions)	42 302 329	43 576 661	+3%

*Estimate

Figure 1.1 Major visitor attractions in Scotland
Source: Scottish Tourist Board (1997).

Quality development

As a concept quality has been with us for millennia but it is only comparatively recently that a quality movement has emerged, with professional bodies devoted to the development of a specialist literature and a technology of the subject. However, the roots lie deeply buried in history. Concern with measurement and with standards can be identified in historical accounts throughout the ages.

The code of law of Hammurabi, King of Babylonia (*c.*1800 BC) has been cited by more than one author as evidence of strict control of quality in a relatively advanced civilization. Certainly the clause quoted by George (1972) puts it clearly: 'The Mason who builds a house which falls down and kills the inmate shall be put to death.' More akin to the tourism industry, in Saxon times officials were empowered to protect purchasers from unscrupulous traders. Standards of weights were introduced first when Mercia was the chief principality of England. Lerner (1970) traced the practice of making fabrics in medieval Europe to identify their origin with a view to ensuring an acceptable standard. Running through these historical examples is the common thread of customer satisfaction, whether the customers were the inhabitants of Babylon or the weavers of medieval clothing.

The three principal theatres for the development of quality during the twentieth century have been Europe, America and Japan. Initially this was in the manufacturing sector and the Japanese progress in quality after the Second World War was spectacular, helped along by gurus, Deming and Juran. Above all, the Japanese success in the postwar global economy was due to the implementation of their national quality policy by a top-down managerial approach. This enabled them in the late 1970s, during the 1980s and in the early 1990s to achieve by peaceful economic means what they had failed to do through war: dominate the world.

The stages in quality development have been:

- inspection
- quality control
- quality assurance
- total quality management.

Inspection involves a simple sorting and grading, and taking corrective action where the standard set for a product or service has not been reached. This simple quality level developed into *quality control* that includes paperwork control, basic quality planning, testing of the product or service and the use of basic statistics to measure performance and standards. *Quality assurance* evolved from these two levels and includes statistical process control for each stage of production or service delivery, the use of quality costs, involvement of services, quality planning and comprehensive quality manuals. These outline details of all tasks and processes from setting standards, listing materials required, methods to be followed, personnel requirements (training and level), measurement, auditing of systems and third party approval. In essence, for many organizations quality assurance is concerned with the adoption of

11

quality standards through the International Standards Organization (ISO) 9000 series, which helps provide confidence that a product or service will satisfy given requirements for quality. The ISO standards were initially adopted by the manufacturing sector, and governments around the globe encouraged its application to the service sector. However, there are many other quality initiatives and systems which are more suited to the service sector and these will be dealt with later in Part One and elsewhere in the text.

The fourth level in the evolution of quality management is *total quality management* (TQM). This involves the application of quality management principles to all aspects of the business. Quality management is defined in the ISO series as 'that aspect of the overall management function that determines and implements the quality policy, and as such, is the responsibility of top management'. The management philosophy of TQM can operate independently of the accreditation system but should follow the principles of Deming (1982), Juran (1988), Crosby (1979) and other quality gurus.

Quality has been defined in a variety of ways:

1 'Quality should be aimed at the needs of the consumer, present and future' (Deming, 1982).
2 'Quality is conformance to requirements' (Crosby, 1979).
3 'Quality is in its essence a way of managing the organization' (Feigenbaum, 1983).

These definitions of quality integrate the needs of the customer with the way in which an organization and its systems are managed. The focus is on satisfying the customer and re-engineering the organization to achieve that objective, not the maintenance of management systems that have evolved over time to suit the organization. Total quality management is looked at more fully later in the next chapter.

The growth in service quality

Quality in service has been the subject of research since the early 1980s. Academics such as Gronroos, Berry and Bateson have undertaken extensive investigations into the issues surrounding service quality. This research highlights the differences between the service and manufacturing industries such as the intangibility of service, the inseparability of the production and consumption of service, and the heterogeneity and perishability of service. This research has been very appropriate for the tourism industry and many organizations in the heritage sector have made good use of the models developed. Examples and adaptations of models such as SERVQUAL will be illustrated in later parts of the text and they provide strong evidence of how this embracing of quality can improve business performance.

Quality and tourism

We are what we repeatedly do. Excellence, then, is not an act, but a habit. (Aristotle)

Tourism is increasingly referred to as the world's biggest industry. As tourism increases in value to each country, so the demands of the consumer for quality in all its related products and services increase. The previous discussion on quality development highlights the importance of the customer and the need to ensure products and services conform to their requirements. However, different customers will expect, want and/or need different things from essentially similar offerings. Heritage visitor attractions, like other tourist products, can be packaged for many different markets, from the mass market to the tailored group and individual. Where similar price and delivery mechanisms are adopted by tourism providers in this global arena it is the focus on quality that can often provide the competitive edge ensuring that growth continues and can be sustained. It is in everyone's best interest, from the large national heritage attraction to the small independent operator, to deliver the customers' required standard of service.

In simple terms it demands:

- talking to the customer (consumer and market research)
- finding out what they want (product and service development)
- setting standards to suit the customer (quality planning)
- operating procedures to achieve the standards (reorganization of the processes)
- providing the expected product and service (quality of resources – human and material)
- control, evaluation and review (quality improvement and development).

The strategic importance of this cyclical approach cannot be overestimated. By investing in people for quality, establishing excellence in service delivery and providing a framework for continuous improvement for growth and delivery, providers of HVAs – public, private, small and large – are able to unite under the same banner and compete on a worldwide stage.

Many tourism organizations in the heritage business sector like to think they have 'Been there – done that' with 'quality'.

The journey to achieve quality is on a never-ending road. It starts in the design and delivery of services and products. Quality should be streamlined, simplified and cost-effective. Many of the quality management techniques pioneered and developed in Japan and the USA can work in a global environment if the ideas and methods are modified to suit local cultures.

Conclusion

The 'quality revolution' has placed more power in the hands of the consumer so continuous quality improvement has become a matter of survival for all organizations in the heritage sector. The growth in service quality has taken many businesses by surprise but knowledge of how to implement it can ensure more than survival – it can provide sustainability and competitive advantage as well.

The structure of the heritage industry is complex and the quality needs are different in each case. However, there are common threads throughout the sector, which enable standards to be set and service quality to be delivered.

Questions

1 Outline the main reasons for the growth in the number of HVAs in general and discuss this growth for an attraction with which you are familiar.
2 What are the main stages in the development of quality and how relevant are these to the heritage visitor?
3 How do you define quality in relation to HVAs?

References and further reading

Bateson, J. (1991). *Managing Services Marketing*. 2nd edition. Dryden Press.
Berry, L. L., Bennett, D. R. and Brown, C. W. (1989). *Service Quality: A Profit Strategy for Financial Institutions*. Dow-Jones-Irwin, and Homewood.
Boniface, P. and Fowler, P. (1993). *Heritage and Tourism*. Routledge.
Crosby, P. B. (1979). *Quality is Free*. McGraw-Hill.
Deming, W. E. (1982). *Quality, Productivity and Competitive Position*. MIT Press.

Deming, W. E. (1986). *Out of the Crisis*. Cambridge University Press.

Feigenbaum, A. V. (1983). *Total Quality Control*. McGraw-Hill.

George, C. S. (1972). *The History of Management Thought*. Prentice Hall.

Holloway, J. C. (1998). *The Business of Tourism*. Longman.

Juran, J. M. (ed.) (1988). *Quality Control Handbook*. McGraw-Hill.

Lerner, F. S. P. (1970). Quality control in pre-industrial times, *Quality Progress*, **3**(6), 22–25.

Pearce, D. (1995). *Tourism Today: A Geographical Analysis*. Longman.

Scottish Tourist Board (1997). *Tourism in Scotland*. Scottish Tourist Board.

Yale, P. (1991). *From Tourist Attractions to Heritage Tourism*. ELM Publications.

Yale, P. (1992). *Tourism in the UK*. ELM Publications.

Zeithaml, V., Parasuraman, A. and Berry, L. (1985). Problems and strategies in services marketing. *Journal of Marketing*, **49**, 33–46.

2

Critical success factors for the organization

Siobhan Drummond

Introduction

This chapter provides an overview of current quality issues in the heritage sector of the tourism industry including authenticity and funding issues among others. A number of case studies are used to illustrate the significance of these issues. The chapter is then developed by an identification of the critical success factors that include every aspect of the visitor experience or 'journey' and concludes by identifying business functions that can be used to ensure success.

Contemporary quality issues

Contemporary quality issues in heritage tourism revolve around satisfying a diverse range of consumers in an ever-changing environment. In the tourism industry we are providing quality of service as well as product and the intangibility and variability of that service makes it difficult to control and understand. Coupled with that there are different levels in the relationship between quality and the operation of HVAs – the strategy and the detail – and much depends on resources and motivation of management when using quality as a means of delivering consistent good service.

Courting the customer as a strategic route for tourism organizations seeking a competitive edge does not require the development of a new science. In practical terms for heritage attractions it means undertaking a business self-assessment, managing variation in a changing environment, setting standards, investing and trusting in people and attempting to ensure that all organizations involved in this growing sector work together. The strength of a united approach through quality provides the key to sustainable competitive advantage as well as profitability, improved performance and value for money. However, with the goal posts constantly shifting and consumer expectations constantly rising quality is an ongoing challenge.

The major quality issues in heritage tourism today include:

- authenticity
- conservation and preservation
- funding issues in the HVA
- understanding the critical success factors of the HVA and the sector
- use of quality tools and techniques to gain advantage and, in some cases, to survive.

This last issue includes a focus on the customer, business self-assessment, benchmarking, setting standards, investing in people – motivation, trust, education and training – managing change and using quality models such as SERVQUAL to bridge the gap between customer expectations and the services offered by the HVA. These issues are dealt with throughout the text but a general introduction will help to set the scene. Some of the ways in which an understanding and utilization of quality improvement tools and techniques can benefit the HVA are outlined later in this chapter.

A key starting point for any HVA is long-term planning and the recognition of the importance of heritage to the tourist industry. This is imperative if the increasingly sophisticated demands of the expanding, discerning tourist market are to be met. In the USA 15 per cent of bookings with travel agents are for special interest travel, including the heritage sector, where quality, not price is the prime factor.

Authenticity

Authenticity is one of the main issues in HVAs today. Do we need the gloss of superficial entertainment? Narrowly defined, heritage is about cultural traditions, places and values. Broadly defined, heritage is about a special sense of belonging and of continuity – this is different for every visitor. On the one hand there is the argument of portraying authenticity to the visitor and, on the other, there are tourism marketeers who are trying to make a successful business venture of heritage. In reality there is usually a difference of views but it is important to maintain a balance. In order to present authentic heritage, and to conserve and preserve it, a substantial amount of investment is required. In order to secure this investment it is sometimes necessary to compromise on some factors if any of the heritage is to be saved. Introducing heritage 'attractions' into the mind of the tourist is often the first step in the process of attracting tourists to a particular location. Controversy surrounds what heritage, historic building, etc. mean. An example is the old market square of Leuven in Belgium, which is viewed as an interesting historic place in the city. It was completely rebuilt after being seriously damaged during the First World War. Urry (1990) and Ashworth (1993) raise the question of these heritage resources. Is the actual age of the building really crucial to the appreciation of the average visitor?

Interpretation and presentation are central to the discussion on authenticity and heritage interpretation provides the key to successful management. Interpretation is the starting point and presentation the culmination. These issues will be discussed more fully in a subsequent part of the book.

Issues such as authenticity and politics also arise in the quality debate. The politics of heritage tourism development and the process are seldom straightforward. The restoration of a historical site or the building of a heritage monument to display cultural richness and heritage are admirable, but there are always a number of groups or interested parties who wish to determine how the story is told or how the information and experience is detailed. Many mainstream museums are now including the work of different groups in their exhibits, but not everyone is happy with the interpretations minorities have placed on heritage sites within their control. For example the National Museum of the American Indian was criticized for giving too much attention to settlers' brutality and too little to American Indian violence. Horne (1984) states that restoration also raises issues of authenticity. Tastes change. He asks whether we would admire the Parthenon if it still had a roof, and no longer appealed to the modern stereotype taste – if we repainted it in its original red, blue and gold and if we reinstalled the huge, gaudy cult figure of Athena, festooned in bracelets, rings and necklaces. We could not avoid the question that threatens our whole concept of the classical: did the Greeks have bad taste?

In essence it is clear that as far as authenticity is concerned the developers and managers of heritage visitor attractions need to apply sensitivity to heritage resources, the community and the visitor. Authenticity and its interaction with heritage and history are discussed in the next chapter.

Conservation and preservation

Conservation is a critical issue. As the age of mass tourism is at saturation point tourism agencies throughout the world become more conscious of the damage that has ensued as a result of tourist activities. There are numerous examples from around the globe. The Balearic Islands of Spain have witnessed a change in the way of life as well as the landscape over the last two decades. Ancient burial sites in Hawaii have been destroyed to make way for more development of tourist facilities. The Great Barrier Reef off Australia has had irreparable damage to the coral because of sightseers and trophy collectors.

Today, more than ever before, countries and organizations responsible for our global heritage require sensitivity to these resources – sensitivity to the community and to the visitor. Assessing heritage attractions in an analytical and critical way opens the way to sustainability and the enablement of different types of heritage to benefit. This cluster approach has been effectively put into practice in Villdieu-les Poeles, Normandy, France. This theme village has developed from its medieval heritage as a manufacturing area of brass, copper and bells. Its success as a heritage centre has been assisted by the optimization of a number of heritage resources, partnership and synergy. As a result many heritage crafts have been preserved and traditional ways of working have been conserved. Other organizations have different approaches.

Case study

One response to the 1992 Earth Summit in Rio de Janeiro was the setting up of Scottish Natural Heritage (SNH) with the aim of conserving and enhancing the richness and diversity of Scotland's natural heritage. It has the support of national tourism agencies in pursuit of this aim, as the tourist organizations that they represent will also benefit. Special areas of conservation (SACs), SSSIs that, incidentally, protect 11 per cent of Scotland, national scenic areas (NSAs – covering 13 per cent of the country), and natural nature reserves (NNRs) were instated. The development of natural heritage zones was encouraged and as a result the corncrake, sea eagle and red kite are now being re-established. As well as conserving the natural heritage there are other benefits – 8000 jobs are directly linked to natural heritage; open-air recreation generates £730 million for the Scottish economy supporting 29 000 full-time equivalent jobs.

Scottish Natural Heritage's role is critical to pump-priming new initiatives, in mounting demonstration projects, grant-aiding key projects and providing quality advice to ensure the economically valuable resources of Scotland's natural heritage are managed wisely. Tasks that they have undertaken include securing the management of the Cairngorms, Loch Lomond and the Trossachs, improving environmental education, improving land management and access, and encouraging sustainable use of maritime areas as well as developing policy which ultimately enhances the quality of heritage for the visitor.

This case study illustrates that quality issues find themselves in a balancing situation.

It is not enough to just preserve heritage, it needs to be made accessible to be interpreted and woven into the wider tourism field and it needs to be marketed – without demeaning it or damaging it and that require long-term quality planning. To put it in context, however, global conservation will become more critical as each year the global population swells by 78 million – that is an increase of about 214 000 people a day. Since 1960 the world's population has doubled and, unless the world's rich nations help the poor ones deal with their burgeoning populations, a series of crises and disasters looks inevitable by the middle of the twenty-first century. Population increases will exacerbate problems such as water shortages, growing deserts, toxic waste, the growth of urban slums and over-fishing, to name but a few.

Conservation of HVAs is put into perspective when the 1999 report from the United Nations Population Fund warns us that, if we do not share wealth, the human race may not survive beyond the next few centuries!

Funding issues in heritage visitor attractions

Funding has a major impact on the development of HVAs and, ultimately, quality is affected by this issue. Economic factors play a major role in steering the major heritage institutions across the world, as there is a need for more self-sufficiency as corporate and government support shrinks. In addition, governments are looking critically at their financial commitment and questioning whether they should continue with the traditionally high level of support. However, if HVAs can demonstrate a relationship between level of support and customer satisfaction then the argument for continued support would be greatly strengthened. It is therefore in everyone's best interests to look at quality programmes, initiatives and management to assist in the process. Costs of resources across the sector have also risen and, if visitors to heritage visitor attractions are increasingly asked to pay higher admission rates to meet these costs, then it is not surprising that their expectations invariably rise.

There are still many heritage institutions that believe their role is mainly to act as preservationist and keepers of educational temples. This stance has resulted in dropping visitor numbers and, in some cases, closure. Increasingly a new approach to funding is required.

Case study

The Museum of Modern Art in New York has redefined its role as an HVA. The museum wants people to visit it more often and stay longer. In order to achieve that objective it now provides an alternative meeting place and it has become an entertainment venue; it has seized the opportunity to become an active participant in community learning and support. This changing audience has led the museum to operate in a different economic environment and, by focusing greater attention on the visitor needs, the management has created a more welcoming environment. There was a need to expand services and programmes to satisfy the new markets. Mail order, dining, social functions and concerts have been added to the portfolio of services and this has required staff to be more skilled and have better understanding of the visitor.

Source: Scottish New Horizons: Enterprise (1999).

Organizational policies and quality systems need to be in place to offer the required visitor service. There are many good global practices that could develop the funding structure of heritage attractions and at the same time improve the quality image of the sector.

The American heritage sector is well practised in beneficiary and endowment development. In addition to admission fees, membership fees and integrating volunteers into the development of many US museums, this additional financial resource enables them to have more freedom in the future direction of the organization. Partnerships can be forged to reduce the cost of some of the managerial functions such as marketing, administration and training, as illustrated by the heritage attractions in Villdieu-les-Poeles, the French medieval village.

Sponsorship can be successful in increasing funds and at the same time widening access and building networks in the wider community – with schools, other groups and the corporate market. Many events at the world-renowned Edinburgh Festival would not take place without sponsorship. Maximizing the visitor spend is another way of improving the funding structure and ways in which this has been successfully undertaken have been through extending the season by putting on heritage events for specific groups, differentiating the pricing structure for pensioners, and generating revenue through quality retail and catering services.

Public sector funding will vary from country to country but the political importance of a nation's heritage has become increasingly valuable and acute as the world becomes a global village and barriers and boundaries disappear. The issue of funding will inevitably become more important, and good use can be made of the quality tools and techniques discussed in the next chapter to improve funding support.

Critical success factors of heritage visitor attractions

The critical success factors to consider for HVAs include every aspect of the whole 'journey' for the customer and the organization, from the initial enquiry for information to the after-service follow-up where appropriate.

At the outset it should be remembered that HVAs do not operate in isolate and there is a strong link with other elements in the 'journey' – transport, accommodation and ancillary services. Organizations also have different visions and objectives – some HVAs operate in a non-profit-making environment, others are in business for profit. There are differences in size and ownership to consider as well – some are publicly owned and of secondary importance to the main business, others are private enterprises and the main business focus. Despite these variations, HVAs can begin to identify the critical success factors by asking the following questions:

- What do we mean and understand by 'quality' in our organization?
- Who has responsibility for setting the standards?
- How do we overcome our quality problems and deliver quality service?

The definition of quality lies with the organization but should be determined by knowledge and understanding of the customer (internal and external), the community and environment (local and national) and the competition (local, national and global).

The customer, constraints on the organization, external parties such as national tourism organizations and other agencies such as the Museums and Galleries Commission (UK) set standards internally and externally.

The delivery of quality service requires the organizations to overcome their quality problems. Tools and techniques, which can be used in this process, are outlined after this discussion. Many international tourism agencies and national and local tourist organizations have undertaken studies in the measurement of customer satisfaction and attitudes to destinations and attractions – these can be useful starting points for HVAs.

The identification of each element in the 'journey' differs for each attraction. Although the HVA is unable to control each stage in the process, it can influence the service quality to varying degrees. An understanding of the customer's reaction to the service offering is vital to see if it is meeting the needs of the target market.

Key critical success factors

Image

A visitor's impression is formed within the first six seconds of entering a visitor attraction but the organization needs to send out a positive image to its market before the 'journey' begins. In operational terms this requires the right design (from websites to physical layout) and effective planning and control of the day-to-day activities.

The physical appearance and layout of the building, spaces and interior rooms has the power to create a positive experience. It can also increase efficiency and facilitate flow of visitors. Attention to the entrance and directional and informational signage can help with the image as can the professionalism of staff encountered, the cleanliness of the attraction, the check-in facilities and the system for admission.

Motivation

Customers must have a reason to go to the HVA. Knowledge of their expectations, needs and desires can help here and the simplicity of Maslow's (1954) hierarchy of needs and Herzberg's (1959) work on motivation can assist in the process. Internal customers (employees) also need to be motivated. Staff should be knowledgeable and trained to be courteous and to engage with the visitor.

Visitors should experience the same quality treatment whether shopping in the retail outlet, buying admission, having coffee or asking for information. Few organizations in the HVA sector would question the level of expertise at the core of their exhibitions and collections, as they are seen to be conceived and researched by professionals, but the same rule should apply to the support staff – in administration, marketing, finance and especially those in direct contact with the public. This issue is dealt with more fully later in this book.

Accessibility

There is a direct link between customer satisfaction and accessibility. Access should meet the needs of the customers. Too many organizations, particularly in the public sector, suit their traditional internal system. For example, UK museums generally close their doors at 5.00 p.m. and visitor numbers are falling, but research indicates that there is a community market – youth, family and specialist groups – who would like access and would make use of the facilities in the evening and during non-peak times.

In the same sector most museum employees with public interaction tend to be employed in a security capacity. These staff could be developed into an enabling and advisory role thus improving access to the exhibits and activities and, at the same time, improving customer service and staff motivation.

Social inclusion is something that concerns every organization today and networks should be built with all types of community groups to ensure that all market needs are addressed. 'Talk and listen' is a good approach for improving access.

24

Many organizations are increasingly concerned with customers obtaining access to the HVA via other media. Development through the Internet and websites has improved access for many HVAs – you can now walk through Monet's garden at Giverny, enjoy a tour of the Sherlock Holmes museum or visit Jane Austen's house without leaving your own home. On a different level, but still very important, physical signposting of directions and information is another access issue that can be addressed at the design stage and through operational management.

Mix of amenities

Elements of the 'mix' may not always come under the management of the HVA itself but should be considered as part of the 'journey'. They would include on-site services such as the attraction itself and products/services vital to the quality offered to the customer – parking, signposting, literature, seating, lighting, disabled access, toilet facilities, litter bins, retail outlets, catering facilities and educational and entertainment activities. Off-site amenities would include signposting from all routes, accommodation and transport services.

Ideas for this mix should come from the broadest possible sources and then these ideas can be turned into experiences.

Mechanisms to purchase

Products and services should be easily accessed and promoted whether they are purchased or 'free'. They need to be appropriate to the HVA's image and market segments as well as easily delivered and transported. This requires staff to be skilled and have more understanding of the customer. It requires services and programmes to be expanded to reflect changing needs and demands. Opportunities need to be exploited as every purchase can provide additional funding for the operation. The purchasing function can be tied in with other elements in the mix of amenities outlined above to develop an entire 'package' for the customer.

Quality visitor service

A service culture exists in every HVA – even if it is not developed. The staff should enjoy helping the visitor as much as the visitor enjoys the heritage attraction.

25

The task of shaping the staff takes place at recruitment once the organization has identified the qualities needed and the attributes necessary to fulfil standards. Induction and training will give staff knowledge of all operations and provide performance standards.

Communication, interpersonal and customer service skills can all be developed through role-playing and taking ownership. Evaluation of their own performance is crucial in this process as are periodical reviews of staff knowledge, pride in their job and the courtesy they extend around them.

Customer service is not just about the human component of staff but the process and setting to support staff. By focusing greater attention on visitor needs, an organization naturally creates a more welcoming environment.

Quality customer service looks at how the physical setting and policies work together to support staff. The system should not act as a barrier and diminish motivation. If the environment is visitor oriented then the organization is effectively nurturing a motivated and courteous staff.

Quality of service can be improved through the use of a quality 'toolkit' and these tools are outlined and discussed in the next chapter.

Other techniques used to identify the quality of service offered by HVAs are addressed throughout this book, from measuring the gaps in the service provided by organizations to benchmarking organizations in the same or different sectors.

However, it must be highlighted that the above critical success factors need to be addressed alongside the following business functions:

- product development and innovation
- marketing and promotional activities
- revenue generation and funding
- education and training
- community and public sector intervention.

Although some of these functions are referred to by authors throughout the text they are worthy of further consideration in any quality debate.

Conclusion

This chapter identified the key quality issues facing HVAs today as authenticity, conservation and preservation, funding, understanding of the critical success factors and the use of quality tools and techniques for survival. Image, motivation, accessibility, mix of amenities, mechanisms to purchase and quality visitor service were seen as the key success factors. The chapter also recognized that other business functions needed to be enhanced to provide a competitive edge and quality service. These business functions include product development and innovation, marketing and promotional activities, revenue generation and funding, education and training and community and public sector intervention.

Questions

1 Suggest ways in which an HVA could improve its funding structure.
2 The chapter identified key quality issues for the heritage sector in general. Choose an HVA and identify what you consider to be the main quality issues.
3 Critical success factors were outlined – use them to measure the success of an HVA of your choice and see if can you identify some others.

References and further reading

Ashworth, G. (1993). Culture and tourism: Conflict or symbiosis in Europe? In *Tourism in Europe: Structures and Developments* (W. Pompl and P. Lowery, eds), CAB International.

Boniface, P. and Fowler, P. J. (1993). *Heritage and Tourism*. Routledge.

Fowler, N. (1987). *Making the Most of Heritage*. HMSO.

Garvin, D. A. (1988). *Managing Quality, the Strategic and Competitive Edge*. Free Press.

Herzberg, F. W., Mausner, B. and Snyderman, B. B. (1959). *The Motivation to Work* (2nd edn). Chapman and Hall.

Horne, D. (1984). *The Great Museum: The Representation of History*. Pluto.

Maslow, A. H (1954). *Motivations and Personality*. Harper and Row.

Murphy, P. (ed.) (1997). *Quality Management in Urban Tourism*. Wiley.

Ryan, C. (1995). *Researching Tourist Satisfaction*. Routledge.

Scottish Enterprise (1998). *New Horizons: International Benchmarking and Best Practice for Visitor Attractions*. Scottish Enterprise.

Scottish Natural Heritage (1999). *Annual Report*. Scottish Natural Heritage.

Scottish Tourist Board (1994). *Visitor Attractions: Keys to Success: A Development Guide*. Scottish Tourist Board.

Urry, J. (1990). *The Tourist Gaze*. Sage.

Yale, P. (1991). *From Tourist Attractions to Heritage Tourism*. ELM Publications

Zeithaml, V. A., Parasuraman, A. and Berry, L. A. (1990). *Delivering Quality Service*. Free Press/Macmillan.

3

Methods of quality improvement

Siobhan Drummond

Introduction

Here we look at ways we can develop the critical success factors mentioned in the previous chapter. The use of this tool kit is one of the cornerstones of continuous quality improvement and, ultimately, business success.

There are a number of quality tools and techniques that can be used by HVAs that can assist organizations bring about success and excellence. We begin by looking at the benefits of quality improvement programmes and quality systems. Motivation, trust and development initiatives such as Investors in People, business self-assessment models and the European Model for Total Quality Management based on the American Baldrige Award and the Japanese Deming Prize are then reviewed. The chapter continues to look at ways of managing change through Total Quality Management (TQM) and considers benchmarking as an additional tool in the process.

Quality improvement programmes

Quality improvement programmes can bring about numerous business benefits and results. The major result is customer satisfaction that can further result in achieving a specific victory for the organization. Victory for different organizations might be defined by a variety of terms, such as survival, more capital, attracting investment, larger market share, more jobs, improved staff morale and market image, improvement in the quality of life and higher profits. Some of the other benefits include the 7 Cs outlined below:

- cost savings with reduced waste and less rework
- communication improvement – internal and external
- comprehension through education and development – personal and professional
- competence in delivering standards through appropriate training
- culture change with improved attitudes for all levels in the organization
- customer focus – internal and external
- commitment and continuous improvement leading to greater efficiency.

Quality systems

Meeting customer requirements at minimum cost is what most tourism businesses strive to achieve and the above benefits can be achieved through the introduction of a simplified quality system. Such a system is invaluable for setting service standards and improving the delivery process. In an ideal world every service standard would be harmonized at international level and perhaps it should be part of everyone's strategy. Systems do not need to be complex – all we need to do is ask ourselves what the customer wants, look at how we provide the products and services and then evaluate each task and stage in the delivery process. This quality issue is considered in greater depth when the SERVQUAL model is discussed later in the text.

Motivation and trust

Investing in people underpins quality in everything a business does. Today all tourism businesses are driven by all kinds of pressure – profits have to be maintained and increased, new business to be won and competitors have to be challenged. One way to meet these growing pressures has been proved time and time again – the right people doing the right job. Government papers have pointed clearly to the need for a highly motivated and well-qualified workforce. In the UK the national standard for effective investment in people is called Investors in People (IIP) and it provides businesses with a valuable tool for continuous quality improvement through people. It promotes good human resources practice with the aim of significantly improving organization performance – improvement in sales, productivity, efficiency, quality, customer care and profitability. The standard focuses on four key principles:

1 *Commitment* – an IIP standard makes a public commitment from the top to develop all employees to achieve its business objectives.
2 *Review* – an IIP standard regularly reviews the training and development needs of all employees.
3 *Action* – an IIP standard takes action to train and develop individuals on recruitment and throughout their employment.
4 *Evaluation* – an IIP standard evaluates the investment in training and development to assess achievement and improve future effectiveness.

These principles have been broken down into 24 indicators that are the basis for assessment. Case studies in Scotland indicate that heritage visitor attractions that have achieved the standard have improved efficiency and performance as the Clan Donald case study illustrates.

- 80% of the overall Scottish IIP in the tourism sector sample experienced improved business performance
- 71% experienced improved employee attitude
- 41% experienced lower labour turnover
- 25% experienced no increase in training costs.

Improving motivation and trust in the workplace are two of the most significant underlying benefits from this investment. Honesty, respect and openness can result from setting time aside to get to know each other, develop a two-way process and provide feedback on a regular basis. These factors were key to achieving a highly motivated and trusting workforce in Japan throughout the 1970s and 1980s when the country's commitment to quality enabled it to achieve world-class status in the service sector of its economy as well as in the manufacturing side.

Case study

Clan Donald Lands Trust is a non-profit-making charitable trust, formed in 1971 to purchase the last remaining acreage of the once vast Clan Donald lands on the island of Skye. The Clan Donald Visitor Centre is the main income source and it attracts more than 40 000 visitors to the area annually. It is a major employer on the island with over 35 full- and part-time staff. With a wide variety of job classifications the training programme at the Clan Donald Centre needed a formal structure. The IIP standard provided this and in addition it identified methods of improving communication lines between management and staff. This in turn helped create a better team spirit, as staff were required to be more involved in developing and achieving business marketing and training goals.

The benefits of IIP have been recognized at the Clan Donald Visitor Centre as:

- helping to identify and target training to meet specific business and staff needs
- the income forecasts were surpassed once the IIP standard was in place while expense figures were on target
- the IIP standard helped to open up wider lines of communications and staff group discussions were scheduled and structured.

The Director for the centre recognized that after two years of involvement with IIP that members of staff were much more professional and aware of the business objectives and, more importantly, of providing quality service and facilities for the visitors. He noticed that staff had a new pride in their work and were willing to suggest ways of improving the product.

Source: Investors in People, Tourism Business Benefits, Scottish Enterprise (1997).

Heritage business self-assessment

Every heritage tourism business must measure up to the best to succeed against hungry competitors in increasingly open world markets. The use of self-assessment is a valuable tool to help all types and sizes of organizations to assess current performance and identify opportunities for improvement. The process allows the business, whether a method of transport like the Orient Express or a privately owned historic inn, to discern clearly its strengths, areas in which improvements can be made and culminates in planned improvement actions which are then monitored for progress. It provides a basis for benchmarking – a process of comparison which can be taken both internally and externally – and shows the progress which has been made. The European Model for Total Quality Management is the model against which most European organizations apply self-assessment – the Baldrige Award is the main model in the USA and the Far East. The nine elements outlined in Figure 3.1 have been identified as the key components of organizational excellence. This model is currently being reviewed.

Managing change and service quality with total quality management

Variation permeates the HVA sector and it is the lifeblood of the industry. However, the business processes within this mixture must be managed in order to ensure that this valuable sector offers consistently good quality across the spectrum. As quality is defined by the visitors then heritage attractions need to know what the visitors want and then produce it within the agreed time frame at minimum cost. This is not a difficult concept to understand but it does require attention from everyone. It embraces how you meet all your visitor requirements including how they are greeted on the telephone, delivery of the HVA's brochure and developing new products and services when required.

However there are a number of visitor implications to consider. What constitutes a quality offering depends on the customer, in other words, what they expect and/or want/need and what the competition can offer affects their view of quality.

Different customers will expect, want and/or need different things from essentially similar offerings, so perhaps there can be no universal standard – over time customer expectations will change, therefore, quality is a dynamic concept. There is no doubt that the rapidly changing environment has greatly increased the need for strategy and top managers at the level of presidents and chief executive officers have linked quality with profitability, defined it from the customer's point of view and required its inclusion in the strategic planning process. The change in the role of quality is divided into four major eras as illustrated in Table 3.1. The stages move from quality inspection to strategic quality management.

The new strategic era that we are in is complex and intensely competitive. Market research on quality, pressure for continuous improvement and high levels of communication and participation are now required. These responsibilities broaden the job of general managers and operators in HVAs. Total quality management is today used to refer to the management approaches being developed in the current era of strategic quality management. Oakland

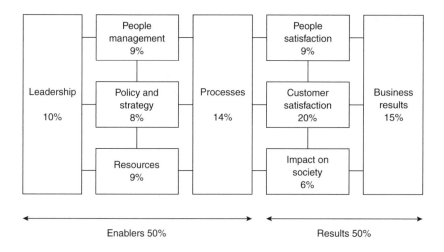

Enablers 50%   Results 50%

ENABLERS	
1. **Leadership**	Behaviour of all managers in driving the company towards total quality.
2. **Policy and strategy**	The company's mission, values, vision and strategic direction – and the manner in which it achieves them.
3. **People management**	The management of the company's people.
4. **Resources**	The management, utilization and preservation of resources.
5. **Processes**	The management of all the value-adding activities within the company.
RESULTS	
6. **Customer satisfaction**	What the company is achieving in relation to the satisfaction of its external customers.
7. **People satisfaction**	What the company is achieving in relation to the satisfaction of its people.
8. **Impact on society**	What the company is achieving in satisfying the needs and the expectations of the community at large.
9. **Business results**	What the company is achieving in relation to its planned business performance and in satisfying the needs and expectations of everyone with a financial interest in the company.

Figure 3.1 The European Model for Total Quality Management
Source: European Quality Foundation (1998).

Table 3.1   The four stages of the quality movement

| Identifying characteristics | Stages of the quality movement | | | |
	Inspection	Statistical Quality	Quality Assurance	Strategic Quality management
Primary concern	Detection	Control	Co-ordination	Strategic impact
View of quality	A problem to be solved	A problem to be solved	A problem to be solved, but one that is attacked productively	A competitive opportunity
Emphasis	Product uniformity	Product uniformity with reduced inspection	The entire production chain, from design to market, and the contribution of all functional groups, especially designers, to preventing quality failures	The market and customer needs
Methods	Gauging and measurement	Statistical tools and techniques	Programmes and systems	Strategic planning, goal-setting, and mobilizing the organization
Role of quality professionals	Inspection, sorting, counting, and grading	Troubleshooting and the application of statistical methods	Quality measurement, quality planning, and programme design	Goal-setting, education and training, consultative work with other departments, and programme design
Who has responsibility for quality	The inspection department	The manufacturing and engineering departments	All departments, although top management is only peripherally involved in designing, planning, and executing quality policies	Everyone in the organization, with top management exercising strong leadership
Orientation and approach	'Inspects in' quality	'Control in' quality	'Builds in' quality	'Manages in' quality

Source: Garvin (1988: 36–7).

(1997) viewed TQM as a new way of managing to improve the effectiveness, flexibility and business as a whole to meet the requirements of customers. The philosophy of TQM stresses a systematic, integrated, consistent organization-wide perspective involving everyone and everything. It focuses primarily on total satisfaction for both internal and external customers, within a management environment that seeks continuous improvement. It recognizes that customer satisfaction; health, safety, environmental considerations and business objectives are mutually dependent. It is applicable within any organization, regardless of size, and the approaches to TQM vary from company to company.

In the tourism industry we can use the TQM roadmap outlined in Figure 3.2 to help us manage change and variation in any type of HVA. The roadmap embraces many of the contemporary issues and techniques already discussed and can be achieved over a five-year period.

Phase 1: Preparation for total quality management

This requires leadership and commitment to be visible and sustained. The management styles will become more participative and from this a clear, long-term mission statement can be developed which will be aligned to the HVA's values, linked to customer needs and involve employees. A quality policy can then be communicated through awareness and training sessions laying the foundations for a quality improvement environment.

Phase 2: Quality improvement

This can be achieved by using a number of recognized tools such as identifying the business's critical processes and the cost of each one. Brainstorming and benchmarking – both internal and external comparisons – are just two of the tools that can help with measuring the business performance and planning improvements through training.

Phase 3: Customer care

Although this phase focuses primarily on the external customer it should also embrace the internal customer. The elements involved are self-explanatory but should be measured regularly by means of surveys, competing products and services, routine inspections, number of complaints and process time.

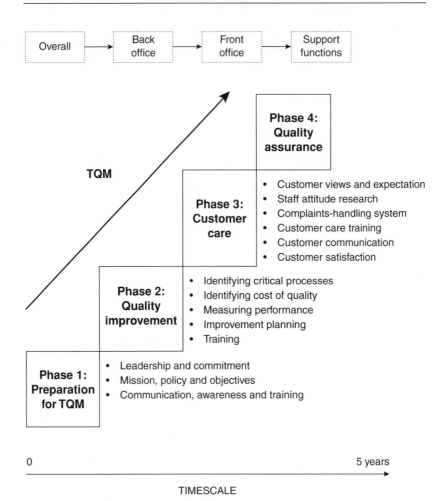

Figure 3.2   The quality roadmap

Phase 4: Quality assurance

Some controls and disciplines need to be placed on each business process and procedure to ensure that the HVA is complying with the standards set by itself or some other affiliated organization. By providing a consistent framework of standards across all functions the organization will also develop cohesion – a very important element in a fragmented business.

Each stage in this process needs to be monitored, evaluated and reviewed in a cyclical fashion, and should be undertaken at regular, defined intervals appropriate to the business.

Total quality management is not just a set of techniques or a list of points to follow. It is a way of managing any business, large and small, as the components – understanding customers, quality management systems and continuous quality improvement – can be readily modified to any operation. We have seen from this discussion that the three cornerstones to achieving TQM are people, systems and quality improvement tools and techniques.

'Best management practice' is a term that can be used almost inter-changeably with TQM. Experience has shown that, mainly due to cultural differences, individual nations have found some practices to be more or less effective than others when applied to their tourism industry. For example, total quality service has emerged from the TQM movement but takes the social structure of the HVA into account. The ultimate goal is to build employee ownership into service excellence, that is, employees should wish to deliver the best service without repeated prompting. This requires empow-ering employees, and in some cultures there are different levels of confidence, education and commitment. For instance, values, freedom of speech and working conditions are very different in North American HVAs than they are in East Asian HVAs. One of the ways in which we can improve quality is by learning what is good and best practice in similar and different HVAs. The technique that is used in this process is called benchmarking.

Benchmarking

In order to undertake this process it is necessary to look at the performance of other HVAs, identify best practice and compare what you have to offer in relation to their development and management. From this information you can identify the critical success factors of these leading edge competitors and assess your performance against them. This can assist your organization or sector of the tourism industry to improve quality at every level and ensure long-term success.

In a recent benchmarking exercise commissioned by Scottish Enterprise (1997) a number of HVAs were studied in ten different countries ranging from Ireland to Singapore. The objective was to identify international best practice that could then be used to enhance the performance of Scottish attractions in these areas.

A number of issues emerged from the study, which have helped HVAs look at their own organization with a view to quality improvement, ranging from consumer-directed technology to seasonality extension and beneficiary and endowment development to community relations.

Conclusion

This chapter has given an overview of some of the common quality tools and techniques that can and are being used in HVAs around the world. These can be used by small and large organizations alike and they can be chosen for implementation at different times. Total quality management is a business philosophy as well as a series of quality stages. The importance of monitoring, evaluation and review is also stressed. The road to quality is a never-ending journey but it can be an enjoyable experience for all involved – from the customer to the organization and its environment.

Questions

1 Suggest ways in which an HVA might carry out Phase 2 as illustrated on the TQM roadmap.
2 Identify the reasons why an HVA might adopt the IIP standard as a means of improving quality.
3 Discuss the usefulness of the European Quality Model in undertaking a business self-assessment in the heritage sector.

References and further reading

Australian Quality Council (1997). *The 1997 Australian Quality Awards Framework*. Australian Quality Council.

European Quality Foundation (1998). *The European Foundation Quality Model Framework*. European Quality Foundation.

Dale, B. G. and Plunkett J. J. (eds) (1990). *Managing Quality*. Philip Allan.

Deming, W. E. (1992). *Quality Productivity and Competitive Position*. MIT Press.

Garvin, D. A. (1998). *Managing Quality, the Strategic and Competitive Edge*. Free Press.

Hewison, R. (1987). *The Heritage Industry*. Methuen.

Oakland, J. S. (1997). *Total Quality Management*. Wiley.

Scottish Enterprise (1997). *Investors in People Tourism Business Benefits*. Scottish Enterprise.

Swarbrooke, J. (1995). *The Development and Management of Visitor Attractions*. Butterworth-Heinemann.

4

Heritage, authenticity and history

Kathryn A. Burnett

Introduction

Heritage as a concept has exploded on to a global stage and permeates the local, regional and national spheres. Prentice's (1993) typology of heritage attractions demonstrates the breadth of heritage today – sporting parks, seaside towns, craft centres, monuments, nature trails, theatres and technology sites – all constitute heritage attractions and sit alongside many more sites, both rural and urban, both educational and entertaining to vie for our attention. Heritage attractions are frequented by many kinds of visitors – people spending leisure time locally, people visiting for education or for business or, in many cases, individuals visiting as tourists. It is fair to say, as Herbert (1995) points out, that there is a definite overlap between leisure, tourism and heritage, and much of our understanding of how people experience heritage can be enhanced with reference to the well-established literature on tourism and leisure practices more generally, as well as the burgeoning amount of material derived from heritage-specific research. In this short discussion I aim to do two things. First, I wish to provide a brief background to the relationship between heritage and authenticity. I will then follow this with a second, related, focus – the relationship between heritage and history. Where appropriate I will make reference to some current examples of heritage attractions to illustrate my point. These examples will be drawn from both Scotland and beyond. To begin, however, I want to briefly introduce three main sociological points that should inform our understanding of heritage management and interpretation today: first, heritage is a contradictory entity; second, heritage is a social institution; and, third, heritage is a politicized process.

Understanding heritage: a sociological view

First, let us consider the idea that heritage is a contradictory entity. Some forms of heritage appear to operate in the name of conservation, preservation and education. One might argue that such heritage occupies the 'high moral ground' as such attractions tend to concern themselves, to varying degrees, with ethical approaches, sustainable practices, the heritage is presented as 'historically accurate' and the site developers would tend to engage with authenticity claims, and in many cases would seek to satisfy the 'authenticity test'.[1]

Other forms of heritage attraction appear to operate with a different value system. The 'heritage industry' is viewed as presenting the past to people in a packaged, commodified form with the emphasis on play and competitive advantage – our site has the 'most attractions', 'the oldest buildings', 'the biggest choice of souvenirs' or, even, 'our site is the most authentic'. Unsurprisingly, the distinctiveness of any attraction is a crucial factor in market advantage (Bachleitner and Zins, 1999: 200). In this ideal type of heritage there is less concern over what is 'authentic' in any accurate historical sense and greater emphasis is given to what is 'attractively authentic'. But as public funding commitment in the British Isles has shrunk and heritage as an industry has markedly expanded all attractions find themselves in a highly competitive, privatized sphere. As a result most heritage attractions are a combination of both of these stances – they seek to attract all visitors from all backgrounds and of all persuasions. No small feat! The tension between being 'historically accurate' or 'truly authentic' and that of the demand to be entertaining and attractive is a headache that just will not go away for heritage providers.

My second introductory point is that heritage is a distinctly social institution. The connection between heritage as a consumer activity and the representation of the past, or in some cases of contemporary existence, is one which must be understood in relation to wider social processes and, more specifically, should be recognized as a process by which we understand our relationships with particular structural frameworks which confer our identity and social position such as our class, gender, family, work, age, ethnicity and so on. For example, Corner and Harvey (1991: 45–6) present the British case that following Thatcherite restructuring of both the economy and society in the 1980s, the once independent concerns of heritage and enterprise became locked together as 'devices of ideological mediation'. These ideological devices continue to inform our sense of 'tradition' and 'modernity' but they have been shaped and reformed as a result of changing class positions and the reassessment of past certainties of employment and status.

Our everyday view of heritage is one which is now deeply entwined with our sense of history and past as well as with our current consumerist tendencies; that is, choice and good value are key factors but so too are the desires to be entertained, to be educated and to be provided with an enhancement to one's very sense of self. This point is important. Heritage – as part of the growth in culture as industry – must be seen to deliver the opportunity for visitors to build, enhance or reorientate their own (and others') sense of identity (c.f. Bachleitner and Zins, 1999: 200). This might be a confirmation of one's national identity such as a visit to a battlefield or a national sporting stadium. It might be the chance to examine one's gender role, sexuality or professional standing. Through heritage attractions men and women's experiences in factories, on farms or in domestic service are presented to us for reflection. We might reflect on our age at museums of childhood, or our class as we tour a stately home or a tenement house. We may examine our claims to be country folk or city dwellers as we move between rural sites and urban attractions. The choices are vast and the heritage and tourism industries work very hard at expanding the choice and stimulating our desire to make those choices. To explore and experience heritage is now part and parcel of our leisure identities. Our engagement with the concept is less an option and increasingly an expectation. We are engaged, as Cohen and Taylor (1992: 40) have suggested, in both 'reality work' and 'identity work'. And life is increasingly rarely 'just lived' but rather we are encouraged to undertake remedial work on who we are and what we accept as reality. Furthermore, how we engage with and how we resist the social structures around us is done with the help of experts and advisers. Heritage is one such culture industry that has expanded its remit to help us reassess our lives, our pasts and our sense of what is real.

The point here is that our experiences of heritage attractions are personal engagements which stimulate us to reflect on who or what we are, and our interpretation of such sites present for us opportunities to reflect on the nature of social relations, value systems and tastes both in the past and in contemporary times. The debates over how 'authentic' or historically 'accurate' any representation is, therefore, is not simply one of intellectual pride or of differences in academic opinion. For the most part the concerns over how heritage is constructed and presented to society at large are important and valid concerns. Debate is healthy and provokes both consumers and providers alike to examine what they desire from heritage and why.

Finally, in this introduction, let us consider the idea that heritage is a well acknowledged politicized process. The choices an attraction makes in how it sells itself, what it appears to promote, value and emphasize, creates the possibility for people to feel included or excluded from its narrative and for the possibility of facts and experiences to be ignored, shaped or enhanced in order to present a particular discourse of 'truth' or 'reality' (Edensor, 1997: 176). Some attractions use interpretation and their promotional material to communicate a public relations message (conservation sites and woodland trails are possible examples) but in some cases the site actively seeks to inculcate the public in a particular 'knowledge'; in short, the interpretation and promotion activities of the site are for the purpose of propaganda. The authors give the examples of nuclear power stations and their visitor centres. Other examples might include military museums where the 'truth' and 'righteousness' of campaigns are carefully presented and the critical reflection of past campaigns and rationales is kept on a tight reign.

The degree to which heritage attractions encompass the diversity of society and the range of experiences is predicated on the extent to which certain experiences or narrative are viewed as acceptable or entitled to expression and, in many cases, to what extent such experiences would be profitably sustained in the marketplace. Corner and Harvey (1991: 49) suggest that while heritage's common form is its association with a sense of shared 'inheritance' this is often weighted towards specific characteristics such as gender, ethnicity or social class. So for example, the shared cultural heritage of England has been seen as predominantly a white Anglo-Saxon Protestant (WASP) tradition and the cultural heritage of Scotland has been accused of being overbearingly masculine. In short, heritage is often guilty of suppressing the history of certain groups such as the historical cover-up of the relationship between past American presidents and slavery and the accusation that 'what heritage does not highlight it often hides' (Lowenthal, 1996: 154–6). But heritage is also worked on to represent more palatable versions of truth such as the animal rights activists determined 'correction' of Eleanor Roosevelt's fox fur to a cloth coat in the Washington memorial to the late president (Lowenthal, 1996: 155) or the careful glossing over of historical reference to the relationship between Finland and Germany during the Second World War at the Suomenlinna Museum, Helsinki. History, then, is often ignored, hidden or improved upon for the sake of a more palatable, entertaining or marketable narrative.

In conclusion to this introduction, then, the extent to which a heritage attraction can offer a 'real' or 'true' experience as opposed to some version or representation of an assumed reality has been well debated. Boniface and Fowler (1993), for example discuss at length the problematic relationships between 'East' and 'West' and indigenous and colonial representations within heritage tourism throughout the globe. Ideological struggles are now common-place within the heritage sphere and claims over what is 'real', 'true' or 'authentic' remain the essence of much of these conflicts. We examine the concept of authenticity below. Furthermore, the basic ideological struggle between history and heritage informs our discussion here and we return to consider this debate in the latter section of this discussion.

Authenticity: what is the attraction?

In order to examine how heritage attractions are meaningfully interpreted by visitors as well as how they are viewed by those who are employed in their name, and the cultural community which they represent, it important that we consider one of the more fundamental issues that underpin the evaluation and experiencing of heritage, namely, authenticity. If we take a global view of how cultural heritage is viewed we can be in no doubt of the importance attached to the concept of authenticity. Throughout the 1990s global conventions attended by leading dignitaries, experts and key organizations such as UNESCO and the World Bank have repeatedly emphasized the need to take account of authenticity concerns. Following the Charter of Venice (1964) authenticity was acknowledged as the essential qualifying factor by which cultural heritage would be considered and valued. The Nara Document on Authenticity (1994)[2] promoted the accommodation of cultural diversity, yet it recognized the potential for conflict between cultures. It encouraged those involved in cultural heritage management, conservation and promotion to work together to understand both the tangible and intangible aspects of heritage and to respect the cultural communities which generated such heritage. This respect must be balanced with possible developments and the requirements of other communities and organizations. The Nara Document went on to state that what constitutes cultural heritage, and indeed authenticity, would vary from culture to culture and would be dependent upon a rich variety of sources of information (e.g. setting, traditions, techniques, spirit and feeling). The complexity of how authenticity is attributed to heritage was therefore clearly reinforced in the Nara Document.

Authenticity is a concept, which has attracted much academic debate. Scholars of both tourism and heritage have concerned themselves with the nature of the concept and the extent to which it remains a goal or concern of today's tourism and heritage consumer. This academic interest is not a recent one. In the late eighteenth century the now classic travel accounts of the time were much concerned with finding a 'real' or true depiction of ways of life and culture at that time thought long gone. In Scotland, for example, Johnson and Boswell's celebrated tour of the Hebrides was underpinned by Johnson's obsession to challenge the authenticity of the Ossian poems and to reveal James MacPherson as a fraud. The whole Ossian affair remains one of the more contentious examples of a desire to identify and revel in 'authentic experiences' of a different way of life which the epic poems describe (Gold and Gold, 1995:42). The Ossian poems despite any 'fakery' claims were immensely powerful constructions of a mythic and emotive past which has served the business of Scottish tourism well. In fact, the debate surrounding the poems has only served to create spin-off effects which draw more upon the controversy than the actual content of the poems themselves. By the nineteenth century, the Romantic response to the expansion of modern industrial capitalism was such that it prompted the expansion of travel and tourism with considerable emphasis on the fulfilment of the self through an engagement with 'otherness' and 'difference'. But even in these early stages of the development of mass-market tourism Buzard (1993) notes that tensions were emerging from within the experience. Individuals sought to draw distinctions between travellers and tourists and within that distinction were implicit references to the ability to 'know' difference and 'real experience' as opposed to engaging with a sight or culture in a 'superficial' unsophisticated fashion. The 'authenticity' discourse was increasingly reinforced at this time as tourists and travellers both searched for 'alterity' – that is, the experience of the unfamiliar – but it was argued that tourists often failed in their attempts as they met with false, distorted and partial representations of 'real culture' on their largely 'guided' travels (Buzard, 1993: 174). Historically, then, we have always had tensions between how sights and cultural phenomena are viewed by individuals in their tourism and leisure pursuits. The early consumers of tourist sites and cultural heritage were just as prone to succumbing to 'the gaze' and as such they often demanded that expectations were matched by 'realities'. The desire to keep their custom ensured that the fledging tourist-heritage industry would do what it could to oblige.

The key debate within the late twentieth century for the consumers of tourist-related experiences such as heritage attractions, arts and crafts or the consumption of food and drink has been the extent to which modern day tourists are viewed as foolishly passive in their acceptance of inauthentic experience and their capacity to embrace a false sense of reality (Boorstein, 1964) or they are (more sympathetically) portrayed as unknowing victims of the industry's tendency to present staged authenticity as the 'real thing' (MacCannell, 1976). Boorstein writing in the 1960s argued that tourists were prepared to settle for inauthentic illusory experiences and thus reinforced one of the more persistent negative stereotypes of the tourist. Later, MacCannell, in his now classic account, suggested that modern tourists of the late twentieth century were not fools but pilgrims on a quest to find and delight in authentic experiences which would fulfil their otherwise alienated existence within modern industrial society. MacCannell suggested that those consumers of the authentic were doomed in their search as the tourism and heritage industries had anticipated the demand for 'glimpses of the real' and the 'behind the scenes' or 'backstage' presentations, and thus created the now widespread possibility of 'staged authenticity' such as 'behind the curtain' experiences of the industrial theatres of manufacturing plants, or being given the opportunity to meet with 'real locals' or to visit an authentic local traditional event. The staging can be subtle or blatant but the upshot is the same. Tourism and heritage industries insist upon the commodification of the authentic experience, for it is in this process of creating an objectified experience – a commodity which can be packaged and sold under the label of 'authentic' – that the industries whet our appetites for attaining the unattainable and experiencing the unexperienced (Crang, 1994; Edensor, 1997; Tunbridge and Ashworth 1996). We are given appetites for the authentic we never dreamed we had. As brochures are acquired, leaflets collected, advertisements lazily scanned, we the consumers are tempted into a wider circle of experience.

But Boorstein and MacCannell's views on authenticity have been questioned. Erik Cohen, writing largely in reaction to these two views, argued that both Boorstein and MacCannell effectively miss a crucial point – authenticity is not a 'known entity'. Authenticity is not an objective phenomenon but, rather, authenticity is a 'negotiable concept' which is open to change and is an outcome of the relationship between tourists and their consumption of cultures and environments. Authenticity is actually a social process – created and open to change through time and space. Cohen's research has been crucial in drawing our attention to the idea that authenticity is not a 'known' entity but rather it is socially constructed; that is, what we consider to be 'authentic' rests on social and cultural norms and relations. The role of history, experts and 'tastes' inform what it is that we view as 'authentic' or what we would like to be 'authentic' (Tunbridge and Ashworth, 1996: 10–11).

It is possible, argues Cohen, for any object, event or experience to be made 'authentic' over time with some careful stage-managing and communication. In this process of 'emergent authenticity' it is possible for cultural producers to create authentic products for a discerning market of consumers by recognizing what consumers want in their quest for 'authenticity'. This has been demonstrated most clearly with research into the production of ethnic crafts whereby the things viewed as 'most authentic' are things which often depict the most exotic otherness – the most exaggerated features of difference – of a particular culture (Cohen, 1988: 380; Littrell, Anderson and Brown, 1993). The meaning of an object, event or experience then can be changed to suit different interpretations and, furthermore, each individual will choose to take their own interpretation from things – their own personal sense of what is authentic will differ from other people's.

This notion that authenticity is a concept which is open to various interpretations and experience is crucial for it then informs our discussion of the nature of commodification of culture. One of the main accusations laid at the door of tourism and heritage is that it negatively 'commodifies' culture. In this process of commodification the industries of tourism and heritage create distorted visions of cultures, traditions, and past realities and experiences. In contrast to this view is the argument that heritage and tourism can actually conserve, re-create and enhance the social and cultural relations. Perhaps of most interest to us here is Cohen's argument that we must be careful not to expect tourism and heritage consumers to have the same expectations of authenticity as cultural experts and 'heritage intellectuals'. The lay person's version of what is authentic may well be a much 'looser' and more 'playful' notion than what has been assumed by some critics of the tourism and heritage commodification processes (Cohen, 1988: 383). Furthermore, as May (1996: 718) has pointed out, we should be wise to the notion that much of our concern over authenticity lies with our response to alienation in our contemporary life. His suggestion that our concerns with authenticity are variable in as much as our experiences of alienation are to a greater or lesser degree also variable and attempts to quantify 'authenticity' as more or less accurate and people's experiences of it more or less valid is rather pointless.

Clearly the recognized shift within the industry towards 'dramatic representation' of experiences as spectacles as opposed to the presentation of historical objects (Corner and Harvey, 1991: 56) has implications for how authenticity can be viewed and valued. And, although much debate still centres on the claims of authenticity associated with historical objects, the move towards heritage as an opportunity to view the past through 'narratives' and thematic portrayals of experiences – such as mining, housework, fishing – has been predicated on the trend toward 'witnessing' the past through engagement and 'experience' at the attraction. Consumers of heritage attractions are encouraged to touch, feel, smell and taste the past – the sensual and 'sensational' nature of the 'newer' style of heritage attractions have, as we know, drawn both praise and fire in almost equal measure. The final point in this section is to take on board the perspective of Barbara Kirshenblatt-Gimblett (1998: 11) who suggests that our knowledge of authenticity is only possible when we do not understand what is before us: 'Authenticity occurred when audiences confronted the incomprehensible.' This claim, that we really only know the authentic when we are most distanced or unknowing of it, has a certain ring to it and is perhaps the main reason why the heritage attraction will continue to be construed as inauthentic from a 'historical truth' position. The main goal of heritage attractions to promote, interest, educate, inform and entertain, and all with the particular goals of widespread appeal and easy comprehension, is such that we recognize and understand quickly what is before us. Perhaps there is something in the claim that only through a laboured process of negotiated understanding can we touch on a sense of authentic.

History and heritage: an uneasy alliance

The meaningful interpretation of heritage by consumers must also be located within the tensions between heritage and history. In the first instance we have the widespread argument that heritage has brought history alive has made it accessible to us all and has fostered an interest in things past and present that might well have been ignored, forgotten or devalued. The view that heritage champions history has widespread appeal as the following statement from Kensaku Morita reveals at the opening of the twenty-second session of the World Heritage Committee in Kyoto in 1998: 'I am convinced that heritage should be essential for the meaningful appreciation of the history and culture of one's country. I believe that it is most important for heritage to foster in the minds and hearts of young people the love of culture and peace.'[3]

But, despite high profile claims that history is known and made better through our heritage activities, tensions remain between the two spheres; history and heritage are two different yet related processes and it is important that we make some reference to how this distinction operates. One of the more widely quoted writers on the relationship between heritage and history is David Lowenthal whose book, *The Past is a Foreign Country*, is a now established classic on heritage study (Lowenthal, 1985). In a more recent commentary Lowenthal points up the basic tension between heritage and history when he writes: 'If historians despise heritage fakery, heritage disdains historians' truth fetishes'. (Lowenthal, 1996: 127).

Lowenthal suggests that we have a tendency now to improve our heritage by endowing the past with 'exemplary perspectives' while endowing the present with 'idealized traits of earlier times' (Lowenthal, 1996: 153). There is a particular trend within the heritage industry to focus on the everyday and familiar aspects of life and through this to connect our past to our present. Furthermore, heritage is an active process whereby the past is reactivated, reanimated, reworked and excavated – the sleeping past is woken up – for present-day consumption (Lowenthal, 1996: 141). But this awakening will change as the tastes and desires of each present change through time and space. As Lowenthal (1996: 143) suggests heritage is the upshot of recognition that we *need to remember* certain things in order to preserve our identities but much is still discarded and rejected along the way. Glasgow needs the Clyde and its history but Glasgow also needs to provide heritage attractions that generate revenue and jobs as well as enhancing the city's leisure provision. The recently opened Maritime Centre has clear reference to the shipbuilding industry but there is a sense in which the centre has reinforced the displacement or decentring of Glasgow's shipbuilding. Located within a new retail park it is starkly iconographic of the heavy industry's decline and with it already suffering from lower than anticipated visitor numbers, it would appear that Glasgow is uncomfortable with a dedicated site celebrating a now spectacularly defunct industry.

Perhaps one of the interesting angles on our relationship with history though heritage is the extent to which history 'got wrong' is ever corrected. The act of recording memories and reflections transforms such representations into a more objectified truth that is much harder to refute, to ignore or to alter (Lowenthal, 1996: 146). There is an 'immunity to correction' which is both practical – no one wishes to take something all apart and start again – and ideological. But in certain cases the realities of history are just too important to ignore and heritage attractions work hard to readjust and 'correct' previous mistakes. Heritage creation is about an imagined past not an actual one and therefore getting it wrong is not necessarily problematic as long as the story provided fits the purpose. Heritage is arguably more about what *should be* than what actually is or was. Some heritage celebrates and some heritage just remembers and there is a difference, argues Lowenthal

(1996: 159), which should inform our reflections on what is taking place in the name of heritage interpretation. This leads us to a final point in this section. Heritage succeeds largely because it is more real than real. This is the postmodern turn of which so much has been written and spoken about (Hoelscher 1998: 371; McCrone, Morris and Kiely, 1995: 45). Much heritage is seen as 'better' than the original because it selectively presents to us the most familiar, the most expected and most 'authenticated' imaginings of past times, spaces and relations. Hoelscher (1998) describes how 'America's Little Switzerland' – the town of New Glarus, Wisconsin – has attracted considerable attention for its creation and redefinition of 'Swissness'. Houses, crafts, events have all been reworked in the constant shaping of 'ethnic memory' in the New Glarus landscape. Johnson (1996) has argued that there is a tendency to become a little overwrought and sensitive in respect of heritage as 'bogus history', furthermore, we should follow the example of Edward Bruner and see heritage sites as presenting the opportunity a 'multiplicity of readings of history'. Authenticity is a struggle whereby different interpretations must compete for attention. Implicit in this is the question of power and the 'political economy of taste' (Appandurai, 1986: 44–5). We know that certain group's tastes tend to 'win out' and others are relegated as too dangerous, or unimportant or unfashionable to be allowed and when heritage sites seek to address the inequalities of such tendencies we should applaud such acts. The Twentieth Century Exhibition at the new Museum of Scotland is an excellent case in point, for here the choices of items which represented the past century were made by the public with a few 'famous folk' thrown in for good measure. The display is not only diverse but also strangely conservative and in some respects you could be tempted to view the selection as disappointing in its lack of imagination, but this is the very substance which invites critical reflection on one's own tastes and positioned identities. The heritage in front of us is someone's history and to them it has been chosen for its very 'realness'.

Perhaps one of the more commendable aspects of heritage is that, in its search to present the 'extra-ordinary' in the ordinary, heritage developers and managers seek to create heritage out of almost anything. We now recognize that almost any site, event, artefact or historical figure is fair play for the heritage treatment and this has resulted in the growth of leisure attraction in fields previously untainted by the pleasure ethic. For example, the attraction of industrial heritage such as the small Gas Works at Biggar.[4] The works, which began operating in 1839, are the only ones of their kind surviving in Scotland. The Biggar Gas Works are, in the words of the site's own promotional material, 'a remarkable example of a virtually complete small gas making plant built in 1839 to supply the town with gas lighting. They were rebuilt and expanded in 1914 and served the town until 1973 and the advent of liquid propane gas'. So this remarkable example has survived but, as McCrone, Morris and Kiely (1995) have pointed out, it is a remarkable fact that contemporary industry is only likely to become heritage when it is proverbially 'down the tubes', 'washed up' or 'rusting' like an old tin can. The Scottish oil industry is given as a case in point; for now it survives and as such its representation within Aberdeen heritage attractions is, for the most part, tokenistic but in decades to come we may yet be furnished with the leisure opportunity to visit rusting oil platforms moored at sea and experience life as it was on a late twentieth-century rig.

There are clearly, many examples whereby heritage has made a particular effort to 'stay true' to historical experience and yet, for the purposes of re-creating the past in the present, there is a need to rearrange time and space. 'Real' buildings or artefacts are displaced from their original setting and relocated elsewhere but this relocation constructs a new past which can be meaningfully interpreted and experienced by both visitor and manager alike. The Scottish Railway Preservation Society, which operates the Bo'ness and Kinneil Railway, on a greenfield site by the south shore of the Firth of Forth near Edinburgh, has had to re-create an authentic traditional railway setting by obtaining and re-erecting traditional buildings from other settings. Their website provides some detail on what this involved:

> Bo'ness station has been built since 1979 on a landscaped site which had previously been occupied by railway sidings, timber yards and coal mines. Buildings have been designed to reflect a traditional railway style, or moved from other locations. The station building was originally at Wormit, the train shed is from Haymarket, the signal box from Gartsherrie South Junction and the footbridge from Murthly.[5]

Similarly the re-creation of historical events by heritage events companies[6] appears to add particular gloss to companies seeking to 'bring alive' the past whether it be glory or gore. Again, the reconstruction is one which makes a virtue of the fact that the performance is a re-creation for it can be shaped and adapted for different audiences – children, overseas visitors, journalists. One Scottish company puts it like this: 'Over the years, the Heritage Events Co. has produced a wide variety of short dramas and presentations tailor-made to serve the needs and objectives of specific clients from the world of business and commerce.' Flexibility and an ability to cater to all are a key element in the industry success. Few commercial enterprises have refrained from embracing the diversification and added value options open to them and for many it is through the purchasing of these replications of our inalienable wealth that provides us with a method for experiencing authentic pasts (Kirshenblatt-Gimblett, 1998: 196).

Conclusion

In conclusion, the demands of the heritage industry are not to present the 'real authentic' but to present the spectacle and sensation of the authentic. This is what 'heritage as industry' does. The debate on the priorities which certain heritage sites might have and to what extent the engagement with history should be more informed on fact and less inclined towards fiction is an ongoing agenda. We should be careful not to deny the possibility that heritage as spectacle and fabricated past can provide the consumer with the possibility of learning, stimulation and a thirst for a deeper knowledge through other avenues and channels. This is perhaps where the supporting literature, promotional material such as websites and, even, the possibility to purchase merchandise on site all come into their own.

But as Ascherson (1994) has argued, heritage is more than just country houses and statues, it is the memory and passions which are passed down from one generation to the next and it is the ordinary folk who inherit something who should decide 'whether they want to cherish it, sell it or wipe their boots on it'. It is the nation, the people who must be consulted and entitled to comment on what constitutes heritage. The extent to which quality heritage management can incorporate the wishes of the people at large is a challenge worth taking up. It is the debate over how and why people are satisfied with an attraction that will lend substance to any claim to the quality of an attraction. As one final example demonstrates, the recent opening of the reconstruction of the Great Hall at Stirling Castle has been met with the lament that the meticulous research and enhancement of the building to its 'authentic glories' has actually been too good. Historic Scotland's decision to reproduce a yellow limewash on the walls has meant that the hall now stands gaudily apart from the aged lichened stones of the historic castle. Irony indeed!

Notes

1 Paragraph 24(b)(i) of the Operational Guidelines refers to the test of authenticity. (b)(i) meet the test of authenticity in design, material, workmanship or setting and in the case of cultural landscapes their distinctive character and components (the Committee stressed the reconstruction is

only acceptable if it is carried out on the basis of complete and detailed documentation on the original and to no extent on conjecture (UNESCO 1996).

2 http://www.unesco.org/whc/archive/nara94.htm
3 Speech of Mr Kensaku Morita, Parliamentary Vice-Minister of Education, Science, Sport and Culture, Kyoto, Japan.
   http://www.unesco.org/whc/archive/repcom98a2.htm
4 http://www.scran.ac.uk/
5 http://srps.org.uk/railway/info.htm
6 http://members.aol.com/heritevent/promo.htm

Questions

1 Explain what is meant by the suggestion that heritage is a social institution.
2 Is it important for heritage attractions to be authentic?
3 Why is there an uneasy alliance between heritage and history?

References and further reading

Appandurai, A. (ed.) (1986). *The Social Life of Things: Commodities in Cultural Perspective.* Cambridge University Press.

Ascherson, N. (1994). Blow up the Duke of Sutherland, but leave his limbs in the heather. *Independent on Sunday*, 9 October, p. 20

Bachleitner, R. and Zins, A. H. (1999). Cultural tourism in rural communities: the residents perspective. *Journal of Business Research*, **44**, 199–209.

Boniface, P. and Fowler, P. (1993). *Heritage and Tourism in 'the global village'.* Routledge.

Boorstein, O. J. (1964). *The Image: A Guide to Pseudo-Events in America.* Harper and Row.

Buzard, J. (1993). *The Beaten Track: European Tourism, Literature and the Ways to 'Culture' 1800–1918.* Oxford University Press.

Cohen, E. (1988). Authenticity and commoditization in tourism. *Annals of Tourism Research*, **15**, 371–386.

Cohen, S. and Taylor, L. (1992). *Escape Attempts: The Theory and Practice of Resistance to Everyday Life.* Routledge.

Corner, J. and Harvey, S. (1991). Mediating tradition and modernity: the heritage/enterprise couplet. In *Enterprise and Heritage* (J. Corner and S. Harvey, eds). Routledge.

Crang, M. (1994). On the heritage trail: maps of and journeys to Olde England. *Environment and Planning D: Society and Space*, **12**, 341–355.

Edensor, T. (1997). National identity and the politics of memory: remembering Bruce and Wallace in symbolic space. *Environment and Planning D: Society and Space*, **29**, 175–194,

Gold, J. and Gold, M. (1995). *Imagining Scotland: Tradition, Representation and Promotion in Scottish Tourism since 1750*. Scholar Press.

Herbert, D. T. (ed.) (1995). *Heritage, Tourism and Society*. Pinter.

Hoelscher, S. (1998). Tourism, ethnic memory and the other-directed place. *Ecumene*, **5**(4), 396–398.

Johnson, N. (1996). Where geography and history meet: heritage tourism and the big house in Ireland. *Annals of the Association of American Geographers*, **86**, 551–566.

Kirshenblatt-Gimblett, B. (1998). *Destination Culture: Tourism, Museums and Heritage*. University of California Press.

Linklater, M. (1999). Scottish history is being vandalised. *Scotland on Sunday*, 24 October.

Littrell, M. A., Anderson, L. F. and Brown, P. J. (1993). What makes a craft souvenir authentic? *Annals of Tourism Research*, **20**,197–215.

Lowenthal, D. (1985). *The Past is a Foreign Country*, Cambridge University Press.

Lowenthal, D. (1996). *The Heritage Crusade and the Spoils of History*. Viking.

MacCannell, D. (1976). *The Tourist: A New Theory of the Leisure Class*. Shocken.

May, J. (1996). In search of authenticity and *on* the beaten track. *Environment and Planning D: Society and Space*, **14**, 709–736.

McCrone, D., Morris, A. and Kiely, R. (1995). *Scotland the Brand: The Making of Scottish Heritage*. Edinburgh University Press.

Pearce, P. L. and Moscardo, G. M. (1986). The concept of authenticity in tourist experiences. *Australian and New Zealand Journal of Sociology*, **22**, 121–132.

Prentice, R. (1993). *Tourism and Heritage Attractions*. Routledge.

Tunbridge, J. E. and Ashworth, G. E. (1996). *Dissonant Heritage: The Management of the Past as a Resource in Conflict*. Wiley.

Part Two

Site Visits

Eric Laws

Introduction

The two chapters in this part examine some of the quality issues arising from the complexity and the significance of the heritage sector of the tourism industry. During the second half of the twentieth century tourism became one of the world's largest industries, and it continues to be one of the most rapidly growing industries. The key characteristic of tourism which distinguishes it fundamentally from other economic activities is that consumers make temporary visits to the locations where services are provided, and consequently their behaviours have direct consequences for those places, and the people who work and live there. Other distinguishing features are the varied motivations of tourists in their decisions on how to spend time and money on leisure activities. This results in a variety of types of tourism, including heritage and cultural tourism. The wide choice of activities also underlies the importance to managers of providing high-quality tourism experiences for clients and for others affected by tourist activities as tourists can readily switch to alternative destinations and activities if they are disappointed by a particular site.

The culture and heritage of a place have long been known to contribute to its appeal as a tourist destination. 'Heritage, as with place, is a social construct . . . Heritage is a major component of interplace competition' (Hall, 1997: 92). The cultural and heritage aspects of place marketing are increasingly used as striking and effective marketing images to attract general tourists as well as those with a special interest in heritage tourism (Zeppel and Hall, 1992). Throughout the world, heritage sites, historic buildings, archaeological monuments and museums have become major tourism attractions. Johnson (1992: 128) notes their 'critical role in the tourist market; they add character to a destination area and are capable of generating tourist traffic in their own right'.

Motivations for heritage tourism

The interest in travelling to see and admire the sites of antiquity and to appreciate the variety of human cultures is not new;

> from about 1500 BC on, we can discern in Egypt sure signs of tourism, of travel for simple curiosity or pleasure . . . when Thutmose and Akhenaton and Ramses and other such renowned figures held the throne, the step pyramid of Djoser at Sakkarah, the Spinx at Gizeh, the pyramid complex at Abusir, and the like, were already over a thousand years old. On their walls, we find messages left by people who had made a special trip to see these impressive witnesses to the might of their past. Each monument was a hallowed spot, so the visitors always spent some moments in prayer, yet their prime motivation was curiosity or disinterested enjoyment, not religion. (Casson, 1994: 32, spellings in original form)

Speculating on why contemporary tourists are drawn to sites such as Stonehenge. Dallen (1997:227) commented that 'heritage restores a sense of time when people were more innocent and had simpler pleasures, reflecting the values longed for in today's complex society'. Approximately 20 per cent of visitors to the Science Museum in London came mainly because they wanted an enjoyable day out with the family, another 20 per cent gave recreation as their main reason for being there, and about half the visitors surveyed were interested in learning while at the museum (McManus, 1991). Moscardo (1996) noted that most heritage visitors wish to learn about the site, while most sought to be educated, a majority wanted to be informed.

The commercialization of heritage tourism

Many heritage managers have responded to the leisure and pleasure orientation of their customers by presenting and developing their sites in ways which appeal and entertain, and also maximize opportunities to benefit from visitor spending on rides, catering, and souvenirs. In some extreme forms, the commercial approach has been castigated for 'Disneyfying' the history and cultures of peoples (Richter, 1997). It can also detract from the authenticity of a heritage site or even from the local cultural identity by simplified or inaccurate interpretation, reducing the enjoyment of those visitors motivated by a strong interest in the particular site (Turner and Ash, 1975).

Hewison (1989) introduced the term 'manufacturing the heritage industry' and criticized the narrow commercial perspectives that result in a shallow consumerist enjoyment of heritage and cultural artefacts, rather than contributing to a deeper appreciation of complex matters in a society's development. The distortion results from two main factors, the need to present the past in visually exciting ways to be successful in a commercial sense, and the need to be selective in what is chosen for presentation. As a result, although the tourist's experience is enjoyable, serious events such as war tends to be trivialized. He gave as an example the Jorvic Centre in York, representing the area's Viking era, which employs technology such as lighting, people movers and smells and sounds to evoke a sense of the Viking era, but with little authenticity.

Important heritage and cultural sites also come under pressure from tourism development. Great buildings including the Parthenon and Notre Dame are literally being eroded by the constant pressure of visitors' feet: in the mid-1990s the stone floor of Canterbury Cathedral had to be replaced for safety reasons. Condensation and dust resulting from the large numbers of visitors has damaged the painted ceiling of the Sistine Chapel, and although this has been restored and remains open to tourists, visitors have been excluded from many other sites including the prehistoric cave paintings in the Dordogne, and from some of the Egyptian tombs in an attempt to halt their rapid, and very recent, deterioration.

Despite its specialist appeal, and the potential for problems in presenting heritage and culture as tourist attractions, heritage and culture have many synergies with tourism, and they support each other well. Tourism draws on the culture and heritage of destination areas for much of its promotional imagery: castles, cathedrals, palaces, and folklore and quaint villages have a vivid popular appeal. More than this, many visitors wish to explore and experience the heritage and cultural features of destination areas, even if their primary motivation is for relaxation and enjoyment. This interest has positive advantages for individual heritage sites and for countries with striking cultural traditions, bringing visitors and their revenue to areas which often have little other economic activity, thereby providing both the funds and the rationale to conserve old buildings and other facets of local culture.

The 1980s witnessed the rapid emergence of the 'heritage industry' in the UK, visits to heritage attractions in Britain rose from 52 million to 68 million between 1977 and 1991 (Hewison, 1989). Easthaugh and Weiss (1989: 58) commented 'as a tourist attraction, our heritage gives Great Britain a comparative advantage over other countries ... our architectural and historic monuments are a major factor in making this country an attractive destination for overseas visitors'.

Managing heritage sites for visitor satisfaction

The view that heritage sites provide assets for the tourism industry raises the issue of how to manage them for visitor satisfaction. Many, such as castles present complex challenges when presented to paying visitors, not least because they were often built to keep people out rather than to entice them in! Castles and other ancient buildings present many hazards, including dark and uneven stairways or other unsafe areas. The simple safety and comfort facilities taken for granted in modern buildings such as adequate lighting, fire alarms, and even heating or toilet facilities, are quite difficult to introduce into many ancient buildings without intruding on their character or structure. However, there is much that managers can do to ensure that tourists enjoy their experiences of visiting heritage sites.

Chapter 5 surveys a range of themes in the service management literature, and provides a case study demonstrating how the management of Leeds Castle, Kent, sets about ensuring the enjoyment of visitors to one of Britain's premier heritage sites.

Tourism, heritage and culture

Tourism is considered to be a fragmented industry, providing its clients with a variety of forms of travel and a wide range of activities are provided by an extensive array of businesses with varied objectives and resources, but with little apparent co-ordination. Tourists themselves have a variety of motives for travel, and adopt differing behaviours during their journeys. The combination of varied motives and many service providers results in a great range of tourism products on offer, with ever more sophisticated ways being developed to segment the markets for particular tourist products.

The resultant complexity is compounded by the overlaps between tourism and a variety of other sectors including hospitality, leisure, transport and entertainment. The temptation is to regard heritage as another of these business sectors, however, heritage is closely linked with the concept of culture, but in regarding heritage and culture as assets for the tourism industry, to be developed and exploited for commercial gain, their social significance is missed. Ashworth (1993) has argued that the success of heritage tourism threatens the survival of those assets on which it is based. Urry (1990) has noted the growing popular interest in heritage tourism, both to traditional heritage sites such as country houses, and to visit recent industrial landscapes such as warehouses, mines and power stations now operated as tourist attractions.

The heritage of a place cannot be seen merely as an economic asset for the present. It is part of the cultural stock of the community, and a number of serious issues arise from this perspective. Prominent amongst these is the question of what aspects of the heritage to present to visitors, and in what form. Decisions on these matters also affect visitor satisfaction, since people expect to see important and interesting artefacts when visiting major museums or historic sites, and they expect explanations that help them enjoy and understand what they see.

Picard (1991) has called for a new focus in research, away from whether or not tourism debases certain cultures, towards what it means to talk of the impact of tourism on a culture. Heritage and culture are specific attributes of a community and a location, so a potential tension arises between visitors whose interest in the locality is temporary and cursory, and residents for whom that heritage is the basis of their own culture. In selecting, presenting and interpreting an area's heritage and culture to tourists, the objective is often to enhance visitor enjoyment, emphasizing visual aspects of the past and giving a simplified account of history. This does not do justice to its complexity and often avoids discussion of contentious aspects of history. Interpretation has become a key feature of heritage site visits, and there is often an attempt to achieve consistent standards of presentation and experience style across a variety of heritage tourism operations. However, the overall effect is to trivialize or commoditize heritage.

Chapter 6 examines the wider quality issues resulting from interactions between tourism and the heritage, culture and communities in heritage areas.

It presents a case study illustrating tourism management issues and practices in Canterbury, one of Britain's most visited historic cities, which is often included in tourist itineraries with nearby Leeds Castle.

References and further reading

Ashworth, G. (1993). *Culture and Tourism: Conflict or Symbiosis in Europe?* In *Tourism in Europe, Structures and Developments* (W. Pompl and P. Lowery, eds), pp. 13–35, CAB International.

Casson, L. (1994). *Travel in the Ancient World.* John Hopkins University Press.

Dallen, T. (1997). Tourism and the personal heritage experience. *Annals of Tourism Research*, **24**(3), 225–242.

Easthaugh, A. and Weiss, N. (1989). Broadening the market. In *Heritage Interpretation* (D. L. Uzzell, ed.), vol. 2, pp. 58–67, Belhaven.

Hall, M. C. (1997). The politics of heritage tourism: place, power and the representation of values in the urban context. In *Quality Management in Urban Tourism* (P. Murphy, ed.) pp. 91–101, Wiley.

Herbert, D. (1989). Leisure trends and the heritage market. In *Heritage Sites: Strategies for Marketing and Development* (D. Herbert, R. Prentice and C. Thomas, eds), pp. 1–15, Avebury.

Hewison, R. (1989). Heritage: an interpretation. In *Heritage Interpretation: The Natural and Built Environment* (D. L. Uzzell, ed.), pp. 15–22, Belhaven.

Johnson, S. (1992). Heritage centres. In *Case Studies in Leisure Management Practice* (J. Buswell, ed.), Longman.

McManus, P. M. (1991). Making sense of exhibits. In *Museum Languages* (G. Kavanagh, ed.), pp. 35–46, Routledge.

Moscardo, G. (1996). Mindful visitors, heritage and tourism. *Annals of Tourism Research*, **23**(2), 376–397.

Picard, M. (1991). *Cultural Tourism In Bali, National Integration and Provincial Differentiation.* ASEASUK, University of Hull Tourist Development in SE Asia.

Richter, L. (1997). The politics of heritage tourism. Paper presented at the International Conference on Tourism Development: Issues for a New Agenda, Melaka.

Turner, L. and Ash, J. (1975). *The Golden Hordes, International Tourism and the Pleasure Periphery.* Constable.

Urry, J. (1990). *The Tourist Gaze.* Sage.

Zeppel, H. and Hall, C. M. (1992). Arts and heritage tourism in special interest tourism. In *Special Interest Tourism* (B. Weiler and C. M. Hall, eds), pp. 47–68, Wiley.

5

The analysis of quality for heritage site visitors

Eric Laws

Introduction

With the development and commercialization of heritage tourism, industry managers, their clients and researchers are increasingly interested in improving the quality of clients' experiences in this sector of tourism.

This chapter summarizes the theoretical analysis of quality in service industries, and then provides a case study analysing some of the challenges in managing a historic building which is one of Britain's major heritage tourist attractions. Historic buildings are central to the cultural identity of European nations, many are also important tourist attractions, but their internal configurations are idiosyncratic, with steep narrow stairways, many passageways and a mix of grand and tiny rooms. These conditions present heritage tourism managers with a range of problems relating to conservation, as well as presentation and visitor management.

Theories of service quality

The study of the market for services is relatively recent. Zeithaml, Parasuraman and Berry (1990) noted their surprise at the limited field of research available to them when they embarked on the project at Texas A and M University which led to the original SERVQUAL model (Parasuraman, Berry and Zeithaml, 1985), discussed later in this chapter. Tourism shares the general characteristics of services (see following list), which underlie the challenges of delivering satisfying experiences to clients visiting heritage sites, but each site also has individual characteristics which acerbated the difficulties of managing it for visitor enjoyment.

- intangibility
- heterogeneity
- inseparability
- perishability (based on Cowell, 1986).

Features of successful service firms

The foundations of effective service quality management are based on the 'emerging service paradigm' (Normann, 1991). Its focus is an organizational concern for the consumer, and in the consumer's interaction with service processes and service staff. In this way of thinking, service managers seek 'a balance between human input and technology, between costs and income, and finally between quality and productivity' (Gummesson, 1993: 40). This approach represents a departure from earlier concerns with the technical aspects of service production, but to be effective it depends on a style of management and an organizational climate that actively supports the philosophy of service quality. Zemke and Schaaf (1989) examined 101 companies providing excellent service and concluded that successful service firms share several features:

- Managers are obsessive about listening to and responding to changing customer wants, needs and expectations.
- They create and communicate a well-defined, customer inspired service strategy.
- They develop and maintain customer-friendly service delivery systems.
- They hire, inspire and develop customer-oriented frontline people (based on Zemke and Schaaf, 1989).

Meanings of service quality

In his benchmark general study of the topic, Garvin (1988) observed that 'quality' can be classified in five ways. *Transcendent quality* varies between individuals and over time, and is represented by the common phrase 'I know it when I see it.' However, this does not contribute much to the effective management of complex services!

A more performance-oriented approach relies on identifying measurable features of the product, this *expert view of quality* results in design specification and drawings. *User-based quality*, while in part based on individual judgement, is also the basis of consumer legislation which introduced the test of merchantability, requiring goods sold commercially to be fit for their purpose: the classic test was that a bucket should not leak. *Manufacturing quality* approaches attempt to minimize deviations from the standards set in technical specifications. These are internal specifications that conform to the company's requirements, whether or not customers are satisfied. The fifth suggested classification is *value-based quality,* but Garvin noted that 'it seems to be difficult to determine a generally valid link between price and quality' (Garvin, 1988: 42). This is a significant problem in tourism as many holiday products are sold on the basis of low price (Laws, 1999). The sophisticated management information systems now available enable organizations to set different prices for a base product or service in given market segments, thus maximizing overall yield (Edgar, 1997; Kimes, 1994).

Garvin's five quality classifications were related to manufactured products as well as services. As Normann (1991) has noted, part of the early challenge in researching services was to distinguish them from manufactured goods. In contrast with manufactured products, consistent standards cannot readily be achieved in service delivery systems. The difficulty revolves around the two bases to services, the technical aspects of managing any service contrast with the interactions between staff and clients that characterize the delivery of services. This dichotomy has been termed 'type A and type B' (Laws, 1986). Differing, though connected, implications flow from a recognition of these two factors in tourism management. While the technical type A factors are generally under the direct control of managers, the type B factors are more complex. These include the skills and motivations of staff, their ability to interact effectively with clients, and the unpredictably variable expectations and behaviour which different clients bring to the service episode and its constituent elements. (However, the point is made later in this chapter that one of the distinguishing features of sites such as historic castles is the relatively limited scope they offer for technical improvements, since managers are constrained by the special nature of these ancient buildings. As a consequence, effective service management techniques are their foremost concern.)

In summary, the challenge for service managers is twofold: to design and operate a service delivery system that achieves customers' judgements that the service experienced is satisfying, and to obtain technical efficiency in the use of resources to create the service. Many organizations emphasize the second goal: Gronroos (1990) has distinguished between two approaches to managing the quality of services: those driven by technology, and those founded on customers' needs.

Technical approaches to service quality

The technical approach to quality is often expressed as performance criteria specified for elements in the service delivery system. Thus, airlines publicize the proportion of their 'on-time' arrivals. For a heritage site, a relevant performance measure would be the timely departure and duration of guided tours. Hollins and Hollins (1991) also advocated a process of continuous improvements, relying on a view which underlies service blueprinting that the service is a chain of events which the customer experiences. The stage of designing the service is its managers' main opportunity to determine the characteristics of the service offered to customers.

One strategy which service managers often adopt in their search for consistent service is to eliminate employee discretion and judgement whenever possible. This approach to service design relies on the specification of tasks to a standard of performance required by management, thereby providing a basis for measuring the effectiveness of staff performing services. An example is the attempt to ensure that a consistent level of detail is provided in interpretative commentaries at heritage sites by all guides. Increased standardization implies a reduction in the discretion allowed to individual employees, although this contradicts clients' expectations of being treated as individuals, with needs that may vary during the many events of which a service is composed. It is common experience on tours of heritage sites that some visitors ask the guide for highly detailed information on specific aspects of the site, while the majority of the group is keen to move on to other features of the site. Efficiency goals may clarify performance targets for staff, but can conflict with the customer's expectation of warm and friendly service. Underlying this approach are the twin assumptions that consumers experience a service as a series of events, while managers see the service as a set of elements which require skilled co-ordination, and resource control, in delivering specified standards to clients.

Customer-oriented service quality

The second approach to service quality discussed by Gronroos (1990) was fitness for use. This can best be understood in terms of customers' expectations of satisfaction, against which they evaluate their subsequent individual experiences during the service. This approach reflects marketing theory that argues that customers' experiences with any purchase give rise to outcomes for them varying from satisfaction to dissatisfaction. This reflects a divergence from the standards of service which clients had anticipated, as the following abbreviated quotations indicate: 'The seeds of consumer satisfaction are planted during the prepurchase phase of the consumer decision process' (Wilkie, 1986: 558). It is against this individual benchmark that tourists measure the quality of their service experiences. 'Satisfaction is defined as a postconsumption evaluation that the chosen alternative is consistent with prior beliefs and expectations (with respect to it). Dissatisfaction, of course, is the outcome when this confirmation does not take place' (Engel, Blackwell and Miniard, 1986: 155).

This type of quality is more difficult to measure and to manage than conformance to specification. Individuals experience varying degrees of satisfaction or dissatisfaction with a given service, for three reasons. First, each individual approaches a service with his or her own set of expectations based on prior experience, immediate disposition and needs. Second, a guide leading a group around a historic building could, in explaining a particular feature, excite and inform one member of the group, but bore or antagonize another. Third, the combination of these two factors, varying expectations and differing experiences, can result in unequal gaps between expectations and experience for customers. Managers who wish to provide services which fit their customers' needs must therefore incorporate flexibility into the design of their services so that staff can respond effectively to their clients' individual needs. This requires skilled staff, operating within an organizational culture focused on clients' needs, and empowered with (limited) discretion by the design of the service delivery system to make immediate judgements about the use of the company's resources to satisfy the clients they are serving.

Masberg and Silverman (1996: 23) have commented on the lack of research to understand what heritage visitors actually want:

> In an industry so dependant upon the satisfaction of visitors . . . very little research into visitor experience at heritage sites has been adequately designed to explore the visitors' perspective rather than that of the

professional or researcher. Research thus far has not elicited and presented visitors' own terms, discussions and meanings related to heritage site visits.

Effective service management depends on the best possible understanding of what clients expect from their service experiences.

The SERVQUAL model

A widely used approach to understanding customer's judgements of service quality seeks to identify gaps between their expectations and their perceptions of the service that they received. This line of enquiry forms the basis of the SERVQUAL model (developed and refined by Zeithaml, Berry and Parasuraman in a series of articles and books spanning more than a decade). It provides a multidimensional scale based on two questionnaires each of 22 items to investigate five key aspects of service: tangibles, reliability, responsiveness, assurance and empathy (see following list). Using Likert scales, one questionnaire measures expectations prior to service, the second records subsequent perceptions of service performance. Perceived performance ratings lower than expectations indicate poor service quality. This principal gap results from five underlying service dimensions.

1 *Tangibles*: physical facilities, equipment, appearance of staff
2 *Reliability*: ability of organization to deliver promised service reliably and accurately
3 *Responsiveness*: willingness of service provider to help customers
4 *Assurance*: knowledge and courtesy of personnel, ability to inspire confidence
5 *Empathy*: level of care and individual attention provided to customers (based on Zeithaml, Berry and Parasuraman, 1985).

SERVQUAL has been criticized both for its underlying conceptualization and its methodology (Brown, Churchill and Peter, 1993; Carman, 1990; Teas, 1994). Some researchers even question the continuing use of SERVQUAL: 'At best, it can be argued that SERVQUAL is applicable to contexts close to its original setting, that is, appliance repair, retail banking, long distance telephone . . . it is questionable . . . whether it is measuring service quality at all' (Robinson, 1999: 29).

Nevertheless, it has been applied to tourism in a number of studies, for example Tribe and Snaith (1998), Saleh and Ryan (1992) and Fick and

Ritchie (1991). Although it has been subjected to severe criticism, SERVQUAL continues to serve us well in two important respects: it highlights unequivocally the centrality of quality in service research and management, and it emphasizes the complexity of managing service experiences (Laws, 2000).

Many contemporary researchers investigating the related issues of service quality and the ways in which customers experience service episodes continue to refer their work to the SERVQUAL model, either by directly employing some or all of its constructs, or by explicitly attempting to differentiate their analysis from what has become the benchmark of modern service management research. Bitner (1992) has suggested that perceived service quality, in contrast to the quality of individual service transactions, may be similar to an individual's general attitude towards the service firm.

Approaches to service quality that equate it with satisfaction have the advantage of being customer focused. Any gaps in the experience – anticipation – provision model suggest that one or more parties are less than completely satisfied. The reasons for any dissatisfaction can be investigated by analysing customer perceptions through interviews, content analysis of correspondence and focus groups, or by evaluating the service design and service delivery system performance using techniques such as service mapping or service blueprinting.

Many experts believe that service quality is closely related to customer satisfaction, and view quality as the outcome when the customer's expectations are met. The process by which consumers understand quality is often regarded as a comparison of service standards expected against their perceptions of their experiences. A close match between the three elements (anticipation, provision and experience) indicates the probability of a satisfied customer and professionally fulfilled service staff and managers.

Events during service consumption

It is also worth noting that customers' experience often embraces a longer time frame than the duration of the service itself. Lalonde and Zinszer (1976) distinguished three phases: pre-transaction, when expectations are formed, selection of the provider is made and clients prepare for the service; the transaction itself; and post-transaction, when clients have concluded consumption of the core service. In the post-consumption phase, customers take their departure, and form a judgement of their overall satisfaction with it. This judgement is later factored into any subsequent decision about repurchasing.

A key difference between manufactured goods and services is that all the production processes for manufactured goods have been completed when the purchase is made but, with services, a series of events occurs after purchase and the customer plays an active role in them. A fuller understanding of customers' service quality perceptions may be gained by regarding a service as a series of events each of which is experienced as yielding greater or lesser satisfaction (Laws, 1986). For example, a visit to a historic castle often spans several hours and includes a range of activities such as shopping for souvenirs, consuming meals and beverages, and strolling in the grounds as well as the 'core' experience of touring the castle itself. Any aspect of these events could create satisfying or dissatisfying experiences for the visitor.

Managing visits to castles

Historic buildings, and castles in particular, are familiar sights throughout Europe, presenting an imposing, solid appearance, with high walls, and fortifications whose original purpose was usually to keep unwanted visitors out. This is part of their attraction to contemporary visitors, but the structure of their interiors, with narrow, uneven and dark staircases, and complex corridors, also presents difficulties to tourists trying to negotiate them. Typically, tourists' experience of visiting most castles is now highly organized, as a result of management decisions about how to control the flow of large numbers of people through a sequence of sights and activities determined by each castle's individual location, configuration and special features. This control is essential to minimize congestion and to ensure safety both for the artefacts on display and for visitors, since many historic buildings have winding, uneven staircases and their many dark corridors can disorient tourists.

Although the contemporary managers of a historic building operate within the physical constraints of its structure, usually heavily protected by conservation rules, they are able to influence their visitors' experiences through the design and resourcing of the visit strategy, that is, to adopt a 'visitor ethic':

> It is important in trying to cater, or 'care' for the visitor, that every step along the way is considered as part of a strategy or *visitor management plan*. Each element is important and a lack of caring, whether it be in the signing, car parking, quality of catering, or the cleanliness of the toilets, can destroy the overall visitor experience. (Parkin et al, 1989: 109, *original italics*).

In most historic buildings, visitors are either accompanied by a guide or encounter custodians located in each major exhibit area. Service management theory recognizes the importance of encounters between staff and clients (Bowen and Schneider, 1985). In castles, these points of contact are important in providing visitors with information to help them enjoy their visit, but also ensure that every visitor follows the predetermined sequence through the building's internal spaces and exhibits. Tourists also come into contact with staff at catering and retail outlets, and when participating in any of the activities which form an increasing feature of visits to historic buildings and their grounds, including displays of traditional skills such as archery or falconry, or crafts, and attending musical or other performances.

Conceptualizing the management of heritage site visits through service blueprinting

This approach focuses attention on the 'moments of truth' (Carlzon, 1991; Normann, 1991) in which the customer judges the quality of his or her experience, and on ways in which deviations from the standards specified for a service may be managed both within the service design concept, and more generally through organizational approaches such as the empowerment of contact staff. Acceptance of the sequential and sometimes fragmented way in which services are experienced leads to analysis of the various phases in the service experience by techniques such as structural modelling (Yale, 1993) and service blueprinting (Laws, 2000; Shostack, 1985).

The set of decisions required to manage service delivery systems can be conceptualized as resulting in components in a customer's overall experience (Lehtinen, 1985). In the case study that follows, service blueprinting was adopted as the main technique to gain an understanding of visitor management at Leeds Castle.

A service blueprint records and maps the events and processes which the customer experiences. At its core is the view advanced by Shostack (1985) that a service can benefit from design techniques as a basis for its management. In essence, a service blueprint is a diagram that shows all the elements that go to make up the service being studied: its purpose is to enable the service to be analysed as objectively as possible. Shostack herself suggested that a service blueprint should have three main features. First, it must incorporate within the design a time dimension, enabling the researcher to follow the progression of the service delivery system that the customer experiences. Second, it should show the main functions that together comprise the service, and show their interconnectedness. Shostack argued that the third feature of a blueprint is that it should incorporate performance standards for each stage of the process. A related technique, service mapping, has been described as a process which

> visually defines a service system, displaying each sub-process within the sequence ... the map should revolve around the explicit actions the customer takes to receive the service ... the specific contacts the customer has with contact personnel are mapped, as are the internal services (invisible to the customer) that support contact services. (Berry, 1995: 83).

Service blueprinting can be used in designing a new service, as this is its managers' main opportunity to determine the characteristics of the service offered to customers. It also provides a way of investigating the issues confronting managers of an established service delivery process, identifying the potential for improvements to services or facilities (Kingman-Brundage, 1989). The option of physical redevelopment is not available to heritage managers, who are constrained by the structure of the building and must usually seek improvements to the service aspects of the visit. A feature of service blueprints is their potential to identify failpoints, the parts of a service, which are most likely to cause errors (George and Gibson, 1988). This provides the diagnostic capability of the method; although it may be expensive to implement quality improvements, these costs should be weighed against the expenses of service failure (Lockyer and Oakland, 1981).

Overview of the service blueprint method

Blueprinting requires the researcher to generate two sets of information, and to compare them. First, the customer's perspective can be studied in a number of ways, including observation and participant observation techniques of the sequence and significance of events (Gummesson, 1991). The experiences are recorded by the research team in diary format, and can be shown diagramatically in the form of a flow chart (Figure 5.1).

Drive to site > park car > pay entrance fee > purchase guidebook > join group tour > tour site > purchase souvenirs > purchase refreshments > use toilets > depart.

Figure 5.1 Generalized flow chart of events when visiting a heritage site

The second set of information is also presented as a flow chart (Figure 5.2), showing the sequence of interlinked technical processes undertaken by the organization to prepare the service; these are largely invisible to the customer. Research to establish this can be based on a combination of techniques including direct observation and interviews with managers and staff, thus eliciting the detail of the service delivery concept (Gummesson, 1991).

Figure 5.3 presents the blueprint of visitor experiences at Leeds Castle (discussed further in the ensuing case study). It rotates the visitor and service delivery flow charts, combining them in the form of a service blueprint that enables the researcher to visualize the managerial tasks underlying each phase of the visitor's experience.

> Promote heritage attraction > organize signposting on roads > locate and organize car parks > set entrance charges and staff pay boxes > plan sequence of tours > maintain and display site > select and train guides > organize catering, retailing and toilets.

Figure 5.2 Generalized aspects of managing visits to a heritage site

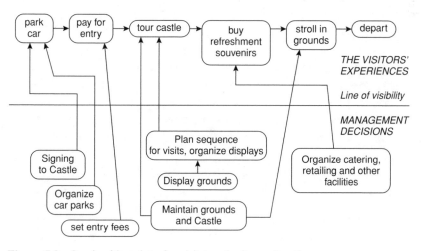

Figure 5.3 Service blueprint of a visit to a heritage attraction

Case study: Leeds Castle

Leeds Castle is one of Britain's leading historic attractions, and is often featured prominently in English Tourist Board and other high profile international promotions. Its striking design and its location in a beautiful lake and country park provide a unique setting for many cultural and other events attracting local, national and international audiences. The entrance to the castle grounds is adjacent to the main motorway linking London with continental Europe, providing easy access for day excursionists from a vast catchment area, as well as the potential of being a stopping point for motorists travelling between Europe and Britain.

The origins of the castle date from Saxon times, when a wooden manor was built for the royal family near the village of Leeds in Kent. After the Norman conquest of England in 1066, the country was subdued by the construction of stone castles, and Robert de Crevecoeur started to build his castle on the present site around 1119. A century and a half later, his great-great grandson fought unsuccessfully against King Henry III at the Battle of Lewis (1246), and was later obliged to yield the castle to Sir Roger de Leyburn, a supporter of the king. In 1287, his son conveyed Leeds Castle to 'the august prince and my most dear Lord Edward the noble King of England and my fair Lady Elinor Queen of England' (Leeds Castle Foundation, 1994: 8).

After parking their cars or leaving their coach, visitors enter the grounds through the ticketing point with adjacent shops, refreshment and toilet facilities, before proceeding to the castle. Visitors can then undertake any of the activities available, in whatever sequence appeals to them, although within the castle their visit follows a strict sequence. This case study concentrates on the management of visitor experiences to the castle itself, and does not deal with the other features of a typical visit such as the maze and grotto, the aviary, the vineyards, or the Culpeper Garden.

Visitor satisfaction management at Leeds Castle

The research on which this case is based has been reported in detail elsewhere (Laws, 1998; 1999). The methodology combined visit diaries, enhanced by previous knowledge of the castle, as background to a semi-structured interview with the managing director of Leeds Castle Enterprises Ltd. The objective of the interview was to validate each item in the visit diaries as being one that other visitors had remarked on as a factor influencing visit satisfaction. The managing director was asked to give rationales for each item, these are summarized in the following list. Following this interview, the notes taken were content analysed, and the 19 separate points identified in the satisfaction diaries were condensed into key factors in the service design, a technique advocated by Ramaswamy (1996). This indicated four key areas for management decisions: a visitor's approach to the castle, signing, interpretation, and visitor flow management.

1 *The approach to the castle*: the castle was opened to paying visitors in 1974, when Leeds Castle Foundation was established. At the outset, it was decided that views of the castle and its lake, set in spacious lawns, were to be sacrosanct. From this, it followed that the car parks and most visitor amenities were located a considerable distance from the castle. A notice is printed on entrance tickets, and the walk is well signposted. A duckery and attractive gardens were constructed to soften and enliven the walk, with strategically located benches, and special transport was provided in the grounds for the elderly, or disabled. However, the use of wheelchairs inside the castle itself is limited to three at any one time because of the many narrow staircases.

2 *Signing*: signs in the grounds are kept to a minimum and are presented in a consistent style, using red or grey lettering on a cream background. However, as people often fail to read the information provided, there is a need for staff to be available to talk to visitors. At Leeds Castle, the ideal is for visitors to see a member of staff at every turning point. All staff are encouraged to interact with visitors, but for some gardeners this may be less easy. They are primarily employed for their trade skills, although some enjoy talking about their skills with visitors who are often very interested in the carefully designed and tended gardens which are also home to the national collections of catmint and bergamot.

Leeds Castle has a higher staff to visitor ratio than most historic attractions, all contact staff are paid on one rate, £3.65 per hour in 1997, the rate is reviewed annually in September. There are about 200 part-time and casual staff, each working two to three days per week. A potential problem at the time this study was undertaken was the proposed introduction of a higher minimum wage, by the European Union. It was anticipated that this could result in higher entry charges.

3 *Interpretation of Leeds Castle*: there is very little signage within the castle, as it is a policy that signs would intrude on the visitors' enjoyment of the building and its contents, giving visitors more the impression of a museum than a lived in house. During normal visiting hours, staff are stationed in each main room or area of the castle and are expected to be proactive, responding to visitors' interests rather than reciting factual information by rote. This system enables people to move through the various parts of the castle at a pace dictated by their own interests, some spend more time in the displays of the heraldry room, others are more attracted by other areas such as the furnishings of the drawing room or the Thorpe Hall room. The castle is regularly opened early for pre-booked coach parties and for special interest groups, and in these cases visitors are guided through the castle by staff using their more specialized knowledge, and if required, in a foreign language.

The Leeds Castle guidebook is now available in nine languages as 50 per cent of visitors are from overseas. One in seven visitors purchase a copy on entry at the ticket boxes, the large print run means that it is profitable at £2.50 per copy: although £250 000 is tied up in three years' stock. The guidebook is particularly useful when visiting the grounds where there are fewer staff, but also helps expand visitor enjoyment and understanding within the castle.

4 *Flow of visitors through the castle*: the structure of old buildings such as Leeds Castle is not ideal for large numbers of visitors, and it was essential that they all followed one route through the building. From the first day of opening the castle to the public, it was decided that visitors would enter through the Norman cellars, thus gaining pleasure from the unique exterior view of the Gloriette rising from the lake. The visit then proceeds in chronological order through the castle. Visitors have no choice but to follow the prescribed route: unobtrusive rope barriers are placed to guide them.

Conclusion

Each heritage site presents a unique challenge in managing it for visitor satisfaction, reflecting its structure, original purposes, state of preservation and its contemporary function (many ancient buildings open to the public are also private homes). Service management theory can inform the decisions of heritage managers to operate in ways that contribute to visitor enjoyment, and help in ensuring that a site is managed in ways that are sensitive to its special character.

The second chapter in this section extends the discussion to a consideration of the quality issues resulting from interactions between visitors to heritage attractions and the local communities' heritage and culture.

Questions

1 Describe the sequence of events you have experienced when visiting a heritage visitor attraction.
2 Identify and discuss the service features of a successful heritage visitor attraction you are familiar with.
3 Draft a report to the managers of the heritage visitor attraction you discussed visitor satisfaction.

References and further reading

Berry, L. (1995). *On Great Service, a Framework for Action*. Free Press.

Bitner, M. (1992). Servicescapes: the impact of physical surroundings on customers and employees. *Journal of Marketing*, **56**, April, 57–71.

Bowen, D. E. and Schneider, B. (1985). Boundary spanning role employees and the service encounter: some guidelines for management and research. In *The Service Encounter: Managing Employee/Customer Interaction in Service Business*. (J. A. Czepiel, M. R. Soloman and C. F. Surprenant, eds). Lexington Books.

Brown, T., Churchill, G. and Peter, J. (1993). Improving the measurement of service quality. *Journal of Retailing*, **69**(1), 127–139.

Carlzon, J. (1991). *Moments of Truth*. Harper and Row.

Carman, J. (1990). Consumer perceptions of service quality, an assessment of the SERVQUAL dimension. *Journal of Retailing*, **66**(1), 33–53.

Cowell, D. (1986). *The Marketing of Services*. Heinemann.

Edgar, D. (1997). The principles of yield management: economic aspects. In

Yield Management, Strategies for the Service Industries (I. Yeoman and A. Ingold, eds). Cassell.

Engel, J. F., Blackwell, R. D. and Miniard, P. W. (1986). *Consumer Behaviour*. Dryden Press.

Fick, G. and Ritchie, J. (1991). Measuring service quality. *Journal of Travel Research*, **30**(2), 2–9.

Garvin, D. A. (1988). *Managing Quality, the Strategic and Competitive Edge*. Free Press.

George, W. R. and Gibson B. E. (1988). Blueprinting: a tool for managing quality in organizations. QUIS Symposium at the University of Karlstad, Sweden, August.

Gronroos, C. (1990). *Service Management and Marketing, Managing the Moments of Truth in Service Competition*. Lexington Books.

Gummesson, E. (1991). *Qualitative Methods in Management Research*. Sage.

Gummesson, E. (1993). *Quality Management in Service Organization, an Interpretation of the Service Quality Phenomenon and a Synthesis of International Research*. ISQA.

Hollins, G. and Hollins, B. (1991). *Total Design, Managing the Design Process in the Service Sector*. Pitman.

Kimes, S. E. (1994). Perceived fairness of yield management. *Cornell H.R.A. Quarterly*, February.

Kingman-Brundage, J. (1989). Blueprinting for the bottom line. In *Service Excellence: Marketing's Impact on Performance*. AMA Chicago.

Lalonde, B. J. and Zinszer, P. H. (1976). *Customer Service: Meaning and Measurement*. NCPDM.

Laws, E. (1986). Identifying and managing the consumerist gap. *Service Industries Journal*, July, 131–143.

Laws, E. (1998). Conceptualising visitor satisfaction management in heritage settings: an exploratory blueprinting analysis of Leeds Castle, Kent. *Tourism Management*, **19**(6), 545–554.

Laws, E. (2000). *The Design, Analysis and Improvement of Tourism Service Systems*. Segamore, Illinois (in press).

Leeds Castle Foundation (1994). *Leeds Castle*. Philip Wilson.

Lehtinen, J. (1985). Improving service quality by analysing the service production process. Research report, University of Stockholm.

Locke, E. A. and Scweiger, D. M. (1979). Participation in decision making, one more look. In *Research in Organisational Behaviour*, vol 1 (B. M. Staw, ed.), JAI Press.

Lockyer, K. G. and Oakland, J. S. (1981). How to sample success. *Management Today*, July.

Masberg, B. A. and Silverman, L. H. (1996). Visitor experiences at heritage sites, a phenomenological approach. *Journal of Travel Research*, **34**(4), Spring, 20–25.

Normann, R. (1991) *Service Management: Strategy and Leadership in Service Businesses*. Wiley.

Parasuraman, A., Zeithaml, V. A. and Berry, L. (1985). A conceptual model of service quality and its implications for future research. *Journal of Marketing*, **49**, Fall.

Parkin, I., Middleton, P. and Beswick, V. (1989). Managing the town and city for visitors and local people. In *Heritage Interpretation* (D. L. Uzzell, ed.) vol. 2, pp. 108–114, Belhaven.

Ramaswamy, R. (1996). *Design and Management of Service Processes*. Addison Wesley.

Robinson, S. (1999). Measuring service quality, current thinking and future requirements. *Marketing Intelligence and Planning*, **17**(1), 21–32.

Saleh, F. and Ryan, C. (1992). Conviviality: a source of satisfaction for hotel guests? An application of the SERVQUAL model. In *Choice and Demand in Tourism* (P. Johnson and B. Thomas, eds), Mansell.

Sasser, E. W., Olsen, P. R. and Wycoff, D. D. (1978). *Management of Service Operations*. Allyn and Bacon.

Shostack, L. (1985). Planning the service encounter. In *The Service Encounter, Managing Employee/Customer Interaction in Service Business* (J. A. Czepiel, M. R. Soloman and C. F. Surprenant, eds), Lexington Books.

Teas, K. (1994). Expectations as a comparison of standards in measuring service quality, an assessment and reassessment. *Journal of Marketing*. **58**(1), 132–139.

Tribe, J. and Snaith, T. (1998). From SERVQUAL to HOLSAT: holiday satisfaction in Varadero, Cuba. *Tourism Management*, **19**(1), 25–34.

Wilkie, W. L. (1986). *Consumer Behaviour*. Wiley.

Yale, P. (1991). *Tourist Attraction to Heritage Tourism*. ELM Publications.

Zeithaml, V. A., Parasuraman, A. and Berry, L. A. (1990). *Delivering Quality Service*. Free Press/Macmillan.

Zemke, R. and Schaaf, P. (1989). *The Service Edge, 101 Companies that Profit from Customer Care*. NAL Penguin.

6

Management of cultural and heritage destinations

Eric Laws

Introduction

However attractive and interesting its heritage might be, a place or a site can only become a destination for modern tourism as a result of two sets of related activities. One is the development of facilities that cater to the needs of tourists including site presentation and interpretation. The second requirement is that effective marketing must be carried out in the areas from which tourists originate. The challenge to sites in an era of global travel and investment is to retain their authentic identity, yet incorporate modern visitor management practices.

Tourism produces pressures to conform to internationally accepted standards of site presentation and interpretation, and also for the wider destination area to meet visitor expectations for accommodation standards, transport, food hygiene and general safety. This produces a tendency to commodify heritage site experiences through marketing and as a result of site interpretation strategies. These approaches are discussed in the light of another stream of research investigating heritage site visitor motivations, and a synthesis is proposed based on managerial objectives for heritage site operations.

While individual heritage attractions present unique problems in their management for visitor satisfaction, other stakeholder groups are affected as the scale of heritage attraction increases. Rojek and Urry (1997: 3–5) point out that 'tourism and culture now plainly overlap . . . tourism as a cultural practice and set of objects is highly significant or emblematic within contemporary "Western" societies organised around mass mobility.' A case study of management issues and practices in a historic city provides the basis for an analysis of these issues.

The value of heritage tourism sites

The ability of cultural and heritage places or artefacts to attract tourists, and the commercial benefits which resulted, were already well understood in antiquity. Casson (1994: 229–36) has recounted how the statue of Zeus:

> competed with Praxitiles' Aphrodite for the distinction of being the most famed work of art of the ancient world. (It) was in Cnidus . . . a wealthy king once offered to pay off the city's entire public debt in exchange for it. The Cnidians turned him down (because) the statue . . . attracted droves of tourists to the island yearly.

Contemporary research confirms the economic value of heritage and cultural tourism. People with an interest in Virginia's rich heritage were found to stay longer and to spend more than other visitors: 'heritage travellers did more of everything: more activities, sites, cities and towns' (Virginia Tourism Corporation, 1997: 3).

Developing heritage sites for tourism

Mallam (1989) has pointed out that costs are incurred in making heritage resources available for visitor enjoyment: the site has to be made safe to visit, equipped with signage and interpretation to assist visitors in understanding its significance, provided with ancillary services such as car and coach parking, all-weather access roads and internal footpaths, catering and toilet facilities. To achieve this level of development requires capital investment, staffing and management. At this stage of development the site is usually fenced, and pay booths are installed in order to collect entrance fees to defray the costs of its operation. This stage in the development of a heritage site is often controversial, as it represents recognition of

> the maintenance, development and management of the public property which forms a substantial component of the attraction for tourists (natural heritage, cultural heritage, the ambience of a historic town etc) and which is considered a 'free good' in economic terms, i.e. one which is not taken into account in evaluating the impact of tourism and its costs. (Grant et al., 1998)

Some development costs associated with presenting heritage sites as tourist attractions occur at all scales and complexity of site, and at all levels of visitation. The early stage of development can be illustrated by the Burke and Wills Dig Tree. This is located in a remote part of far southwest Queensland, and still bears a message carved in its bark in 1861, telling the two explorers that food supplies were buried a few metres away. Burke and Wills died a few kilometres from the tree, after being the first recorded explorers to cross the Australian continent from south to north.

> A living part of Australia's history has been fenced off by a pastoral company and people now have to pay to see it ... Although isolated, the Dig Tree is a favourite among 4WD travellers. The property manager defended the $10 fee and estimated it cost about $30,000 a year to maintain the site that was visited by about 2000 vehicles a year. 'We want to maintain the site for future generations ... There has been a lot of rubbish left behind ... there have been cases of vandalism ... The fee would include overnight camping. It would cost between $10,000 and $20,000 to construct a toilet and shower amenities. (Edmonds and Lawrence, 1998: 24)

The development of heritage sites for paying visitors brings them into the domain of the consumer market. Consumption of the culture of a place can be justified on three economic grounds: it is a driver of economic regeneration; it funds site preservation and development; and it may be less damaging than alternative uses, or neglect.

Commodification and the marketing of heritage tourism sites

It is a basic premise of marketing that the needs and expectations of consumers must be understood in developing and presenting products. However, despite the appeal of exotic cultures and histories, one of the characteristics of the tourism industry has been a marked tendency to commoditize products, experiences and destinations. Williams and Shaw (1992) consider that commodification of place occurs in one of two ways: by controlling access to a site so that a rent can be collected from visitors; or by commodification of other aspects of the visit, either essential tourist services such as hotels and restaurants, or the site-markers which tourists purchase there to take home. A similar trend is apparent in heritage tourism. Jansen-Verbeke (1997: 2), has noted that:

> convergency on the demand side and standardisation of products on the supply side fit well into the current views on and the practice of economies of scale. This also explains why the option of diversification and divergency in tourist product development, with an emphasis on uniqueness and cultural identity of resources, places and people is regarded as the more risky option.

Despite the diversity of supply and demand in European cultural tourism, there is a widespread convergence of cultural tourism development and marketing policies. Richards (1996: 311–12) explained this in terms of 'the changing relationship between cultural consumption and production' and the growing competition for 'the consumption power of the service class . . . and . . . the mobile consumer'.

Traditionally, tourism marketing has been viewed as the development of attractions and facilities in a destination, linked to the promotion of holidays which will satisfy tourists. In contrast, societal marketing is an approach that respects and protects the integrity of the culture and environment of the destination, while satisfying the needs of tourists (Christie Mill, 1996). Societal marketing differs from traditional marketing in several key respects:

- a shift from increasing demand to altering its character and managing its flow
- providing meaning and fulfilment rather than emphasizing facilities and services
- shifting from standardized tourism to distinctive experiences
- respecting rather than exploiting the environment
- adaptation rather than general solutions
- a long-term view
- an optimization approach in place of maximization
- network rather than a hierarchical approach viewing employees as hosts (based on Christie Mill, 1996; Jansen-Verbeke, 1997; Poon, 1993.

Its approaches are very relevant for destinations which actively promote their heritage and cultural attractions. The philosophy emphasizes the meaning of the place, and the objectives are to enhance visitor experiences and to develop a long-term approach to managing the special features of the place.

Heritage tourism site management philosophies

Despite the economic benefits of heritage tourism, the heritage of a place should not be seen merely as an economic asset for the present. It is part of the cultural stock of the community, and a number of issues are apparent from this perspective. Tensions may arise between visitors with a temporary and casual interest in the locality's heritage and the residents for whom that heritage is the basis of their own culture. Seale (1996: 487) has noted certain requirements if an area is to become a significant tourist destination, generating benefits for a small community.

> First, heritage professionals involved in the identification, planning, development and operation of the site must accept an all encompassing definition of historical/cultural heritage. Second, because a culture's (aboriginal) perspective of historic and cultural significance are of great importance in the selection of heritage resource, the people in question must be meaningfully involved in the entire process.

Ashworth (1993) has argued that the success of heritage tourism often threatens the survival of those assets on which it is based. Hewison (1989) referred to the 'manufacturing' approach to the heritage industry, criticizing narrow commercial perspectives that result in a shallow consumerist appreciation of complex matters. The distortion results from two main factors, the need to present the past in visually exciting ways to be successful in a commercial sense, and from the need to be selective in what is chosen for presentation. He cited the Jorvik Centre in York, which represents the area's Viking era through the use of sophisticated lighting, people movers and artificial smells and sounds thought to be evocative of the era. The presentation lacks authenticity and, although it provides an enjoyable location to visit, the issues of the time and the complex realities of the daily life portrayed have been trivialized.

Managers are faced with the challenge of preserving the structural and aesthetic features of heritage sites. One approach is to 'harden' the site to make it able to withstand the physical impacts of visitors (Hall and McArthur, 1993) by techniques such as designated walkways or closing areas by barriers.

The purpose is to keep visitors separated from sensitive areas, and also to help them appreciate the delicate nature of the environment. However, the style of presentation adopted may alienate the traditional, more knowledgeable visitors who resent the way the site is being presented. In some cases, inappropriate materials may be used for paths and barriers or incongruous interpretation facilities installed, further increasing a sense that the significance of the site has been reduced to a spectacle for enjoyment.

Another approach is to enhance the appreciation of visitors for a heritage site's intrinsic values through interpretation and the quality of its presentation. A key feature distinguishing the heritage sector from other forms of tourism to an area is the emphasis on site interpretation and visitors' interest in learning about it. However, an appropriate style must be used for the interpretative commentary.

> One could imagine a tourist interpretation as being selective, both in its content and in its appearance . . . a well defined and synoptic description of the artefact's characteristics, always in relation to its quality as a tourist attraction . . . made in such a way as to simplify without detracting from the substance or from the value of the artefact . . . presenting . . . its social and cultural importance and the social influences . . . that are revealed in it. (Daskalakis, 1984: 27–8)

Pelaggi (1996) and Timothy (1997) consider that the tourist's individual experience of the site is what determines their notion of its authenticity. Similarly, Teo and Yeoh (1997: 199) cite Ashworth and Tunbridge (1990):

> While authenticity derives from the intrinsic aesthetic or historic value of an object/place for its sake, heritage derives its meaning from the user.

Visits to authentic heritage sites such as palaces or castles are increasingly marketed as enjoyable activities during which historical places and artefacts can be seen, but many modern commercial attractions also promote the theme of enjoying history. Thus, the marketplace for heritage related visits is increasingly contested by sites offering varying degrees of authenticity and with differing managerial objectives, values and resources. It is ironic that authentic sites are generally the least well endowed financially, yet the motivations and expectations of many visitors to authentic heritage sites are at least partly derived from their experiences at visitor attractions which are purely commercial in their focus and which can afford sophisticated and exciting presentations.

Bennet (1988) has noted the problematic gap between heritage professionals and consumers with regard to perceptions and evaluations of heritage products. She discussed interactive technology as one way of adapting the product, allowing visitors to choose freely the media they can best relate to. Table 6.1 presents a typology summarizing the discussion of heritage visitor motivations, and suggests site management approaches appropriate to each group, although it should be noted that many sites seek to cater to a range of visitor motivations.

Discussion

The rapid increase in tourism during the second half of the twentieth century has been noted by many authorities, growth of the industry has been accompanied by a diversification in the forms in which tourism is organized. In particular, there has been a polarization between mass tourism with its often hard, high-impact consequences for destination areas and alternative forms that are considered to offer more potential for harmonious interaction with destination areas and residents. Heritage tourism appeals to those who advocate protection of the integrity and environments of a destination. While providing opportunities for the development of facilities and a basis for the promotion of the area in ways which will satisfy many tourists, these forms also meet some of the criteria suggested for societal destination marketing, as was noted earlier.

Table 6.1   Heritage visitor motivations and the management of sites

Main motivation for heritage site visit	Managerial approach	Examples
Formal learning	Interpretation; site presentation; trained guides; emphasis on authenticity	Interpretative signing, guides trained in heritage, discreet lighting, period furnishings
Curiosity; informal learning	Simple interpretation, development of other attractions and activities	Signing, visitor flow management, themed exhibits evoking period style, souvenirs relevant to heritage site
Entertainment; enjoyment	Development of site to maximize commercial opportunities	Themed activities and restaurants, extensive retailing and catering facilities, programme of varied exhibitions and events to attract visitors

However, with regard to heritage sites and an area's culture primarily as assets for the tourism industry to be developed and exploited for commercial gain, there is a risk that their social significance will be minimized. Richter (1997: 1) warns that heritage

> appear(s) to be a potentially important source of national identity, a form of political communication and socialisation ... Benign, militaristic, jingoistic or 'Disneyfied,' the heritage tourist experience may also help form attitudes and values that shape individual orientations towards groups, institutions and issues. Even the very substance of a heritage is a political construction of what is remembered – different for many groups in society.

As the heritage and culture sectors of tourism continue to evolve and to attract large numbers of visitors with varying levels of knowledge and interest, it becomes increasingly important to ensure that management policies contribute to the protection of these fundamental aspects of civilization, their development and presentation as tourist resources, and their enjoyment by visitors. Table 6.2 draws together many of the points discussed so far in this chapter.

Tourism in historic cities

Cities rank among the cultural treasures of civilization, occupying strategic sites, presenting the attractions of varied streetscapes with religious, military, civic and domestic buildings spanning several centuries. They provide entertainment and artistic outlets for the surrounding population, and function as

Table 6.2   Philosophies of tourist heritage site operation

Managerial objectives for heritage site operation	Style of interpretation	Style of site presentation
Authenticity; preservation	Scientific, informative, a variety of emphases and methods	Conservative, unobtrusive.
Commercialization	Popular, simple, flow management and revenue opportunities	Heritage as a setting for paid activities and events staged to attract visitors

administrative and shopping centres. These attributes, combined with cities' nodal role in local area transport networks make many cities and towns magnets for tourists (Ashworth and Tunbridge, 1990; Murphy, 1997; Page, 1995), particularly when they are marketed appropriately (Kotler et al., 1993; Law, 1993).

The culture and heritage of historic cities have long been known to contribute to their appeal as a tourist destination. More specifically, three conditions are necessary for a city to succeed as a heritage centre for tourism: it needs a number of attractive and reasonably well preserved buildings from a range of historical periods; these should be used for activities consistent with tourism (not, for example, as a prison); and the city should have played a significant role in national or local history (Urry, 1990). Murphy (1997: 1) points out that 'urban tourism has become a major trip purpose', and he focused analysts' attention on the ways in which tourism uses the community as a resource, and in turn affects the lives of everyone.

Tourists and other city space users

The concentration of large numbers of people in a small geographic area has always imposed significant management and policy problems for cities, not least in terms of the maintenance of the health and economic welfare of residents and their visitors (Ashton, 1992). In contemporary society, cities face a variety of pressures including demographic trends, changing preferences for city centre or urban living, and transportation, retailing and tourism developments, (Jacobs, 1972; Le Pelley and Laws, 1998; Leontidou, 1990; Soane, 1993). A number of issues arise for policy makers seeking a balance of benefits for a city's main stakeholder groups, the tourists themselves, residents and the business community. These problems are exacerbated by the complex and often urgent conservation or restoration needs of many historic cities (Godfrey, Goodey and Glasson, 1994; Le Pelley, 1994).

The different users of city spaces include heritage tourists, residents who choose to spend part of their leisure time in the city; visitors on family or business visits; and non-recreating residents using the city spaces in the normal course of their lives. Each of these groups has a different pattern of behaviour, and makes somewhat different use of the city's spaces (Ashworth and Tunbridge, 1990). On the other hand, visitors share many basic needs with a city's habitual space users, including parking, restaurants, cafés, toilets and shopping, but the numbers of tourists increase the pressure on these facilities beyond the level which is required to provide services to the inhabitants, thus increasing the area's dependency on tourist spending.

Problems also arise because tourists are temporary visitors and, therefore, they are often are unfamiliar with a particular destination, they have limited time at their disposal, but many shared general interests. As a result, they tend to cluster around specific heritage attractions. This concentration of tourists provides opportunities for businesses such as catering and retailing, but also results in localized congestion. Tourists are often conducted to the main sites in groups (whose size is usually determined by the capacity of the coaches in which they travel) and this acerbates pressures around honeypot sites. Other tourists wish to wander, stopping to gaze at varied features of the city scape and its heritage, but in so doing they may intrude into spaces which residents regard as 'private', creating tensions between these groups (MacCannell, 1976; Urry, 1990).

Case study: Canterbury

In the challenges to tourism facing Canterbury, Le Pelley and Laws (1998) have drawn attention to the general issues facing Europe's walled historic cities. These cities are by nature compact. For example, Canterbury is less than half a mile in diameter; consequently, the different patterns of space usage overlap significantly, resulting in congestion and conflict. The historic walls themselves are a significant constraint on the potential for structural change. In other cities such as Bruges where the walls have disappeared, the historic street layout and the presence of such features as a moat continues to act as a controlling factor on the economic life of the city.

Canterbury is one of the most important historic cities in Britain. Its key role in Europe's Christian heritage, and its strategic location near the English Channel gateways linking Britain with the European continent, make it one of Britain's main tourist centres. Canterbury City Council, and its predecessors, have been actively involved in tourism since pilgrims were attracted in large numbers immediately after the murder of St Thomas Becket on 29 December 1170. Its original 'touristic' importance was celebrated in Chaucer's *Canterbury Tales*, first published in 1380.

The city has only 36 621 residents but it receives in excess of 2 million day visitors annually, and over 500 000 visitors staying overnight (*Canterbury District Tourism Profile*, 1994). The rate of increase has risen from an average increase of 50 000 per year over the last 20 years to an estimated 100 000 annual increase in 1995, primarily in the form of groups making day visits by coach. The consequences can be understood from the combined perspectives of the tourist destination life cycle (Butler, 1980), and the causation theory of visitor–resident irritants (Doxey, 1975). Canterbury may be approaching the peak of its life cycle, as the large number of visitors is beginning to drive local people away from the city centre.

The council has long considered it important to provide a good experience for all visitors in the expectation that they will encourage friends and relatives to come. Their approaches have included promotional activities, visitor surveys, and the development and implementation of programmes for visitor management and visitor amenity improvements. However, by the late 1980s, it had become apparent that a piecemeal approach was no longer sufficient, and a more systematic approach to the long-term management of Canterbury's tourism industry was made more urgent by a number of impending developments. The catalyst for change in the South East of Britain was the construction of the Channel Tunnel (progressively opened to services during 1994 and 1995), and an accompanying series of major improvements to the area's roads. Improved access held the promise of more visitors in the area, but also implied a threat to Canterbury's tourism industry from a range of competing destinations in Kent, the Nord Pas de Calais, and further afield.

Visitor management initiatives in Canterbury

A sensitive approach is required to the key problem in Canterbury, the physical constraints imposed by its narrow medieval street patterns and its buildings. In order to develop a sustainable policy approach to Canterbury's tourism, the city council set up a partnership with the commercial sector, amenity groups, the cathedral, the county council and a local college. The Canterbury City Centre Initiative (CCCI) has been established as a legal entity which aims to develop a sustainable management strategy for tourists and shoppers which complements the qualities of life of Canterbury's residents by involving the tourist trade and residents in its evolution.

The CCCI has four main objectives:

1 To identify and respond to the needs of residents and visitors.

2 To stimulate the prosperity of the business community.

3 To add value to the experience of visiting Canterbury.

4 To preserve the character of the city.

As a result of forecasts during the early 1990s of an increase in coach group visits, it was decided to move the coach park. The only available large site, capable of holding in excess of 100 coaches, was on the east of the city centre. Logistically, this is not the ideal location as the main coach arrivals to the city come from the west. The new coach park was seen as a temporary solution while a more permanent arrangement was investigated. Nevertheless, it presented an opportunity to test the efficacy of various visitor management techniques, and to see whether good quality facilities would attract coach drivers to the new coach park: it is hoped that they will no longer drop passengers illegally in the streets. The effectiveness of the four tourist trails is also being evaluated, as is the contribution made by the Shepherds to the success of Canterbury's visitor management strategies. The project also included the development of a methodology for pre-booking tour coach visits to Canterbury, in collaboration with partner cities Bruges in Belgium and St Omer in France on the development of proactive approaches to tourism hosting strategies. This involves market research, especially on parties arriving from Nord-Pas de Calais, focus groups with schoolteachers in France and coach operators' workshops, held in Bruges, Canterbury and St Omer. The objective is to involve coach tour operators and their drivers in accepting the concept and benefits to be achieved by pre-booking and a move towards general acceptance of the idea that it is not unreasonable for tourists to expect a 20-minute walk to reach the centre of any of Europe's historic towns.

Congestion

Tourists are often unfamiliar with the cities they visit, and they tend to congregate in specific areas. In Canterbury, these are particularly the cathedral precincts and the main shopping street. In the 1960s a bypass was constructed around Canterbury and the High Street was pedestrianized. This has encouraged tourists to spread further afield within the city, rather than limit their visit to the area around the cathedral. Further pedestrianization and additional initiatives are encouraging tourists to experience different areas of the city. In many towns, local traders have objected to the exclusion of vehicles from shopping streets during the day. In a community newsletter, Canterbury City Council justified pedestrianization in the following way, 'The Council has (also) been implementing a policy of pedestrianization and general street refurbishment. This is not a luxury item. It makes sound economic sense to keep the town centre in good order as this is what attracts shoppers to Canterbury'.

The cathedral itself experiences severe pressures from visitors, in response to which it has developed visitor management policies appropriate to a church. The first recorded visitor management task was to ensure that the medieval pilgrims approached St Thomas Becket's tomb on their knees! The contemporary challenge is to ease the flow of visitors around the main points of interest in the cathedral. The religious and architectural importance of the cathedral attracts many school parties, both from Britain and abroad, and these groups were identified as a major cause of complaint by others who used the cathedral. A scheme known as 'Operation Shepherd' was developed to control the entrance of groups, for example by pre-booking group visits in order to limit the impact of groups on worshippers and each other. In the first year, only 13 per cent of groups booked their visit to the cathedral but within two years nearly half of school groups pre-booked.

Stakeholder analysis of the Canterbury initiatives

The quality of a tourism system's operations can be assessed by examining the outcomes for each stakeholder group, (Laws, 1995; Ryan, 1995). Table 6.3 presents a summary of responses to various problems and the improvements made for selected stakeholders in Canterbury's tourism system.

Analysing historic city tourism systems

The complexity of managing tourism in a historic city can be appreciated using perspectives from systems theory. This concept argues that selected inputs are combined in a series of processes with the intention of producing specified outputs, each process stage adding accumulating value to the service. Efficiency in the system's operation can therefore be evaluated by measuring outputs

Table 6.3   Improvements for Canterbury's stakeholders

Stakeholders	Indicative tourism problems	Responses
Stakeholder		Improvements
Residents	Congestion	Attract tourists into less visited areas
Tourists	Congestion	New walks; signing; maps; pedestrianization
	Limited range of attractions	New attractions
Coach operators	Restricted and undeveloped parking	New coach park; Shepherds
Cathedral	Crowds detract from experiences of visitors and worshippers	Shepherding scheme; entrance charges
Environment	Pollution	Air quality monitoring at selected sites; park and ride scheme to reduce cars in city; new location for coach park
	Inappropriate changes to historic buildings	Special planning controls

against the inputs required to produce them, by examining the quality of those outputs, and by considering the way each process contributes to the overall service. Kirk (1995) has noted that although systems thinking has mainly been applied to 'hard' engineering situations, where outcomes are unambiguous and highly predictable, the concept can also be applied in 'soft' situations where human behaviour is a significant factor in business activities which combine social and technical processes (Checkland and Scholes, 1990).

The interdependency of the elements which together make up tourist destinations can best be understood from the perspective of a soft, open, systems model (Checkland Scholes, 1990; Leiper, 1990; Mill and Morrison, 1985). The 'systems' aspect of this type of model has the advantages of focusing attention on all the major inputs needed to provide tourism services, and on the outcomes of tourism processes for all groups with interests in the destination. The 'soft' feature of the approach is concerned with the interactions of tourists and residents in tourist destination areas.

The model is 'open' because it recognizes the legislative, cultural and technological contexts for tourism processes. A further aspect highlighted by this analytical framework is the consequences of tourism for the area's environment. On a theoretical level, systems theory provides a way of focusing the insights from many social sciences on destination processes and their consequences.

Systems theory argues that the efficiency of the destination's operations will be affected by changes to any of the elements of which it is composed. For effective management, three aspects need to be clearly understood:

■ the effects on outputs of any change to its inputs

■ the ways in which its *internal* subsystems and processes are linked

■ how the subsystems and processes are controlled.

Application of a soft, open systems framework to Canterbury

All tourist destination systems consist of elements (or subsystems) in the form of natural or primary attractions such as climate, supported by secondary features such as hotels (Jansen-Verbeke, 1988). Figure 6.1 indicates that, in Canterbury, the primary elements are the historic city itself and particular attractions, especially the cathedral. The secondary elements include hotels, guesthouses and the range of attractions, shopping and catering in the city centre. Additional elements are the information services available to visitors, catering, and car and coach parking. Destination inputs are managerial and technical skills, including recognition in the local planning process of the need for a positive framework for tourism management leading to a continuity of approach, investor's resources, and the expectations and attitudes of its tourists and residents.

The model recognizes the significance of external factors such as changing competitive conditions or improvements to the transport network. The method focuses attention on the outcomes of the system's functioning for particular stakeholder groups during a given time period. Evaluation of the outcomes against the costs of inputs and policy objectives provides the basis of feedback, thus introducing a future-time dimension to the model.

INPUTS	THE CANTERBURY DESTINATION SYSTEM	OUTCOMES	FUTURE
Tourists Expectations	PRIMARY ELEMENTS	IMPACTS Economic Community Environment Ecology	The Canterbury City Centre Intitiative
ENTREPREN- EURARIAL CREATIVITY	Cathedral		
	Historic city centre		
EMPLOYEE SKILLS	SECONDARY ELEMENTS		
INVESTORS CAPITAL	Hotels	STAKEHOLDERS OUTCOMES (selected)	PEACE and
LOCAL AUTHORITY planning	Catering		PATHS projects
	Retailing	Tourists Residents	
Residents' expectations and attitudes	Attractions	Employees Retailers	
	Information services	Coach operators Local authority	
	Parking		
	Infrastructure		
	EXTERNAL INFLUENCES		
	Transport developments Competition Tastes		
	Legislation		
	Tastes Competition Legislation Demographics Politics Transport developments		
Present			

Figure 6.1 A soft, open systems model of tourism in Canterbury

Conclusion

The positive side of the tourism industry is well documented. Tourists' spending can contribute to site and area development by bringing wealth and stimulating employment, enterprise and infrastructure development. The interest which drew tourists to a particular area can encourage the preservation of its unique features of local heritage and culture (as well as giving a persuasive rationale for the protection of natural environments or the ecology of

93

the area) while providing a source of finance to improve access to them for visitors and residents alike.

The sites that attract leisure visitors are highly varied, and each faces a unique set of problems and opportunities. Consequently, it is rather difficult to make generalized statements about heritage visitor attractions which are universally applicable: it is precisely the differences between places, and the individuality of visitors, residents and the heritage and culture of each destination which makes tourism both an exciting human activity and a fascinating field of study.

Questions

1 Compile and pilot test an interview instrument designed to explore the motivations of visitors to heritage attractions.
2 Interview residents near a heritage centre and summarize their views of the benefits and problems resulting from tourism in the area.
3 Draw up and discuss a systems model of a heritage visitor attraction you are familiar with.

References and further reading

Ashton, J. (1992). *Healthy Cities*. Open University Press.

Ashworth, G. (1993). Culture and tourism: conflict or symbiosis in Europe? In *Tourism in Europe, Structures and Developments* (W. Pompl and P. Lowery, eds) pp. 13–35, CAB International.

Ashworth, G. J. and Tunbridge, J. (1990). *The Tourist Historic City*, Belhaven.

Bennet, T. (1988). Museums and the People. In *The Museum Time Machine: Putting Cultures On Display* (R. Lumley, ed.) pp. 63–85, Routledge.

Butler, R. W. (1980). The concept of a tourist area cycle of evolution: implications for management of resources. *Canadian Geography*, **24**(1), 5–12.

Canterbury District Tourism Profile (1994). Canterbury City Council.

Casson, L. (1994). *Travel in the Ancient World*. Johns Hopkins University Press.

Checkland, P. and Scholes, J. (1990). *Soft Systems Methodology in Action*. Wiley.

Christie Mill, R. (1996). Societal Marketing – implications for tourism destinations. *Journal of Vacation Marketing*, **2**(3), 223–237.

Dallen, T. (1997). Tourism and the personal heritage experience. *Annals of Tourism Research*, **24**(3), 225–242.

Daskalakis, G. (1984). Tourism and architectural heritage – cultural aspects. *Proceedings of the 34th AIEST Conference*, Prague, pp. 23–36.

Doxey, G. U. (1975). A causation theory of visitor–resident irritants, methodology and research inferences. *Travel and Tourism Research Association, Conference Proceedings*, San Diego, pp. 195–198.

Economic Development Strategy (1997). Canterbury City Council.

Edmonds, M. and Lawrence, E. (1998). Dig deep or miss history. *Brisbane Sunday Mail*, 20 September.

Godfrey, K. B., Goodey, B. and Glasson, J. (1994). Tourism management in Europe's historic cities. In *Quality Management in Urban Tourism, Balancing Business and Environment* (P. E. Murphy, ed.) pp. 192–202, University of Victoria.

Grant, M., Human, B. and Le Pelley, B. (1996). Canterbury City Centre Initiative: visitor destination management in practice. In *Insights*, English Tourist Board.

Grant, M., Human, B. and Le Pelley, B. (1998). Who pays for the free lunch? Destination management and the 'free good' factor. *Insights*, **9** (January), A95–A101, English Tourist Board.

Hall, M. and McArthur, S. (1993). *Heritage Management in New Zealand and Australia: Visitor Management, Interpretation and Marketing*. Oxford University Press.

Hewison, R. (1989). Heritage: an interpretation. In *Heritage Interpretation: The Natural and Built Environment* (D. L. Uzzell, ed.) pp. 15–22, Belhaven.

Jacobs, J. (1972). *The Economy of Cities*. Pelican.

Jansen-Verbeke, M. (1988). *Leisure, Recreation and Tourism in Inner Cities*. Geographical Studies.

Jansen-Verbeke, M. (1997). *Developing Cultural Tourism in Historical Cities: The Local Challenge in a Global Market*. Discussion paper at the International Academy for Tourism Studies Conference, Melaka.

Kirk, D. (1995). Hard and soft systems: a common paradigm for operations management? *International Journal of Contemporary Hospitality Management*, **7**(5).

Kotler, P., Haider, D. H. and Rein, I. (1993). *Marketing Places*. The Free Press.

Law, C. M. (1993). *Urban Tourism: Attracting Visitors to Large Cities*. Mansell.

Laws, E. (1995). *Tourist Destination Management, Issues, Analysis and Policies*. Routledge.

Le Pelley, B. (1994). Canterbury: managing tourism and heritage. In *Quality Management in Urban Tourism, Balancing Business and Environment* (P. E. Murphy, ed.), proceedings of conference, University of Victoria, Victoria.

Le Pelley, B. and Laws, E. (1998). A stakeholder-benefits approach to tourism management in a historic city centre: the Canterbury City Centre Initiative. In *Embracing and Managing Change in Tourism: International Case Studies* (E. Laws, B. Faulkner and G. Moscardo, eds) pp. 70–94, Routledge.

Leeds Castle Foundation (1994). *Leeds Castle*. Philip Wilson.

Leiper, N. (1990). *Tourism Systems*. Massey University Press.

Leontidou, L. (1990). *The Mediterranean City in Transition*, Open University Press.

MacConnell, D. (1976). *The Tourist: A New Theory of the Leisure Class*. Macmillan.

Mallam, M. (1989). Can heritage charities be profitable? In *Heritage Interpretation: The Natural and Built Environment* (D. Uzzell, ed.) pp. 44–50, Belhaven.

Mill, R. C. and Morrison, A. M. (1985). *The Tourism System*. Prentice Hall.

Moscardo, G. (1996). Mindful visitors, heritage and tourism. *Annals of Tourism Research*, **23**(2), 376–397.

Murphy, P. (ed.) (1997). *Quality Management in Urban Tourism*. Wiley.

Page, S. (1995). *Urban Tourism*. Routledge.

Pelaggi, M. (1996). National heritage and global tourism in Thailand. *Annals of Tourism Research*, **23**(2), 432–443.

Poon, A. (1993). *Tourism, Technology and Competitive Strategies*. CAB International.

Richards, G. (1996). European cultural tourism, trends and future prospects. In *Cultural Tourism in Europe* (G. Richards, ed.) pp 311–333, CAB International.

Richter, L. (1997). The politics of heritage tourism. Paper presented at the International Conference on Tourism Development: Issues for a New Agenda, Melaka.

Rojek, C. and Urry, J. (eds) (1997). *Touring Cultures: Transformations of Culture and Theory*. Routledge.

Ryan, C. (1995). *Researching Tourist Satisfaction*. Routledge.

Seale, R. (1996). A perspective from Canada on heritage and tourism. *Annals of Tourism Research*, **24**(3), 484–488.

Soane, J. (1993). *Fashionable Resort Regions, their Evolution and Transformation*. CAB International.

Teo, P. and Yeoh, B. (1997). Remaking local heritage for tourism. *Annals of Tourism Research*, **24**(1), 192–208.

Timothy, D. (1997). Tourism and the personal heritage experience. *Annals of Tourism Research*, **24**(3), 751–754.

Urry, J. (1990). *The Tourist Gaze*. Sage.

Virginia Tourism Corporation (1997). *Heritage Tourism National Omnibus Study*. Virginia Tourism Corporation.

Williams, A. and Shaw, G. (1992). Tourism research, a perspective. *American Behavioural Scientist*, **36**(2), 133–143.

Yale, P. (1991). *From Tourist Attraction to Heritage Tourism*. ELM Publications.

Part Three

Concept Development

Graham Black

Introduction

The two chapters in this part explore the specific issues involved in developing a concept for a heritage attraction. They are written from the point of view of the heritage professional and so reflect dominant concerns for conservation and the retention of the integrity of the site.

Heritage sites and collections, by their very nature, are assets of immense natural, historical, cultural and social value. For the purpose of these two chapters, the term 'heritage site' has been used in a generic sense to include ancient monuments, cathedrals and churches, collections in museums and galleries, historic houses and gardens, nature reserves etc. and relevant visitor centres.

The chief exclusion from this definition has been those locations whose *primary* function is to make a profit and/or to act as a public relations exercise. Many of the elements covered in the chapters are of direct relevance to these types of presentations. However, a key underpinning factor is normally missing from them – that is, the recognition of the exceptional heritage value of the site (or building, or landscape, or collection, etc.) and, as a corollary to this, an understanding that there is a primary duty of care, a responsibility to protect and preserve the resource for the benefit of this and future generations.

Heritage managers, therefore, view the unique nature of the assets for which they are responsible – and the established concept that we do not 'own' our heritage sites and collections, but hold them in trust for future generations – as a non-negotiable background which conditions the purpose of and approach to their presentation.

Yet no heritage manager can exist in isolation from the 'real' world. There are enormous pressures to increase visitor numbers, both to enhance revenue generation and to reflect and meet the needs of the full range of, particularly, their local population. Most heritage managers also believe strongly in the need to improve the visitor experience and, thereby, enthuse more people about their site or subject – but, equally, they fear being accused of 'dumbing down' the academic content of their site presentation.

There are many similarities, therefore, between the objectives of the heritage manager, those of the general visitor and those of the tourist industry, but also differences in emphasis. While the tourist industry, as Part Two illustrates, places considerable emphasis on quality in service provision, heritage managers ultimately see quality in terms of the opportunity for the visitor to engage directly with the site or collection. This part seeks to illustrate how these differences can be balanced by the use of interpretive techniques. Heritage interpretation *per se* is defined in the second chapter, but its principles, in terms of the development of an audience-led approach, permeate the whole section.

It must be emphasized that quality, in the development of the concept, is first and foremost a management issue, gives primary responsibility to the protection of the site and depends ultimately on good planning. It is also a team effort and must take into consideration the long-term strategy for the site and its operational, curatorial, educational and marketing requirements. However, it remains, ultimately, a creative exercise, evoking in visitors an intuitive 'gut' response – the 'wow' factor – which means they know they have been engaged in something special and have gained something memorable from the experience.

At its simplest, the interpretive approach to the development of a concept is based on an outline *interpretive plan*. This seeks to define:

- *what* you wish to present – specific site/resource issues, themes etc. to be presented
- *why* you wish to develop/change the attraction – specific objectives
- *who* you are targeting the presentation at – nature of target audience, needs of audience; expectations of audience
- *how* you intend to present the attraction – the *concept*.

The concept should be developed as the most appropriate response to the answers you define to the questions What?/Why?/Who?, but will also be influenced by other factors such as the overall policy or ethos of the heritage organization involved, the available budget and the scale and nature of the proposed space.

The objective of these two chapters is not to provide a specific framework for 'How to do it?' This would be impossible, as every site and its audience are unique. Rather, the chapters set out to explore the factors that influence concept design and to define some principles that should assist in ensuring the quality of the end product.

7

Whats, whys and whos of concept design

Graham Black

Introduction

The nature, strengths and weaknesses of the site or collection, the aims and objectives of the responsible organization and an analysis of the projected audience together provide a structured framework for the development of the concept. This chapter sets out to explore each of these factors in turn, concentrating on the impact each has on the concept design.

What?

The development of a concept for the presentation of a heritage site begins with the nature of the site and its management requirements. It must take into account:

1 *The resource audit*: the resource in terms of its natural, cultural, historical and social importance.
2 *Managing the site*: the resource in terms of its protection and in the definition of a realistic future.

3 *Access to the resource*: how best to achieve this while maintaining its integrity and aesthetic appeal and striking an acceptable balance between access and conservation.
4 *Managing the organization* responsible for the resource. This includes definition and management of the budget for the creation of the presentation and meeting operational needs.

Quality in concept development for a heritage attraction must be based on these considerations. Organizational management is considered elsewhere within this book. Operational issues directly relevant to the presentation will be referred to when appropriate. This section will concentrate on quality issues relating to the development of the concept for the presentation of the site.

The resource audit

Having decided that the site or collection should be made accessible to the public, the starting point lies in analysing the special characteristics that define its significance. This is usually approached through the carrying out of a 'resource audit'. In the case of a nature reserve, for example, this would include the identification of its geology, geomorphology and specific animal and plant life. For a monastic site, it would include surviving architecture, ground plans and objects recovered during archaeological excavations, documentary evidence, etc. In a museum, it would be the collections and other support material. Not all of these elements need be physical. The Sherwood Forest Country Park, in Nottinghamshire, for example, is not only an SSSI, including almost 1000 historic oak trees; it is also associated with the tales of Robin Hood, a key element in any resource audit of the site.

The audit should identify not only those aspects of the site seen by its management or curatorial team as being distinctive but also attempt to define the elements most likely to attract a response from the visitor. It plays a central role in defining the objectives for the concept design and is key to the establishment of the main messages, themes and storylines used in the presentation. It also provides a basic inventory or record for the site which can be accessible to all *and* can act as a framework for the conservation strategy which must underpin the presentation.

Managing the site

The primary responsibility in managing a heritage site or collection has to be its *protection*. Any concept for the presentation of a heritage site must establish an approach that balances the needs of visitors today with this primary responsibility of conservation. What we do on or to a site now cannot be allowed to reduce its future value or integrity. The presentation must be seen as part of a co-ordinated approach to the management of the resource.

This ideal has come under increasing pressure since the early 1970s, with a growing emphasis on the need for 'efficient' management (not least the application of commercial criteria rather than public service ones) and, particularly, on the ability of individual sites to raise a much larger percentage of their total running costs. For many heritage managers the pressure to ensure a realistic and, by definition, viable future for their sites has resulted in a disproportionate emphasis on income generation. This has meant not only developing strategies to increase both the numbers of visitors and the spend of each visitor on site, but also seeking to develop other income strands, not least through a special events programme, corporate events and weddings. Increased numbers of visits can cause serious conservation problems. For example, many historic houses now receive more visitors each year than in their entire two or more centuries in private ownership, with an obvious impact on the condition of the historic fabric. As an extreme example of this, Mount Vernon, the home of George Washington, had over 17 000 visitors on the first day of its 1999 season alone!

Inappropriate, or too frequent, events can destroy the atmosphere of the site itself and ruin the experience for the general visitor – try soaking up the atmosphere of a historic site, such as Newstead Abbey in Nottinghamshire, with its connections to the poet Lord Byron, while surrounded by wall-to-wall wedding parties.

However, it has not been all bad news. Increased visitor numbers should mean that the heritage organization has an opportunity to put its message across to audiences from a wider social spectrum than the white, middle-class one normally associated with heritage sites. The pressure to increase numbers has also led frequently to a re-evaluation and subsequent improvement of the visitor experience, starting with the quality of the basic service provision and moving on to improvements in interpretation. This is important in its own right but can also be used by heritage sites and organizations to help to retain and enhance public support for their conservation work and satisfy politicians and other fund-giving bodies of the continuing benefit of public subsidy.

The challenges in the current highly commercial environment are not to lose sight of the underlying conservation needs and to prevent piecemeal encroachment (or 'neglect' in the case of artefacts). This is why concept development must be seen as part of the overall management strategy for the site. The presentational approach should be *part of* the conservation scheme for the site, not fighting against it.

Managing physical access

Access is a physical, emotional and intellectual issue. This section concentrates on factors relating to physical access. Emotional and intellectual aspects, the means by which visitors are assisted to engage directly with the site, will be explored in Chapter 8 through the discussion of heritage interpretation.

For many practitioners, the term 'access' continues to mean the provision of measures to enable people with physical disabilities to enter and use a heritage site and, preferably, follow the same route as all other visitors. This is certainly an important issue, made more so in the UK by the impact of the Disability Discrimination Act 1995, which sets out to give equal rights to disabled people in the areas of employment, obtaining goods and services and buying or renting land or property. Its provisions are being phased in over a number of years. All heritage sites in the UK will have to respond fully to the requirements of the Act by 2005.

Most planning for major heritage presentations now includes the carrying out of an 'access audit' to define present conditions and develop appropriate solutions to ensure equal access for all. In the UK, the Heritage Lottery Fund and the Arts Council Lottery Fund already require full consideration of access for disabled people in grant applications. The author believes this is an issue which is relevant worldwide and would recommend that an 'access adviser', a specialist in this field, is appointed as a full member of the team developing the concept. The adviser's role should go beyond commenting on physical access to include interpretation, marketing, staff training, public programmes and employment. Inclusiveness for the disabled rightly goes well beyond physical access to involve representation within exhibitions and among the staff.

A full analysis of the implications of access for those with disabilities is beyond the scope of these chapters. The Disability Discrimination Act has numerous exemptions, including giving priority to the integrity of an historic building or site over the access requirements of disabled visitors, for example, in not being able to widen historic doorways or install a lift. However it is frequently possible to find creative solutions. Relevant publications, with case studies, are included in the reference section at the end of this chapter.

A key point to note, however, is that improving facilities for disabled visitors normally benefits *all* visitors. For example, the most common disability among heritage site visitors is sight impairment – from those wearing glasses, to the blind. All of us, not just the visually impaired, want to be able to *touch* and enjoy 'hands-on' opportunities. Clear graphics, with the use of a minimum 16-point type size, assist all of us. Good, targeted lighting and no glare or reflections within cases help us all to appreciate exhibits more. The provision of seating is appreciated by everyone, not just those with difficulty walking. Lifts do not only benefit those in wheelchairs. Many visitors, not least parents with buggies, appreciate their presence.

The issue of physical access, however, is not simply about facilities for the disabled. Heritage managers must take into account:

1 *Access to the site*: from the availability of public transport to issues of traffic congestion and parking. The means by which visitors come to the site can have a real impact not only on the immediate environs of the site but also on local communities. For example, if high visitor numbers are anticipated, should the concept consider parking away from the site, with transport, themed or otherwise, to it?

2 *Site carrying capacity, both physical and perceptual*: this includes the threshold at which the quality of the visitor experience is diminished and/or the special 'spirit' of the site is lost; that at which the site itself is put at risk; and the level at which the quality of life of the local community deteriorates. Recent research on different types of carrying capacity has shown that perceptual capacity – that at which visitors feel the site is overcrowded and/or its special spirit lost – may be exceeded long before physical capacity is realized. This is, perhaps, most obviously recognizable in our great cathedrals and in some areas of our national parks. In terms of concept development, physical capacity is a function of site management, but perceptual capacity is largely a function of visitor expectations.

3 *Access to all parts of the site and balancing this against conservation requirements*: for example, if there is likely to be serious overcrowding, should concept proposals include timed tickets – as at English National Trust properties such as Snowshill Manor in Gloucestershire – with a need to occupy visitors elsewhere (in this case in the gardens) while they wait? Or should the manager seek to develop facilities that disperse visitors around more of the site? Chester City Council, for example, faced with a huge concentration of visitors on small sections of its medieval city walls, has developed an interpretation strategy targeted at spreading people more evenly around the whole route. Or should the concept be used to *manage* visitors, taking them away from more sensitive areas or

accepting damage in one area by concentrating visitors there while the rest of the site is largely untouched? These two alternatives are both used frequently in nature reserves and national parks.

Overall, the concept must reflect principles of *sustainability*, meeting the needs of the present visitor without compromising the long-term protection of the site and the needs of future generations.

Why?

The aims and objectives behind the development of a concept for the presentation of a site will be unique to each location or collection. It is essential, however, that they are spelt out clearly as part of the initial brief:

1 It is impossible to develop a concept unless there is a full and approved understanding of what it is meant to achieve, and who will benefit. It is essential that all the different bodies and/or individuals involved in promoting the site agree what the project is for. The aims and objectives provide the basic framework for the project – imagine the impact on the development of a heritage attraction of people with different agendas attempting to pull it in different directions. There is little point in attempting to move forward unless and until the aims are spelt out, realistic and agreed.
2 It is necessary to have clear aims and objectives against which to *evaluate* the concept proposal (see Chapter 8).
3 One of the key definitions of quality in concept development is clarity of message and clarity in the presentation of the message. Unless initial aims and objectives are defined clearly, this is impossible to achieve.

In terms of quality, *aims* should include:

1 The continued conservation and protection of the site itself. This is likely to involve a strategy for managing visitors on the site and for monitoring visitor impact, but links also to influencing visitor behaviour.
2 A definition of the services you seek to provide, in the context of the overall aims of the project. Will there be exhibitions, guided tours, an education service, an information point supporting other facilities in the area, catering and retail facilities? Will the project support research? Will it actively develop collections? Will there be an opportunity for people to become actively involved, for example through a Friends group? Will it disseminate information, and support staff contact with similar sites elsewhere?

105

3 A clear understanding of the outcomes anticipated for the visitor. Beyond providing an enjoyable experience and appealing to all sections of the community, these are likely to include enhancement of the opportunities for both structured and informal learning. However, aims will normally also reflect emotional and behavioural outcomes. The former may include, for example, enhancement of public awareness of the distinctiveness and/or importance of the site or collection or developing pride amongst local people in the special nature of their own area. Behavioural outcomes could include anything from dropping less litter in a nature reserve to supporting the policies of the heritage organization responsible for the site – perhaps encouraging them to become members or even to take an active role in the organization's activities or in conservation in general.

Other aims, linked to the protection of the site, may include the necessity to ensure its financial viability by increasing its visitor attendance and spend. Equally, the site may be seen as having an important role in the economic regeneration of its region by acting as a tourist draw.

Objectives may include:

1 A specific annual audience target, or income target – not simply from admissions but from support activities such as corporate events or Friends' fundraising. For most heritage sites today, spreading the income base beyond admissions is essential.
2 An average length of stay, for example one and a half hours in a city centre site or over three hours if the site is expected to act as a 'stand-alone' attraction.
3 Targeting specific groups within the local community, perhaps as part of an overall strategy of broadening the audience base and combating social exclusion.
4 Defining the education market, for example the potential to attract primary school pupils studying the Key Stage 2 History Study Unit on 'The Victorians' under the UK National Curriculum. You may even set a specific target educational audience.
5 Defining a specific message or messages as the key themes for the presentation.

Who?

One of the great advances of the last 30 years in the planning and management of heritage sites open to the public has been an increasing awareness of the needs, expectations and behaviour of the audience – resulting in an increased sensitivity to these factors in the way sites are presented. Partly, this has been necessitated by the emphasis placed on income generation and the pressure of competition. However, there has also been a genuine desire to enhance visitor enjoyment and understanding, reinforced by rising visitor demands that reflect expectations raised by their experiences at other sites. Whatever the cause, an understanding of the audience is central to any strategy targeted at quality in presentation.

Substantial market research has been carried out on the *nature* of the heritage audience, in terms both of direct surveys at sites and also in the application of more general tourist research. There are, however, still huge gaps in this work, not least in the fields of return or repeat visitors, under 16s and minority groups.

What we are left with, at present, is a classic breakdown into market segments: demographic, geographic, educational groups and special interest groups.

Demographic factors

- Age
- Gender
- Education
- Class/occupation.

Unfortunately, but not surprisingly, published results of this type of analysis, such as Davies (1994), show that, currently, the average heritage visitor is seen as white collar (ABC1), with a high educational achievement. The two genders are relatively equally represented, with perhaps a slight majority of females, although this is dependent on the nature of the site.

People tend to visit in groups, as a social outing, rather than on their own. Most age ranges are represented relatively equally, but with smaller percentages at 16–24 and over 55 years old. Potentially, up to 33 per cent of heritage visitors are under 16, making it highly likely that over 60 per cent of visitors include children in the group – either as families or on organized school trips. Percentages will, however, vary from site to site. For example, there is likely to be a much higher percentage in the older age categories at English National Trust properties, reflecting the trust's membership breakdown.

The evidence available also suggests, however, that the nature of the audience will be influenced by the approach taken to the concept, marketing and operation of the site. It is vital, when planning the concept, to take into account not just the existing audience for the site, or that type of site, but also your objectives in terms of the audience you want to attract. This need not simply be to enhance revenue income. For example, as referred to above, heritage sites in the UK are currently heavily involved in developing strategies to encourage 'access', both physical and intellectual, by those with disabilities, not least as a response to the Disability Discrimination Act 1995. There is also a continuing challenge, particularly for sites that receive public subsidy, to develop support and use by local communities, not least by seeking to overcome aspects of social exclusion.

Geographical factors

- Resident/local, living within 30-minutes' drive time.
- Day-tripper.
- Visitor staying with friends or relatives.
- Tourist – independent, organized party, domestic/international.

Crucially, local people and day-trippers make up a substantial majority of visitors at most heritage sites in the UK, except for those in some of the major tourist destinations, including London. From the limited research available, they represent an even higher percentage of return visitors, reflecting an unwillingness to travel long distances to revisit a site.

The research suggests most visitors prefer to travel no more than one hour to a heritage site. This can vary depending on the scale and popularity of the site and whether it is on a greenfield location with easy access or in a traffic-packed city centre. A market survey of museums in the East Midlands, carried out in 1994–95, one of the largest of its type carried out in the UK, showed that 83 per cent of visitors travelled less than one hour, with 60 per cent travelling less than half an hour (East Midlands Museums Service, 1996).

Much also depends on a tradition of travelling in a certain direction. For example, about 3 million people live within one hour of Nottingham city centre. However, this figure includes many who live in Coventry and north Birmingham. There is no tradition of travelling to Nottingham from these areas and over a decade of marketing effort has failed to make much impact on this situation.

An assessment of visitor potential is one of the most basic elements in defining the concept:

■ to define whether the attraction will be viable
■ to assist in drawing up the revenue budget
■ to ensure that the approach taken to the presentation will cater for the likely visitor numbers and type.

All three of these factors are crucial to the development of the concept:

■ the first to ensure a long-term future
■ the second because the presentation must operate within the available budget – there is no point, for example, in requiring a high staff level if the budget to pay for it is inadequate
■ the third because the concept will influence the speed at which visitors go through the presentation and, therefore, its carrying capacity. The influence of visitor *type* on the concept will be explored in the next chapter.

It is vital to consider not only how many visitors the attraction will receive but also *when* they will come and how long they are likely to stay (or how long you *want* them to stay). Seasonal variation in visitor numbers through the year can be extreme and, in the UK at least, is normally linked closely to school holidays. While Easter Monday is likely to be the busiest day, the peak month is normally August, with 17–20 per cent of the annual total. The worst months are November and December, where 2–3 per cent is not uncommon, reflecting the poor weather and our annual engagement in the purgatory of Christmas shopping. Some sites, however, are beginning to cash in on Christmas: Hampton Court, near London, for example, has Tudor cookery demonstrations, music and late night shopping with special 'seasonal' merchandise.

Space requirements and budgets may well dictate that you cannot plan to cater for the absolute peaks of the bank holidays at Easter and in August. Quality in the development of the concept should, however, ensure that the attraction can cope reasonably comfortably with an average August day. This is made more difficult by the fact that people will not arrive evenly through the day. The peak time is 11.00 a.m. to 12.30 p.m., when 35–40 per cent of the daily total may arrive.

This may mean, for example, developing the concept to reflect *design day* estimates. This begins with an equation such as:

Estimated annual audience = 100 000
Estimated August total (17.5%) = 17 500

Average August week (22.5%) = 3937
Peak day of week (est. 20%) = 787
Peak arrival period (est. 35%) = 275

Can your concept cope with this?

Educational group: structured educational users

'Building in' structured project work will be discussed in the next chapter. In developing the concept, however, you must also consider the impact of educational groups on other visitors – for example, the noise and bustle of a primary school group in a country house; or small children with clip-boards preventing people viewing displays; or the seemingly turbocharged effect of 120 hulking adolescents, representing an entire GCSE group, in small museum galleries.

Most heritage sites are committed to both types of user, and have no choice but to admit them at the same time. For these sites, 'building in' project work can be vital both to enhance the educational value of the visit and to break down educational groups into manageable numbers. However, there may still be a need to restrict educational use to specific days or times, making other potential visitors very aware of these.

Special interest: subject specialist

- Self-directed learning.
- Booked group, e.g. a local history group or a group from National Association of Decorative and Fine Art Societies (NADFAS).

Heritage presentation is not about the creation of displays targeted at the lowest common denominator. While many visitors will have little or no back-ground knowledge of the subject area, the nature of the heritage audience is phenomenally variable. Quality demands both a basic exploration and ease of access to a depth of information, or the full range of a collection etc., for those who wish it.

Audience needs

If we want our visitors to gain from their experience of a heritage site, we must ensure that their *needs* are catered for. Quality requires that users be in the 'right frame of mind' for their visit. Human needs are an important area of study. It is beyond the scope of this chapter to explore the subject in depth. However, because of the ease with which we can apply it to the issue of concept development, the hierarchy of needs originally defined in Maslow (1954) is used as a starting point (Figure 7.1).

There have been considerable developments in the field since Maslow's hierarchy was first published, not least in expanding and extending the range of needs at each ladder level, for example: the need to escape; the need to satisfy curiosity and to seek mental stimulation; the need to explain the world; and the need for peak experiences. See, for example, the brief analysis in Pearce (1995). However, the basic principle for concept development remains that, if we wish visitors to involve and engage themselves with the site/resource and to leave with their understanding and appreciation enhanced, we *must* ensure that the right environment is created to make this possible.

Many of the factors referred to below could be viewed as operational issues rather than as being of direct concern to the developer of the concept, but anyone involved in concept design would be very unwise not to seek to be actively involved in them.

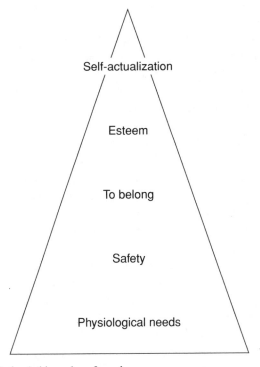

Figure 7.1 Maslow's hierarchy of needs

Physiological needs: our most basic needs are for a comfort break, food and drink, a suitable temperature, seating, etc. If these are not properly catered for, the need can take control of the visitor and make the quality of the site and its presentation irrelevant. This is as important in planning guided tours, for example within a nature reserve (try engaging an audience if they are freezing, soaked or attacked by Scottish midges), as it is for displays in a museum.

Any concept must take into account:

1 *Toilet provision*: a common need on arrival, not least for children, who could be described as 'mobile urinary experiences', but also within larger sites and by the café at the end. Why are there always too few women's toilets? Remember also facilities for the disabled and for nappy-changing, accessible by both genders.

2 *Catering facilities*: particularly if the average visit exceeds one hour. This may be less important if there is a good range of choice within easy reach. The provision of catering can be a real problem, as its poor quality frequently lets a site down. There is substantial anecdotal evidence that what people remember most about a site are its toilets and catering, especially if these are poor!

3 *Climate*: from temperature in a museum to the impact of weather on an open site. Consider factors like visitors wearing heavy coats in winter but coming into a warm gallery. Warmth (or lack of it) can be a major issue in historic houses, where there can be a real problem in balancing conservation requirements and visitor needs.

4 *Noise levels*: the use of interactive exhibits, for example, leads naturally to noise and bustle among visitors, and can cause congestion. Concept development must take factors like this into account. Quality means careful planning/location of exhibit types to prevent congestion; to provide clear signals to visitors on how to behave in different display types; to separate interactives from fragile non-touchables, etc.; and to allow for the fact that visitors in 'hands-on' displays are more likely to select their own circulation path.

5 *Disability*: in addition to suitable toilets, can those with disabilities physically get into and around the gallery/site, the café and to objects? Can they follow the same route as everyone else? Is there a good provision of comfortable seats?

Safety: this should be seen not only in terms of actual danger, but also in relation to orientation to, from and at the site.

Any concept must take into account:

1 *Relief of trip stress*: good pre-visit information; road signage; on-site orientation; ease of exit. If in doubt about the impact of this on the visitor experience of your site, try being lost in your car in a town you have not previously visited, with three children on the back seat. Equally, good orientation within a site is essential to enable visitors to plan their time (or find the toilet).
2 *Visitors feel physically safe*: confidence in the quality and training of the staff; clear evidence that fire regulations and health and safety factors have been properly catered for; light levels, etc. Be very aware that the fire officer can have a dramatic impact on the concept and the visitor route – involve him or her at the earliest possible stage and work together to achieve the best result. Health and safety can be a particular issue for working museums, for example with operating machinery or steam trains.
3 *Visitors put at ease*: if visitors are to be involved/challenged by the presentation, they must feel safe about, or 'comfortable' with, the approach taken. This links directly to the need for a real understanding of the *nature* of your target audience and the development of a sense of belonging.
4 *Disability*: will disabled visitors also feel safe, and certain that they will not be trapped? Can they be certain they will not fall over, or walk into unseen obstructions (such as glass casing with no obvious edging)? Does the fire alarm have a visual signal? Are guide dogs and hearing dogs allowed?

Sense of belonging: most visits to heritage sites are social outings. All visitors should feel welcomed to the site, not have a feeling of exclusion.

Any concept must take into account:

1 *Warmth of welcome* – quality of staff; signage; orientation at beginning; colour schemes. The external architecture of many Victorian museum buildings can be off-putting, as can the colour schemes and 'atmosphere', for example, in contemporary art galleries. Many heritage sites were once renowned for their scowling, old-fashioned museum attendants, in a quasi-Victorian police uniform, or for blue-rinsed harridans acting as room stewards. This situation has now largely been transformed as can be seen, for example, in the new breed of custodians and guides employed at English Heritage sites, the enablers who help visitors to the Tate Gallery, Liverpool, or the 'living history' exponents at sites all over the world, from Old Sturbridge Village in Massachusetts to the Black Country Museum, Dudley, England.

2 *Presentation matches target audience*: media used; language levels, foreign languages if appropriate. The presentational approach taken can vary from contemplative to highly experiential – what is most suitable for your audience?

3 *Communicating a 'sense of place'*: ensuring visitors are able to comprehend what is special or unique about your site and its relevance to them?

4 *Disability*: are disabled visitors welcomed and treated the same as everyone else? Can they interact with friends and family, not just through following the same route, but also, for example, by using the same audiotapes etc.?

Self-esteem: for the site manager this means recognition of the visitor's worth. Our visitors are not there purely as income generators; nor are they granted token access as a means of ensuring continued public subsidy; nor can they be patronised as inferior, ill-educated beings. Visitors are equal participants, there to share our enthusiasm for the quality of the site and there to offer their support and commitment in its conservation.

Any concept must take into account:

1 *Authenticity and integrity*: the visitor has the right to assume that everything in the presentation is accurate and reflects the latest research. It should be clear where reproductions or reconstructions are used and what the evidence for these is. The site or collection, as well as the visitor deserve no less.

2 *Professionalism of execution*: an essential means of demonstrating the worth of the visitor lies in the sheer professional quality of the presentation and its maintenance. Broken down or peeling exhibits, ill-trained or badly behaved staff, dirty washrooms etc., all reflect on the site's attitude to its visitors.

3 *Freedom of movement*: our visitors are not a 'herd'. Enabling a visitor to move at his or her own pace recognizes individual worth. This is particularly true in enabling the visitor to choose voluntarily when to leave. Clearly, this is a problem for 'dark rides' such as the Jorvik Viking Centre in York. In such circumstances, the presence of a freeflow exhibition after the ride (as at Jorvik but not, alas, everywhere) is crucial to visitor satisfaction. It gives the visitor the choice of whether to explore in more depth and of when to leave.

4 *Hierarchy of information*: our visitors will have differing levels of knowledge and interest about the site. We must provide an opportunity to explore the subject matter to a greater or lesser degree, depending on the visitor's individual inclination. We must also ensure that there is an overall clarity of intent within the presentation – that the objectives are clear and that visitors can follow these through.

5 *Provision for children*: catering for children is not just about developing the future audience. They are people in their own right and deserve to be treated as such. This does not mean that everything must be suitable for child use, but concept development must ensure that their specific requirements are taken fully into account.

6 *Meeting expectations*: the concept must reflect visitor expectations. This is easier said than done, particularly if the development is a new one. However, once again, we are back to the issue of understanding the target audience. It also links to the way in which the site is promoted. The marketing programme should not raise expectations beyond what can actually be delivered.

7 *Disability*: is information presented in an accessible format and can it be understood without help? Can labels be read independently? Are there a variety of ways to learn about/access the site or collections? Is the same information or experience offered to all? Will the disabled visitor be able to see the presentation as an affirmation of his or her competence/achievement in understanding?

Self-actualization: Maslow argues that we can never achieve full self-actualization, i.e. our full potential, but are always working towards that end. Our challenge in a heritage site is *not* to attempt to ensure that the visitor leaves knowing 'everything there is to know' about it. That is impossible. Any attempt to do so would demoralize all but the most extreme specialist visitor.

Concentrating on a purely information-led approach also implies that self-actualization is solely knowledge based. We need to take into account the personal benefits that can be gained in other ways, for example through enjoyment, emotional involvement, social interaction and the actual process of discovery. Any concept must be geared to engaging the visitor, to encouraging individual and group stimulus, enlightenment and discovery.

Any concept must seek to achieve:

1 Visitor enjoyment and satisfaction.
2 Stimulus.
3 Enlightenment.
4 That 'gut' feeling of experiencing something unique.

Audience expectations

Much less research has been carried out on this aspect of audience requirements. As the heritage audience is so diverse, expectations may vary depending on the individual or group involved and the precise circumstances of their visit.

What will unite all visitors is the opportunity to gain access to the site, involving:

- ease of transport, including good parking facilities and public transport
- convenient opening hours
- a feeling of 'inclusion'
- as much as possible of the site and collections being accessible
- an expectation that what is presented will be accurate and reflect the latest research
- access to staff, additional information etc., if required
- good value for money.

For most informal visitors, a trip to a heritage site is a social outing. Expectations will include:

- the visit will be enjoyable, interesting and even 'fun'. It will provide family entertainment. There will be things to do together – visitors want to be more than passive recipients of written information
- there will be something for everyone, including good facilities for children
- the visit will provide an opportunity to learn something
- the site will provide good quality facilities and a high standard of service (a picnic site is a real bonus for families).

The 1994–95 survey of East Midlands museums already referred to (East Midlands Museums Service, 1996) included an assessment of public perceptions of museums which can be looked at afresh, if the words 'Heritage sites' are substituted for 'Museums', to suggest what a quality heritage presentation should include:

1 Museums are *educational* – 96 per cent agreed.
2 Museums are *interesting* – 84 per cent agreed – a much smaller but unstated percentage said they were *fun*.
3 Museums *provide family entertainment* – 70 per cent agreed 'in some form'
4 Museums provide *good quality facilities* and *good quality service* – 60–70 per cent agreed in some form, although 37 per cent felt they did not provide good cafés.
5 Museums have *convenient opening times* – 58 per cent agreed.
6 Museums offered *good value for money* – 61 per cent agreed.

When asked what would encourage them to visit more often, responses included children's facilities (14 per cent), cheaper admission charges (11 per cent), more audiovisual and interactive displays (10 per cent), changing exhibits (9 per cent), better catering (6 per cent) and more convenient opening hours (4 per cent).

What is clear from both anecdotal evidence and the research available is that the demands and expectations of informal visitors are rising and there is continuing pressure to further improve the heritage product.

Will the expectations of children be different from those of their parents?

There is much less information available on children, not least because of the UK code of conduct for survey workers which mitigates against interviewing young people under 16 years of age. A key publication (MGC, 1997), which is based on interviews with children aged 7–11 years and their parents, suggests that:

1 Children enjoy *experiencing* the past, including the 'atmosphere' and opportunities to participate and dress up.
2 Children like to be able to *touch and 'do'* – to feel involved.
3 Children like interactive exhibits, computers, creative activities, competitions and trails – all very *active* elements.
4 Children see heritage visits, at their best, as an opportunity to *learn* as well as have fun. They gain an enormous amount from visits relating to their schoolwork.
5 Children who have been to the site on a school trip like to come back to show their family.

To these the author would add:

1 Children tend to hammer 'hands-on' exhibits they like. These must be capable of withstanding full frontal attack.
2 Children get frustrated if the experience is disappointing, if there are large queues for popular 'hands-on' exhibits or if key exhibits are broken. Their boredom threshold is low.
3 Children do not want to read much. It can be too much like school and brings in issues of reading ability and reading age.
4 Parents often need help and encouragement in assisting their children.
5 Children need to be able to let off steam.
6 The approach of children who are regular heritage site visitors may be different. Studies by Hein (noted in Jensen, 1994) showed that children's

concentration and self-confidence increased with regular visits, replacing more rowdy and aimless behaviour.

7 Children's expectations are likely to be highly subjective, reflecting their feelings for the place and who they have come with.

8 Children of 7–11 have a terrible habit of having siblings who are either under 5 years old or are suffering from adolescent angst. They need to be provided for also.

9 Children know what they want in the café and it is rarely quiche and salad!

10 The shop is an important part of the visit for children and must include an exciting and affordable range of small items, targeted at their age range.

Regular visitors may seek:

1 An incentive ticketing scheme.

2 A Friends group, with special events, 'behind the scenes' sessions and the opportunity to participate, perhaps as a volunteer. Active involvement is not necessarily the only issue. For the regular, there is the chance to meet 'their kind of people' and to extend their emotional involvement with the site.

3 If relevant, a programme of changing exhibitions.

4 A different type of experience. The available evidence suggests that infrequent museum-goers value most highly the opportunities for social interaction, active participation and entertainment. Frequent museum-goers, however, seem more likely to show a preference for learning and enhancing their understanding and appreciation.

Structured educational groups are likely to require:

■ precise and focused strategies aimed at schools and, in the UK, related to the National Curriculum
■ facilities such as designated schoolrooms and lunch areas
■ access to specialist staff
■ educational project work built into the presentation
■ the availability of education resource materials and packs.

Providers of public subsidy may seek:

■ Outreach work within the local community and a strategy to widen the range of local people visiting the site
■ an active role in a local tourism strategy

- prestige
- evidence of 'best value' in terms of the application of resources.

This outline list above does not include such potential audiences as the elderly, people with specific disabilities or those from particular ethnic minorities, all of whom will have their own requirements. However, it is extensive enough to make it clear that pressure to enhance the presentation of heritage is coming from a number of directions, including:

- the need to increase visitor numbers and, therefore, income
- the need to diversify the visitor base
- rising visitor expectations
- the need to meet the requirements of the educational sector.

No heritage site reliant on public subsidy and/or visitor income can afford to ignore visitor expectations. Viewing concept development through the eyes of the target audience is an essential part of an integrated approach to strategic planning for the site, based on the continuing need to build a relationship with the audience.

Questions

1 Evaluate the visitor experience of a heritage site known to you in terms of Maslow's hierarchy of needs.
2 Having selected two differing types of heritage site or collection, compare and contrast the types of aims and objectives likely to underpin their presentation to the public.
3 Heritage can be defined as 'those things of value that we have inherited and wish to keep for future generations' (Brisbane and Wood, 1996: 4). How important is it to balance conservation requirements with the need for public access?

References and further reading

Arts Council/MGC (1997). *Children as an Audience for Museums and Galleries*. Arts Council/Museums and Galleries Commission (MGC).

Bicknell, S. and Carmelo, G. (1993). *Museum Visitor Studies in the 90s*. Science Museum.

Binks, G. et al. (1990). *Visitors Welcome*. HMSO.

Brisbane, M. and Wood, C. (1996). *A Future for our Past*. English Heritage.

Davies, S. (1994). *By Popular Demand*. MGC.

DoE and DNH (1994). *Planning & Policy Guidance Note 15*. Department of the Environment and Department of National Heritage.

Earnscliffe, J. (1992). *In through the Front Door: Disabled People and the Visual Arts*. Arts Council.

East Midlands Museums Service (1996). *Knowing our Visitors: Survey 94/95*. East Midlands Museums Service.

English Heritage (1995). *Easy Access to Historic Properties*. English Heritage.

English Tourist Board (1991). *Tourism and the Environment: Maintaining the Balance*. English Tourist Board.

Foster, L. (1996). *Access to the Historic Environment*. Donhead.

Foster, L. and Coles, A. (eds) (1996). *Perspectives on Access: to Museums and Galleries in Historic Buildings*. MGC.

Foundation de France and ICOM (1991). *Museums without Barriers: a New Deal for the Disabled*. Routledge.

Gooding, C. (1996). *Blackstone's Guide to the Disability Discrimination Act*. Blackstone.

Hall, C. M and McArthur, S. (1998). *Integrated Heritage Management*. The Stationery Office.

Harrison, R. (ed.) (1994). *The Manual of Heritage Management*. Butterworth.

Her Majesty's Stationery Office (HMSO) (1995). *The Disability Discrimination Act*. HMSO.

Hooper-Greenhill, E. (1994). *Museums and their Visitors*. Routledge.

Jensen, N. (1994). Children's perceptions of their museum experiences: a contextual perspective. *Children's Environments*, **11**(4), 300–324.

Maslow, A. H. (1954). *Motivations and Personality*. Harper and Row.

Merriman, N. (1991). *Beyond the Glass Case*. Routledge.

Museums and Galleries Commission (MGC) (1992). *The Guidelines on Disability for Museums and Galleries*. MGC.

Museums and Galleries Commission MGC (1994). *The Disability Resource Directory for Museums*. MGC.

Museums and Galleries Commission MGC (1997). *Access to Museums and Galleries for People with Disabilities: Guidelines for Good Practice*. MGC.

National Trust (1996). *Information for Visitors with Disabilities*. National Trust.

Pearce, P. L. (1995). Pleasure travel motivation. In *Tourism: Principles, Practices, Philosophies* (R. M. McIntosh, C. R. Uvelder and J. R. B. Ritchie, eds), pp.167–178, 7th edition, Wiley.

Swain, J., Finkelstein, S., French, S. and Oliver, M. (eds) (1993). *Disabling Barriers – Enabling Environments*. Sage.

Young, V. and Urquart, D. (1996). *Access to the Built Heritage*. Historic Scotland.

8

Hows of concept design

Graham Black

Introduction

Having explored in the previous chapter the operational side of concept design, finally we come to the *creative* aspect of the process – the actual development of the concept. Let us assume that the objectives are clear, that the condition of the site is safeguarded, that the academic research has been incorporated, that we have a detailed appraisal of the scale and nature of the likely audience, that the physical requirements of the visitors have been taken fully into account, that the site and/or space is suitable, that the capital and revenue budgets are adequate and that the local population is content, etc.

The task now is to seek a concept that stimulates that elusive 'wow' factor in the visitor. This chapter explores the elements involved in this task: building the team; developing an understanding of the personal context of the visitor; using an approach based on the principles of 'heritage interpretation'; building in structured educational use; involving the exhibition designer at the concept stage; and planning in evaluation as part of the process.

A multidisciplinary approach

From the material in the previous chapter, it should be clear that developing the concept for a major new heritage presentation is a truly multidisciplinary activity:

1 *Governing body and director*: to set the objectives and monitor proposals to ensure these are met. The director also has to relate the proposals to the business plan and ensure that the operational requirements of the presentation can be met – particularly maintenance and the role envisaged for the front of house staff.
2 *Architect, English Heritage, English Nature, planning officer, conservation officer, access adviser etc.*: to define and approve any building alterations, etc. They have a key role to play in negotiating the balance between conservation requirements and visitor access. Agreeing the visitor route, whether within a building or around a site or nature reserve, is the first key step in establishing presentation content without losing 'atmosphere'.
3 *Curator, etc.*: to provide expertise, define collection availability, ensure both conservation and security requirements are met and have a major input into all other aspects of the project.
4 *Interpreter*: to create a concept which meets the objectives set and the perceived needs of the audience and, with the curator/reserve warden etc. and education officer, write the final presentation.
5 *Education officer, teacher advisers, etc.*: to devise quality investigative education project work which is built into the presentation rather than grafting 'death by worksheet' activities on afterwards. Also to have input into the overall exhibition or presentation content to help to meet the learning needs of the entire audience.
6 *Access adviser*: to help work towards equal access for all, contributing not only advice on physical access issues but also on interpretation, marketing, staff training, public programmes and employment (see Chapter 7).
7 *Academic team*: to ensure that content, even at its most simplified level, is accurate and reflects up-to-date research.
8 *The wider community*: this has become particularly relevant in the UK in recent years, due to the current political debate targeted at the combat of 'social exclusion', but many heritage sites and organizations have long

recognized the importance of involving, and seeking input from, local communities – not least when the site seeks to reflect that community or a particular culture. Many sites are, of course, developed by local communities themselves, and we are seeing this increasingly among, for example, indigenous peoples both to promote local culture and at times as part of an act of reconciliation, such as at the Umeewarra Mission in South Australia. The alternative to inclusion in such circumstances is exploitation. But consultation has a wider role than this, from developing practical solutions to traffic problems to developing the resource audit (see Chapter 7) and engendering local pride.

9 *Marketing officer*: to provide input on the nature of the target audience and on the other potential uses of the site as well as exploring marketing opportunities during exhibition construction and planning for the opening.

10 *Other outside bodies and individuals*: these will depend on the individual site or project. The aim of their involvement should be to bring greater depth and potential to the presentation. One key individual whose agreement can be essential, particularly for building-based proposals, is the Fire Officer. A concept is irrelevant if the route and/or other aspects do not meet fire regulation requirements.

11 *Designers, audiovisual specialists etc.*: to bring their own creative input into ensuring the objectives and concept can become a reality.

12 *Staff trainers*: to guarantee the quality of service provided to visitors. Their role expands if it is intended that exhibition staff act as third person or first person interpreters. In these circumstances you must not only create suitable tour routes, or locations for staff within the displays, but also devise detailed briefs and advance training schemes.

13 *Project manager*: to make it all happen on time and within budget.

The co-ordination and welding together of the team responsible for the creative development of the concept and the eventual presentation itself is a different role to that of project manager whose tasks are largely about risk assessment, timetabling and financial controls. The person who performs this role will vary from scheme to scheme but it is a vital task.

Personal context

While the physical and social context of the heritage visit is relatively straightforward to analyse and respond to, the real challenge comes in defining the personal context of the heritage visitor – the personal baggage we all bring with us and which is unique to each of us:

1 We each bring our past with us – our experiences, interests, prior knowledge etc.
2 We each have our own feelings, attitudes and perceptions about heritage sites – in fact, every one of us sees the world uniquely.
3 We each attach our own meanings to what we see and do.
4 We are each an individual mixture of the extrovert and the introvert.
5 We each have different learning styles – like to read, do, experience etc.

This background will have a considerable influence on the *expectations* (see Chapter 7) each individual has of the visit and on the *responses* he or she will make to the presentation. If we want to assist the individual to engage with the site emotionally and intellectually, and gain from the experience, we must use this baggage as a positive element in the approach taken to the development of the concept.

Clearly, for most types of heritage site the personal baggage of the audience will be as varied as the number of people visiting. Equally obviously, while staff giving guided tours or interacting with visitors on-site have an opportunity to respond directly to an individual's needs and motivations, this is not possible when interpretive media other than person-to-person contact are used. The challenge is to develop a concept flexible enough, and audience-aware enough, to grab and hold the attention of the bulk of visitors – to meet individual needs in terms of different entry and exit points; presentation through a range of types of media; and a 'layering' of material, to be used as the individual prefers.

The experience of the last 40 years would suggest that the most effective way to achieve this is through an approach now defined as 'heritage interpretation'.

Heritage interpretation

This section concentrates on the idea of heritage interpretation as the essential basis for quality in the development of the concept itself. Heritage interpretation is a particular approach to the presentation of a site. The term itself has been subject to a number of definitions. As a member of the Association for Heritage Interpretation, the author recommends that society's catch-all definition: 'The process of communicating to people the significance of a place or object, so that they enjoy it more, understand their heritage and environment better, and develop a positive attitude to conservation'. This definition has the benefits of embracing all aspects of the natural and human-made environment and of combining an objective of enhanced understanding for visitors with concern for sustainability and conservation. But what does it mean for concept development?

Too many heritage presentations are *information led*. Interpretation twists the approach to make it *audience-led*. The challenge is to arouse the visitors' curiosity, to involve and engage them with the site. Through this, visitors are encouraged to think for themselves and to want to discover more: 'revealing . . . something of the beauty and wonder, the inspiration and spiritual meaning that lie behind what the visitor can with his senses perceive' (Tilden, 1977: 3–4).

The methods by which interpreters normally attempt to achieve this are by the following means.

Emphasis on the site or collection

The concept should lead with what is unique about the site. Too often heritage presenters become overwhelmed by the media at their disposal. The site, collections etc. become little more than window-dressing. Interpreters describe this as placing the equivalent of 'a dirty window' between the visitor and the site. The media should be used only where needed to engage visitors with the site, drawing them to its features, objects, etc.

Self-referencing

This builds on the visitor's personal context, the individual baggage (or history) which every visitor brings, by relating the site to our own lives, experiences, interests and knowledge: 'Any interpretation that does not somehow relate what is being displayed or described to something within the personality or experience of the visitor will be sterile' (Tilden, 1977: 9).

Tilden's book, *Interpreting our Heritage*, first published in 1957, is still viewed as the 'bible' for interpreters with its emphasis on this need to relate; on the need to provoke thought; and on the need to take a different approach for children. Self-referencing is basically a means of supplying new information and ideas in a way which encourages visitors to connect these with themselves and their own experiences.

At the Thackray Medical Museum in Leeds, for example, visitors are encouraged to follow individual characters through their lives in an 1840s slum, and their responses to the onset of disease. By meeting the characters in their homes, witnessing for themselves the range of causes of infectious disease, selecting specific medical treatment and being confronted with the outcomes, the visitors gain a real insight into the living conditions for the poor in early Victorian England.

Since the early 1990s, English Heritage has been introducing audio-tours as a key means of interpretation at their most popular sites. These have proven to be both highly effective and relatively cheap. They also have the advantage of not requiring new build, which would intrude on the setting or fabric of the sites. Most of these tours are 'character-led'. An audio-tour of the site of the Battle of Hastings, at Battle Abbey, in Sussex, allows the visitor to choose to hear from any one of three characters: a Norman knight; a Saxon soldier; or Edith Swanneck, the common-law wife of Harold, the Saxon king. At Hailes Abbey, in Gloucestershire, a lay brother 'accompanies' you. At Hailes the audio-tour is also available in a form suited to wheelchair users, covering those areas where access is possible, as well as in versions targeted at the partially-sighted and in basic language.

Active visitor participation

Based on the principles of learning through doing, It is generally recognized that people retain about:

10 per cent of what they hear
30 per cent of what they read
50 per cent of what they see
90 per cent of what they do. (Lewis, 1994: 27)

Active participation does not necessarily mean pulling levers or pressing buttons. Physical involvement is only a means to an end. The real aim is to engage the visitor's mind, to generate a sense of discovery. At Barnwell Country Park, in Northamptonshire, a simple 'nature adventure trail' for children encourages them to use each of their senses in turn, at a series of planned stopping points. At the first, they must find a minty-smelling leaf, at the second 'something that stings, something that prickles, something smooth and something that tickles', and so on – wonderfully effective in stirring young children's imaginations.

We should, through active participation, be encouraging people to interpret for themselves, assisting them to develop the appropriate skills and confidence that enable interpretation in the first place. The challenge is to make this ideal effective in a context where, as shown in the previous chapter, the bulk of general visitors are on a social outing in family or friendship groups. It is, however, essential that the key messages can be conveyed without a lot of effort from the audience. There is a serious risk that recreational visitors will switch attention if they feel they are being made to work too hard.

The Galleries of Justice, in Nottingham, includes a range of examples of this process in action. A computer interactive uses a series of 'trivial pursuits' type questions to encourage visitors to observe and examine objects relating to the history of the police. The same Police Gallery includes objects on open display for *all* visitors, not just the partially sighted, to touch and explore. The Crime and Punishment Gallery includes a section on the social and political background to changes, over time, in the nature of punishment for crime in England. Here, all visitors are given a 'criminal identity number' rather than being tied to an individual convict. The number relates to single characters in each chronological phase of the exhibition, enabling visitors to explore how the nature of punishment for similar crimes changed over time. This combines a self-referencing approach with an active intellectual engagement in developing an understanding of why changes occurred and what their impact was. Clearly, this is a very complex issue, not the sort of thing you would regard as an entertainment on a wet Sunday afternoon. Its effectiveness with the audience shows that heritage exhibitions *can* confront the major issues of today. The *selection* of the specific criminals and crimes was crucial to maintaining visitor interest – what happened to children; what was the punishment for the theft of one pound of black pudding (three months' hard labour in the 1860s); what happened to transportees once they arrived in Australia?

Encouraging social interaction

Research on the audiences for heritage sites emphasizes the social nature of the experience, with at least 90 per cent of visitors coming in family or friendship groups. Most of the research on the heritage site social context, such as that by Blud (1990), has focused on families. However, overall, the evidence suggests that the exhibits which most effectively engage an audience are those which encourage social interaction within and beyond the groups involved – using the interpretation to encourage discussion and involvement. This, in turn, both broadens and deepens their understanding. Thus, at the Thackray Medical Museum groups share information on their characters. At the Galleries of Justice they discuss the fate of their criminal identities and can also visit the museum's 'activity centre' for sessions in object handling. At the Archaeological Resource Centre, in York, groups perform a series of tasks together, such as sifting for fragments of bone.

Practical issues include encouraging conversation (but not making the site so noisy that conversation becomes impossible), varying exhibit heights so that all of the group can use them (important for those with disabilities as well as children), creating exhibits which the group can explore together (a major problem for computer interactives which tend to be devised for use by one person at a time), enabling 'people watching' between groups, so they can learn from each other and, as at the Galleries of Justice, building staff into the exhibition to interact with the audience.

Impact on the senses and emotions

Given the individual nature of every heritage site, we should seek to go beyond knowledge – to engage the senses and emotions of the visitor as a means of conveying a sense of the spirit of the place: 'This is what art does to you. It enraptures and arouses . . . it circumnavigates the brain and appeals directly to the senses' (Januszczak, 1998: 2).

It is not only great art which does this. One only has to think of the impact on entering the nave of a cathedral or viewing an outstanding landscape. Equally, the appeal to the senses and emotions does not come only from the most magnificent aspects of the heritage. It is, in fact, as likely to arise from a detail, something which affects us directly on an individual level – the smell of a peat fire; the volume of noise from a textile machine in operation; the sight of a mummified baby; touching a cat's paw print on a Roman tile.

Thematic approach

Quality in the development of the concept should ensure that there should be clear themes, reflecting the stated objectives. Good presentations are organized – that is, easy to follow. The themes selected should provide a limited number of 'take-home messages' (the author recommends a maximum of *five*, reflecting research on the brain's limited capacity to handle new information at a given time). Reflecting the importance of self-referencing, noted above, the themes used should normally have a strong human interest content – people relate to people. This provides an angle through which more complex or abstract issues can be explored. This approach is superbly applied at The Conservation Centre in Liverpool, where issues concerning the need for, and scientific approach to, the conservation of museum collections are conveyed through the personalities, enthusiasm and expertise of the conservators themselves.

The tool box

The approach taken should reflect the nature of the audience in the appropriateness of the language and media used. The range of media available is extensive, including:

- guided tours
- self-guided trails
- audio tours
- interpretation boards
- graphic panels and flip-books
- cased displays: object based
- objects on open display, including some to touch, or thermoforms for use by the visually impaired
- room sets: from created to 'in situ'
- reconstructions: from small sets, to 'dark rides', to whole sites
- film, video, audiovisuals
- interactives: from simple to computer
- artworks
- staff providing explanations, demonstrations, handling sessions, living history and drama.

Interpreters normally refer to these as their 'tool box'. The approach should avoid information overload. The emphasis should be placed on conveying underpinning meaning rather than facts. There should be a hierarchy of information available, so that those who want to 'find out more' can do so. Crucially, the language used should be 'active' rather than 'passive'.

In major exhibitions, the concept should allow for a 'paced' approach. We should vary the presentational style to retain interest, enthusiasm and concentration. This is a tried and tested method. Shakespeare's tragedies used the same approach. There is a range of possibilities, from experiential through interactive to contemplative. Those selected should be related to the nature of the site and audience. See, for example, Black (1999) for a case study on the pacing of the displays at the Thackray Medical Museum in Leeds.

Fun

The approach taken should be imaginative, interesting and fun. A heritage site should not have a funereal atmosphere. Our visitors want to learn, but want to enjoy doing so. They are there of their own free will. A sense of humour can encourage involvement and learning. The concept should also ensure that the presentation finishes on a high note rather than fizzling out – we need our visitors to leave on an emotional and intellectual high, supportive of the work we are doing and ambassadors on our behalf to other potential visitors. Look at the small size of heritage marketing budgets – word of mouth is the most important element in most site marketing strategies.

Structured learning

While heritage interpretation is targeted particularly at the recreational visitor, who is seeking an opportunity for informal learning in an entertaining setting, the needs of the structured educational visit can be quite different.

The impact of the national curriculum in the UK, with its emphasis on the use of a range of sources of evidence, has been dramatic. Those heritage sites that have been able to demonstrate their relevance to specific study units have witnessed a massive increase in school use. It is a double-edged sword, however, as changes in the curriculum can extinguish demand as swiftly as it was created. Currently, the heritage world is studying with trepidation the effects of the enhanced emphasis on literacy and numeracy in primary schools. This has meant that subjects like history and geography are no longer compulsory. Even before this change, these subjects had no more than 30 minutes per week in the primary curriculum. Given the tightly controlled timetables, visits to heritage sites had to include work that was cross-curricular – fortunately, heritage sites are uniquely able to provide this.

For secondary schools, particularly for age groups approaching national exams, the visit is more likely to be single subject and tightly focused on the syllabus. As secondary school visits tend to involve entire year groups, with anything from 80 to over 120 pupils arriving at once, the concept must enable the site to cope with these numbers. This usually means 'carouseling', that is starting groups of pupils at different points around the site or exhibition rather than attempting a single file circuit which all of them do at one go. The effect of this on the concept will probably be to place emphasis on the different themes or elements of the site rather than producing a single storyline that must be followed in a fixed order.

Teachers prepare detailed schemes of work defining learning objectives, potential activities through which these can be achieved, and the means by which the learning objectives will be assessed. Visits to heritage sites must fit within this structure. Concept development, in terms of structured educational use, must go beyond the allocation of designated educational spaces and the availability of an education officer, to the incorporation of project work, based on active learning principles, within the presentation. It must also include provision for the creation of support materials to assist in the development of high quality pre- and post-visit work, and in preparation for the on-site activities.

Working with the designer

Up until this point, the development of the concept has been treated in words and abstractions. For concepts involving exhibitions, the designer will take these and transform them into three-dimensional ideas. This is when the 'hot air' has to stop and the project takes on an air of reality:

- transforming/organizing space
- defining the surface and atmosphere
- final selection/creation of interpretive media
- lighting
- meeting specific needs, e.g. conservation, security
- ensuring it is achievable within budget and deadlines.

It is a creative input – the designer must be involved at as early a stage as possible as a full member of the team, to become aware of the ethos of the project and to have an input into the ideas process. It is also highly practical, particularly in helping to define the most appropriate approaches, not least in terms of what is actually achievable or affordable, but also in relation to proven effectiveness with audiences.

There is not the scope here to explore the relationship with the designer. It must be emphasized, however, that the concept will only be complete when your ideas are accompanied by a creative solution that will achieve them.

Selection of the designer is clearly crucial and should involve visits to other work he or she has done, a request for references from previous clients and detailed discussions to ensure you are on the same wavelength. What you do not want is a 'yes person' who will bring little to the project beyond your own proposals. Equally, an egotist who believes he or she has the answer to everything is to be avoided at all costs. Beware also the design company where you meet the key person once and find later that all the work is being done by inexperienced juniors. If in doubt, seek advice.

Evaluation

So, at last there is an initial concept! This is the time for the first stage in the evaluation process when all members of the team, the director and governing body and, preferably, a focus group from the potential audience and some co-operative schoolteachers, are given copies to review or taken on prototypes of tours. Their feedback should lead to any necessary changes before development moves forward.

This is a process that will continue as the project progresses. Where the concept is based around a series of talks and guided tours, or through living history demonstrations, for example in a country park or re-created site, it is relatively easy to devise and 'road test' new versions, while a good interpreter will evaluate each session as it takes place, seeking ways to improve and develop it. This is a never-ending process, reflecting gradual social change in the audience as well as growing expertise among the staff, both in the subject area and in ways of responding to the needs of different audiences. From a management point of view, it is also an important way of ensuring that staff do not lose their enthusiasm and commitment, turning into dull machines which repeat the same text indefinitely.

Constant change is possible for this form of 'live' interpretation, because there will be little additional capital cost involved. It is a very different matter for exhibitions, where change will involve major expense. Most exhibition professionals still rely on experience, intuition and assumptions about how visitors are likely to respond to help determine the appropriateness of the design, the effectiveness of the exhibits and whether visitors are likely to use the presentation as intended. A quest for quality should ensure that you go further. A formal evaluation process seeks to apply objective judgements to define strengths and weaknesses in the proposals. To be more than subjective, it must be planned in at the initial stage when the aims and objectives are defined. The task at this stage is to assess whether these are met by the concept. Remember, this *front-end evaluation*, i.e. carried out at the planning stage, is cheap compared to having to make changes during production or after the exhibition has opened.

In ideal circumstances, front-end evaluation is followed by a period of prototyping when mock-ups of individual exhibits and sections of the proposed displays are tested on elements of the target audience. This *formative evaluation* process is common for guided tours and major interactive exhibits but all too rare for general displays, with lack of budget and time the most frequently given reasons. For them, evaluation tends to take place after opening (called *summative evaluation*) when it is normally too late and too expensive to make any necessary changes.

Conclusion: principles

Quality in concept design will come down in the end to a creative process geared to the needs of the individual site and its audience. However, it is not good enough to describe this purely as an art, whose quality cannot therefore be evaluated objectively. In the UK alone, many millions of pounds are spent each year on developing heritage attractions. There must be some means by which their quality can be judged.

Part Three has attempted to define some basic principles that can be applied to concept design. It is appropriate, as a conclusion, to summarize them. Concept design:

1 *Recognizes a primary duty of care*: a responsibility to protect and preserve the heritage resource for the benefit of this and future generations. Quality means striking an acceptable balance between meeting the needs of visitors today and conserving the site for the future.
2 *Will ensure that it is the site, collections etc. which are to the fore, not the media used in the presentation.*
3 *Ensures that a belief in, commitment to and enthusiasm for the site shines through* the presentation, engaging and involving the audience emotionally and intellectually in the special qualities of the site. Visitors should leave with their understanding and appreciation enhanced, rather than being treated as passive recipients of information.
4 *Recognizes that an understanding of the targeted audience*: its intellectual and emotional needs and expectations plus its personal, social and physical context – is central to any presentation strategy. The concept for the presentation must be in direct response to this understanding.
5 *Should ensure clarity* in both the messages presented by the site and the way in which they are communicated.
6 *Demands authenticity and integrity* in the presentation.
7 *Depends on good planning*: there must be clear aims and objectives. Concept development must be seen as part of a co-ordinated approach to the management of the resource.
8 *Reflects the carrying capacity of the site.*
9 *Recognizes that first impressions are especially important.*
10 *Should dictate that the presentation can meet the physical needs of the audience* across the site and throughout the year.

11 *Should ensure that the presentation is fun.*
12 *Demands the highest standards in the execution and maintenance* of the presentation. Quality in concept design means setting production standards and ensuring maintenance needs can be met.
13 *Demands that the requirements for structured educational use are built into the presentation.*
14 *Demands a formal evaluative process* as a key element in developing the concept.

This chapter began by stating that its function was to explore the elements involved in devising a concept 'that stimulates that elusive "wow" factor in the visitor'. At the end, it must be stated that there is no guarantee that this can be achieved. Similarly, it is far easier to define the *principles* required for a successful pop record than to produce a hit. In heritage attractions, much depends on the unique qualities of the particular resource and the way individual visitors respond directly to these. The task of the concept is to help to provoke that response and to support the visitors in their path to a memorable experience.

Questions

1 Why is it important to use a range of media in the development of the concept for a heritage attraction? Make reference to examples you know of different media being used effectively.
2 How would you assess quality in the presentation of a heritage site?
3 For a heritage site or landscape of your own choice, how would you use the principles of heritage interpretation to generate a 'sense of place' among visitors?

References and further reading

Alderson, W. T. and Low, S. P. (1985). *Interpretation of Historic Sites.* 2nd edition. American Association for State and Local History (AASLH).
Anderson, J. (1991). *A Living History Reader: Volume 1 Museums.* AASLH.
Beck, L. and Cable, T. (1998). *Interpretation for the 21st Century.* Sagamore.
Binks, G. et al. (1988). *Visitors Welcome: a Manual of Presentation and Interpretation.* HMSO.
Black, G. (1999). The Thackray Medical Museum. in *Heritage Visitor Attractions: an Operations Management Perspective* (A. Leask and I. Yeoman, eds), Cassell.

Blud, L. M. (1990). Sons and daughters: observations on the way families interact during a museum visit. *Museum Management and Curatorship*, **9**(3): 257–64.

Carter, J. (ed.) (1997). *A Sense of Place: an Interpretive Planning Handbook*. Tourism and Environment Initiative.

Falk, J. H. and Dierking, L. D. (1992). *The Museum Experience*. Whalesback Books.

Freeman, R. (1989). *The Discovery Gallery: Discovery Learning in the Museum*. Royal Ontario Museum.

Ham, S. H. (1992). *Environmental Interpretation: a Practical Guide for People with Big Ideas and Small Budgets*. North American Press.

Harrison, R. (ed.) (1994). *The Manual of Heritage Management*. Butterworth.

James, J. (1999). Culturally sensitive research: interpreting Umeewarra Mission. *Journal of Interpretation Research*, **4**(1), Winter, 77–78.

Januszczak, W. (1998). Art history is not all it's painted. *Sunday Times*, Culture Section, 29 November, pp. 2–3.

Knudson, D. M., Cable, T. T. and Beck, L. (1995). *Interpretation of Cultural and Natural Resources*. Venture.

Lewis, W. J. (1994). *Interpreting for Park Visitors*. Eastern Acorn Press.

Lord, G. and Lord, B. (1991). *The Manual of Museum Planning*. HMSO.

McClean, K. (1993). *Planning for People in Museum Exhibitions*. Association of Science-Technology Centres.

McManus, P. M. (ed.) (1996). *Archaeological Displays and the Public*. Institute of Archaeology.

Scottish Natural Heritage (1996). *Visitor Centres: a Practical Guide to Planning, Design and Operation*. SNH.

Tilden, F. (1977). *Interpreting our Heritage*. 3rd edition. University of North Carolina Press.

Trapp, S., Gross, M. and Zimmerman, R. (1992). *Signs, Trails, and Wayside Exhibits*. University of Wisconsin Press.

Uzzell, D. (ed.) (1989). *Heritage Interpretation*. 2 volumes. Belhaven.

Uzzell, D. (1998). Interpreting our heritage: a theoretical interpretation. In *Contemporary Issues in Heritage and Environmental Interpretation* (D. Uzzell and R. Ballantyne, eds), The Stationery Office.

Part Four

Operations Management

Isabelle Frochot

Introduction

Service quality seems to have become a 'buzz' word of the 1990s and nowadays there does not appear to be one industry unconcerned by this issue. However, if service quality has often been simply defined as 'meeting customers expectations', it remains a complex construct to conceptualize and measure. Furthermore the fewer applications of services marketing research in Europe compared to America, and its lack of representation in heritage attractions, necessitates a careful observation of the existing constructs in order to assess their potential strengths and weaknesses in analysing the specific provision of quality service for heritage sites. Before addressing this issue it is therefore necessary to first examine the notion of service quality by reviewing its definition and its different measurements as it has been addressed by the services marketing literature. This is undertaken in Chapter 9. Chapter 10 lays down the general principles involved in service quality and satisfaction evaluations as it has been portrayed in the services marketing literature.

9

Service concepts and issues

Isabelle Frochot

The importance of delivering a quality service: why does it matter?

The challenge of evaluating service quality has been motivated by recent research that has demonstrated the significance of service quality as a central factor in business success. Service quality has consequently become a focus for any marketing strategy and high levels of service are seen as a means for an organization to achieve a competitive advantage and position itself more effectively in the market place (Lewis, 1993). Customers are also becoming more aware and critical of the alternatives on offer and rising standards of services, prompted by competitive trends, have increased customer expectations (Lewis and Mitchell, 1991). Research shows that the benefits of good service quality relate to customer loyalty and attraction of new customers, positive word-of-mouth communication, employee satisfaction and commitment, enhanced corporate image, reduced costs, and increased business performance. It has also long been recognized that it is particularly important for a company to understand its customers' feelings towards its services since most unsatisfied customers will not come back and, more importantly, those consumers will rarely report their complaint. Moreover a satisfied customer will usually spread the news to four customers while an unsatisfied customer will tell on average ten people. It is therefore crucial for managers to undertake studies and surveys to identify potential faults in their services.

The services marketing field: development and principles

Service quality issues have been addressed by the services marketing literature, an area of research which has grown rapidly in the last 15 years as a result of the recognition by academics and executives of the necessity to generate a new approach for this fast-growing sector of the economy. Despite the ever-increasing importance of services in contemporary economies, it is only in the early 1980s that a specific interest in services marketing appeared. This increased interest can be attributed to several factors among which the rise in services expenditures in the USA, the deregulation of service industries and the acceptance of the unique requirements for effective services marketing played a significant role. Services marketing is now a fairly well established field of research which has developed principally from the USA to spread later to Europe and the rest of the world. Service quality issues have become a common theme in a world increasingly turned towards service industries and its research background is a rich area of interlocking theories and models. The first services marketing conference was organized in early 1980 by the American Marketing Association and much of the research produced at this time aimed at building an argument for the distinctiveness of services from products (Uhl and Upah, 1983). The goods marketing versus services marketing debate represented a fundamental challenge to establish the relevance of the services marketing field. The argumentation was based on the belief that the traditional concepts developed in the marketing field were biased toward product marketing and were not necessarily applicable to a service context. By then, most scholars accepted that the marketing of services was sufficiently distinctive from the marketing of physical products to deserve separate treatment and, since 1986, the debate has shifted to the study of the adaptations necessary to develop effective marketing strategies for services (Edgett and Parkinson, 1993). This evolution has led to an explosive growth in research with the literature focusing on specific issues such as service quality, service encounters, relationship marketing and the acknowledgement of the services marketing literature in leading marketing journals (Fisk, Brown and Bitner, 1993).

The nature of services

The development of managerial and academic interest in services has led to a plethora of definitions that would be impossible to relate integrally. A definition retained here is the one proposed by Kotler (1994: 588) which defines a service as 'any activity or benefit that one party can offer to another which is essentially intangible and does not result in the ownership of anything. Its production may or may not be tied to a physical product'. Originally, the intangible aspect of a service was commonly seen as its most distinctive feature, yet other characteristics also appeared to define its specificity and these can be summarized into four key traits (Bateson, 1979; Berry, 1980; Lovelock, 1983; Payne, 1993; Shostack, 1977; Wyckham, Fitzroy and Mandry, 1975; Zeithaml, Parasuraman and Berry, 1991):

1 *Intangibility*: services are performances rather than objects and, although they might include some tangible support, the core product delivered remains intangible and therefore cannot be evaluated physically. This trait has traditionally been recognized as the fundamental distinguishing characteristic between services and products from which all other differences would emerge (Bateson, 1979; Shostack, 1977; Zeithaml, Parasuraman and Berry, 1985). Intangibility also implies that a service is experienced and ownership is rendered impossible. In the case of heritage services, this means that visitors pay for a service which is the experience they will gain from 'consuming', i.e. visiting a museum, but visitors can only remain at the stage of 'gazers' since they will never own the museum or the artefacts displayed they are experiencing.

2 *Inseparability of the production and consumption*: the processes suggests that services are sold, produced and consumed simultaneously (Kotler, 1982). This also indicates that the consumer is involved in the consumption and production process (Booms and Bitner, 1981).

3 *Heterogeneity*: this relates to the high variability in the performance of services and the difficulty to standardize services (Zeithaml, Parasuraman and Berry, 1991). Hence, the quality of a service is difficult to control since it can vary greatly from producer to producer, customer to customer and day to day.

4 *Perishability*: means that services cannot be stored to be sold at a later date, implying that a service unsold is a service lost. On the contrary one can also argue that a service can be 'oversold' in a sense that there might be too many visitors in a place at once, with for instance the problems of overcrowding often encountered in some visitor attractions.

The service experience and service encounters

The identification of the four traits described above has proved in fact to have substantial implications which required the rethinking of traditional product-based marketing principles to accommodate these particularities. Indeed, by comparison to a product where customers usually receive a good whose quality can be easily evaluated on tangible cues, services involve a mixture of interactions and benefits which all together form the final service received. Therefore, compared with products, services need to be considered more broadly, by conceptualizing their consumption process as a whole experience: although the service performance is aided by tangibles 'What the consumer purchases when he or she purchases a service is an experience' (Bateson, 1991: 495). For example, a visitor to a castle would appear to be *de facto* consuming a physical entity (the castle itself) while he or she would in fact purchase through the entrance ticket the whole experience which include all his or her contacts with the range of different elements provided in the service. Booms and Bitner (1981) also reported that in the consumption of goods, the firm environment had little impact on consumers while in the case of services it took a completely new dimension. The authors' argument was based on the viewpoint that since consumers were present while the service was being produced and consumed, 'the potential impact of total surroundings can sharply influence the consumer's behaviour' (Booms and Bitner, 1981: 50). Therefore, the authors advocated that the traditional four Ps of the product marketing mix (Product, Place, Price, Promotion) should be reconsidered by adding three new dimensions: Participants, Physical evidence and Process of service assembly.

The concept of service encounters relates to the services' second characteristic of inseparability. Since services are produced and consumed simultaneously, the consumer is 'in the factory', often experiencing the total service within the firm's facility (Bitner, 1992). The concept of service encounter refers to this interaction between the consumer and the firm (Surprenant and Solomon, 1987) and is commonly defined as 'a period of time during which a consumer directly interacts with a service' (Shostack, 1985: 244). The service encounter therefore includes all the customers' interactions with a service firm such as the personnel, physical facilities, tangible elements and other customers.

Concerning the first encounter, the *physical surroundings*, the intangibility of services implies that consumers search for tangible cues concerning the firm's capabilities and quality, and therefore the surroundings can in fact be very influential in communicating a firm's image (Bitner, 1992). The physical surroundings have also been denominated the servicescape, by reference to the built environment (as opposed to the natural or social environment) and various research has been conducted on the servicescape (Bitner, 1990: 1992; Booms and Bitner, 1982), the atmosphere (Kotler, 1974), and some studies have extended the concept of the servicescape to the natural environment particularly in the case of leisure services (Clarke and Schmidt, 1994; Peterson, 1974; Wakefield and Blodgett, 1994).

In fact, services theorists have often underestimated this aspect in the service provision since they have tended to study commercial services (such as banks) whereby the physical surroundings were not as important as they might be in the case of heritage services. Indeed, in the case of tourism and heritage services, physical surroundings might take a whole new dimension since it often also represents the core product upon which visitors will gaze. Whether it is a museum collection, a historic house or even a feature of a landscape, this will most often represent the core element of the visit and other factors such as interpretation are then added to it in order to facilitate the experience but the physical environment remains central. It is therefore important that it is very well kept since this will translate the willingness of the property to provide a quality product. However, this is not the only component of the product since the presentation and interpretation of a collection/building will also allow customers' access and understanding of a property. Again this will translate the efforts invested by the management in caring for customers who have made the choice to 'consume' it. The physical surroundings will therefore group a wide variety of elements ranging from the collection, buildings, interpretation to side services such as retailing services, restaurant and toilets. Again, all these aspects are part of the visitor experience and it is therefore important that they are provided with quality in mind. As trivial as it might seem, a dirty toilet or an undercooked dish might appear secondary but all will leave a bad impression on consumers.

Another encounter heavily researched concerns *interactions with other customers*, which concerns the effect of other customers' presence on an individual service perception. One aspect particularly examined is the perception of crowding which is understood as the 'negative subjective experience of certain density levels' (Rapoport, 1975: 134). Research includes work by Hui and Bateson (1991) and most of the research has been established in the recreation field (Hammitt and Patterson, 1991; Pearce, 1991; Shreyer, 1978). Crowding is a problem which can characterise the day-to-day operations of a property but can also occur when organizing large-scale events or specific exhibitions and some kind of visitor control might need to be imposed to remediate crowding problems. Pricing strategies can be introduced in an attempt to manage numbers by offering reduced rates at certain times of the day or days of the week. However, although this practice has been very much applied in traditional commercial services, it remains rarely used among heritage properties. Issues of sustainability and the effect of numbers on a heritage site have also led to some form of crowd control as for instance in the case of Stonehenge in England or the cliffs of Moher in Ireland.

The encounter with service *employees* is seen by other researchers as the core of most services. The necessity of a high level of contact between consumer and service employees legitimates the importance of this service encounter. In terms of training, this recognition has led to the development of staff training courses to improve their customer care techniques. For instance in Scotland different courses have been developed such as Scotland's Best or Welcome Host and have been very popular among visitor attractions' staff training. These training schemes cover general customer care issues as well as more specific aspects such as handling irate customers, special care for disabled visitors and they also provide trainees with a good understanding of the importance of customer care.

The importance of service encounters

The understanding of service encounters and their influences on the service experience is an aspect which has been intensively researched. This academic interest has been stimulated by the underlying belief that 'customer satisfaction depends directly and most immediately on the management and monitoring of individual service encounters' (Bitner, 1990: 69). The interactive process linked to service encounters is seen as an important step in shaping the customers' perceptions of the service received and is often referred to as the firm's 'moment of truth'. This has major implications on visitors' satisfaction evaluations since any incident that might happen during a service encounter will be fully experienced by the visitor and it will sometimes be difficult to rectify a problem on the spot. Furthermore, because consumers will be in contact with a vast range of service aspects, all of these can represent potential sources of satisfaction or dissatisfaction. For instance, if a visitor has come a long way to admire a specific Picasso painting at a museum and this painting has been on loan to another museum, the whole experience of this visitor might be felt very negatively. Equally the fact that a specific exhibit might not work, that a staff member has been unpleasant or that a dish in the restaurant was not hot enough might all spoil an individual's perception of a service. Of course, there are always possibilities to compensate the visitor in some ways, for instance by replacing a dish in the case of the restaurant or offering refunds, discounted or free tickets for a forthcoming visit, but some visitors will still find that their own experience has been spoiled. It is therefore important that all these elements are taken into consideration when evaluating service quality, in other words quality evaluations should not be limited to the core product (the artefacts, or a building for instance).

The constructs of service quality and satisfaction: underlying principles

Although the words 'satisfaction' and 'service quality' have been used interchangeably both these terms refer in fact to different constructs.

Satisfaction

Satisfaction is usually understood as an evaluation of what is obtained in comparison to what was expected. For instance, Engel and Blackwell (1982: 501) defined satisfaction as 'an evaluation that the chosen alternative is consistent with prior beliefs with respect to that alternative'. Others have referred to an experience: 'Satisfaction is not the pleasurableness of the experience, it is the evaluation rendered that the experience was at least as good as it was supposed to be' (Hunt, 1977, cited in Westbrook, 1987). Empirical investigations of this principle started with the work of Oliver (1980) and the introduction of the disconfirmation paradigm, a leading concept ever since.

The disconfirmation paradigm

Since the 1970s, the vast majority of customer satisfaction research has used some variant of the disconfirmation paradigm. Oliver (1980) posited that one perceives stimuli only in relation to an adapted standard therefore in the pre-purchase stage consumers would form expectations of product performance and in the purchase stage would then form perceptions of performances. The concept of confirmation/disconfimation was then defined as the degree to which the product or service performance would deviate from the pre-purchase expectation level. Oliver also advised that such measurement should be done via a single comparative statement using a better than/worse than heuristic. The disconfirmation of expectations paradigm posited that customers' expectations are:

- confirmed when a product performs as expected
- negatively disconfirmed when the product performs more poorly than expected (in which case dissatisfaction occurs)
- positively disconfirmed when the product performs better than expected (satisfaction occurs) (Churchill and Surprenant, 1982: 492).

If such model were to be used to measure quality of the services provided in a heritage site, it would then suggest that visitors would be provided with a list of questions covering the different service encounters of the site evaluated (buildings, interpretation, side services, staff attitude, etc.) and then requested to indicate, for each item, if the service provided was 'better' or 'worse' than what they were expecting. Therefore, one would obtain a score for each item which would represent the degrees of difference between expectations and perceptions, in other words degrees of satisfaction/dissatisfaction.

Expectations and perceptions have been defined as:

1 *Expectations* are shaped by prior exposure to the service, word-of-mouth communication, expert opinion, publicity, communication controlled by the company as well as prior exposure to competitive services (Zeithaml, Berry and Parasuraman, 1991). It is therefore important that heritage site managers are cautious about the type of promotion displayed by their property, since if the promotion promises too much (more that it can offer) this will raise expectations level above perceptions and lead to potential dissatisfaction. Equally word of mouth should not be disregarded since it is a powerful source of information for customers both positively and negatively since it has long been recognized that customers will spread negative word of mouth to more customers than they would positive comments.

2 *Performance* refers to the customers' evaluation of the service they are receiving and is set as the standard used in the comparative process which determines satisfaction judgements. The determinants of perceptions are presumably influenced by the attributes of the service delivery process.

The difference between satisfaction and service quality

So far, we have mostly mentioned the word 'satisfaction' and this term was used in relation to transaction-based evaluations of quality, in other words an evaluation of the quality provided during a service encounter. 'Service quality', on the other hand, has often been used to refer rather to a general attitude towards the firm and is the result of the degree of satisfaction experienced during encounters with the firm. For instance after consuming a service over time a consumer would shape a general impression of the firm's services' quality and this will depend on the satisfaction/dissatisfaction experienced every time the consumer has come in contact with the company. However, both terms are still used to mean the same thing by many writers and new evolution in research has allowed for a clarification of those concepts.

The evolution of the services marketing literature: emergence of new concepts

It has now been relatively well acknowledged that there is still confusion between the satisfaction and service quality constructs since different researchers do not appear to have similar definitions of those constructs and their relative relationship also remains dubious. In fact, the centre of this conflict comes from the doubts surrounding the long-term assumption that perceived quality leads to repeat purchase and patronage behaviour. The clarification of this issue is in fact of central importance since it is critical for practitioners to ascertain whether customers make purchase decisions for an organization which delivers the 'maximum level of perceived service quality' or one with whom they are 'satisfied' (Cronin and Taylor, 1992). In fact, several authors have demonstrated that the presumed link between perceived quality and purchase/patronage behaviours was flawed. In 1984, Olshavsky warned scholars that: 'Little, if any direct evidence exists to support this assumption (*perception of quality is related to purchase/patronage behaviour*); conversely, considerable indirect evidence exists that the alternative with the highest perceived quality is frequently *not* the purchased or patronised alternative' (Olshavsky, 1984: 4).

More recently, Cronin and Taylor (1992: 65) argued that: 'Service quality is an antecedent of customer satisfaction and customer satisfaction exerts a stronger influence on purchase intentions than does service quality.' This study was corroborated by Oliver (1993) who defined quality as only one of the dimensions leading to satisfaction judgements therefore suggesting that the service quality provided by a service would only partly influence the potentiality of customers purchasing the product again from the provider. In 1994, Parasuraman, Zeithaml and Berry identified that other factors such as price and product quality also influenced the satisfaction with a service consumed (Figure 9.1).

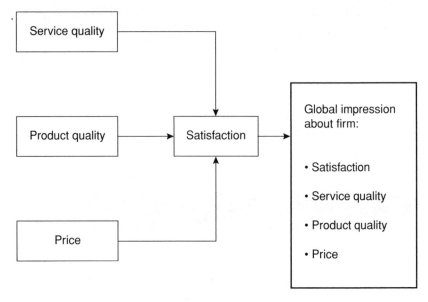

Figure 9.1 The service quality model revisited
Source: Model simplified from Parasuraman, Zeithaml and Berry (1994: 122).

On their side, Cronin and Taylor (1992) also suggested that consumers do not only use service quality but, rather, make their purchase decision on the basis of their assessment of the value of a service. The concept of perceived value is becoming increasingly accepted in the services marketing literature and was defined by Zeithaml (1988: 37) as 'the customer's overall assessment of the utility of a product based on perceptions of what is received and what is given'. The antecedents of value included both the perceived quality and the cost involved. Service value was hypothesized to influence purchase intentions and was considered as a trade-off between customers' evaluation of the benefits of using a service and its cost (Bolton and Drew, 1991). Therefore, the concept of perceived service value represents a step forward in the recognition that service quality, interpreted as the evaluation of a service attribute, is not the sole determinant of purchasing evaluation.

To reiterate, service quality should now be considered as a transaction-based evaluation of the quality provided in a service. It has also been recognized that this is not the only element which will determine consumers purchasing behaviour: although service quality will influence consumer behaviour intentions, product quality, price and value for money are also likely to impinge on this.

If applying these new principles to heritage 'consumption', it would therefore suggest that visitors would evaluate the service provided upon three dimensions: the quality of the service provided (supposedly staff, interpretation, side services), the quality of the product (the buildings) and an evaluation of value for money.

Quality in practice

This chapter reviewed the notion of services and how quality is defined and measured in relation to their own specificities. However, if some precise criteria have been established to measure service quality and satisfaction, they only measure the outcome of an organization provision. This measurement process operates as a barometer of the performance of a company and is therefore intuitively linked to the managerial and operational performance of the organization supporting it and its ability to match consumers' expectations closely. Therefore, an understanding of service quality measurement is not an end in itself but rather the starting point to a deeper investigation into the reasons behind the strengths and weaknesses of an institution.

Indeed, service quality has not solely been defined from the consumers' perspective but it has also been linked to various gaps in the services provision (Parasuraman, Zeithaml and Berry, 1985). The current and following chapter focused on one gap of that model, that occurring between customers' expectations and perceptions of the service consumed. However, other gaps are equally important such as the gap relating the difference between customers' expectations and the managerial perceptions of those expectations. More importantly, it is the translation of managerial perceptions of customers' expectations into service quality specifications and the related service delivery that has a central position. The measurement of customers' perceptions of service quality, therefore, does not bear much use unless it is then translated into specifications that will guarantee high levels of customers' quality perceptions.

The types of service specifications in a heritage context are extremely varied and need to be adapted to the specific and at times rigid service environment within which they operate. The specifications fall within the three categories of service encounters: physical surroundings, employees and contacts with other customers. They will therefore include anything from the handling of food in the restaurant, to the front-office staff at the reception, specifications for the rangers looking after the park, the operation of a queuing system, etc. However, as was noted earlier in this chapter, one distinction that should not be forgotten is that that exists between direct and indirect service provision. The direct service provision relates to all direct contacts between staff and their customers but the dimension of indirect service provision is often disregarded despite its particularly important place in the provision of heritage services. Indeed, because in most cases visitors will be left to their own devices to enjoy and consume the service offered, all the services aspects allowing for that aspect of consumption are equally important. Consequently the service specifications will also include all aspects pertaining to the indirect provision of for instance information signs, path and property upkeep, provision of guidebooks, etc. This implies that those aspects have been appropriately conceived in the first place and that procedures have been installed for their constant monitoring.

Conclusion

To summarize, the search for quality arguably has become the most important trend of the 1980s and service quality is nowadays seen as a key strategic weapon (Berry, Bennett and Brown, 1989). Unfortunately, services quality cannot be objectively measured as can technical quality for manufactured goods and it therefore remains an elusive and abstract construct. The characteristics of intangibility, heterogeneity and inseparability constitute a challenge for managers because they do not allow for an easy process of quality evaluation. More importantly, customers' judgements of a service depend as much on the service process as on the outcome, therefore, customer satisfaction can be seen as depending on the production of services as well as on their consumption (Bateson, 1991). Generally, service quality has been conceptualized as a comparative process in which expected and perceived products or services were compared. The complexity of this comparative process has been studied in depth by Oliver (1980; 1993) and other approaches have developed simplified versions of this model, SERVQUAL serving as an example. However, recent developments in the services marketing field have extended the notion of the evaluation of a firm by including not only the service quality evaluated but also the product quality and price, leading to the notion of value and the repositioning of the concept of satisfaction. The next chapter will provide an overview showing how all these concepts can be 'tied up' into one scale designed to measure service quality in historic houses services.

Questions

1 Identify at least three reasons which justify why providing quality service is vital to a company's success.

2 Explain how the three types of service encounters might differ between commercial services (such as banks, insurance companies) and heritage services.
3 What are the differences between the service quality and satisfaction constructs?

References and further reading

Bateson, J. (1979). Why we need service marketing. In *Conceptual and Theoretical Developments in Marketing* (O. Ferrell, S. Brown and C. Lamb, eds), American Association of Marketing.

Bateson, J. (1991). *Managing Services Marketing*. 2nd edition. Dryden Press.

Berry, L. L. (1980). Services marketing is different, *Business*, **30**(3), 24–29.

Berry, L. L., Bennett, D. R. and Brown, C. W. (1989). *Service Quality: A Profit Strategy for Financial Institutions*. Dow-Jones-Irwin.

Bitner, M. J. (1990). Evaluating service encounters: the effects of physical surroundings and employee responses. *Journal of Marketing*, **54**, April, 69–82.

Bitner, M. J. (1992). Servicescapes: the impact of physical surroundings on consumers and employees. *Journal of Marketing*, **56**, April, 57–71.

Bolton, R. N. and Drew, J. H. (1991). A multistage model of customers' assessments of service quality and value. *Journal of Consumer Research*, **17**, March, 375–384.

Booms, B. and Bitner, M. (1981). Marketing strategies and organization structures for service firms. In *Marketing of Services* (J. Donnelly and W. George, eds), pp. 47–51, American Marketing Association.

Booms, B. H. and Bitner, M. J. (1982). Marketing services by managing the environment. *Cornell Hotel and Restaurant Quarterly*, **23**, May, 35–39.

Churchill, G. A. and Surprenant, C. (1982). An investigation into the determinants of customer satisfaction. *Journal of Marketing Research*, **19**, November, 491–504.

Clarke, I. and Schmidt, R. A. (1994). Beyond the servicescape: the experience of place. Working paper presented at the CIRASS/EIRASS conference on Recent advances in services, Banff, Canada, 7–10 May.

Cronin J. J. and Taylor, S. A. T. (1992). Measuring service quality: a reexamination and extension. *Journal of Marketing*, **56**(3), 55–68.

Edgett, S. and Parkinson S. (1993). Marketing for services industries: a review. *Service Industries Journal*, **13**(3), 19–39.

Engel, J. and Blackwell, R. D. (1982). *Consumer Behaviour*. 4th edition. Dryden Press.

Fick, G. R. and Ritchie, J. R. (1991). Measuring service quality in the travel and tourism industry. *Journal of Travel Research*, **29**, Fall, 2–9.

Fisk, R. P., Brown, S. W. and Bitner, M. J. (1993). Tracking the evolution of the services marketing literature. *Journal of Retailing*, **69**(1), 61–98.

Hammitt, W. E. and Patterson, M. E. (1991). Coping behavior to avoid visitor encounters: its relationship to wildland privacy. *Journal of Leisure Research*, **23**(3), 225–237.

Hui, M. K. and Bateson, J. E. (1991). Perceived control and the effect of crowding and consumer choice on the service experience. *Journal of Consumer Research*, **18**(2), 174–184.

Hunt, H. K. (1977*). Conceptualisation and measurement of consumer satisfaction and dissatisfaction*. Marketing Science Institute.

Kotler, P. (1974). Atmospherics as a marketing tool. *Journal of Retailing*, **49**(4), 48–64.

Kotler, P. (1982). *Marketing for Non Profit Organizations*. 2nd edition. Prentice Hall.

Kotler, P., Armstrong, G., Saunders, J. and Wong, V. (1996). *Principles of Marketing: European Edition*. Prentice Hall.

Lewis, B. R. (1993). Service quality measurement. *Marketing Intelligence and Planning*, **11**(4), 36–44.

Lewis, B. R. and Mitchell, V. W. (1991). Defining and measuring the quality of customer services. *Marketing Intelligence and Planning*, **8**(6), 11–17.

Lovelock, C. H. (1983). Classifying services to gain strategic marketing insights. *Journal of Marketing*, **47**, Summer, 9–20.

Oliver, R. L. (1980). A cognitive model of the antecedents and consequences of customer satisfaction. *Journal of Marketing Research*, **17**, November, 460–469.

Oliver, R. L. (1993). A conceptual model of service quality and service satisfaction compatible goals, different concepts. *Advances in Services Marketing and Management*, **2**(4), 65–85.

Olshavsky, R. W. (1984). Perceived quality in consumer decision making: an integrated theoretical perspective. In *Perceived Quality, How Consumers View Stores and Merchandise* (J. Jacoby and J. C. Olson, eds), Lexington Books.

Parasuraman, A., Zeithaml, V. A. and Berry, L. (1994). Reassessment of expectations as a comparison standard in measuring service quality: implications for future research. *Journal of Marketing*, **58**, January, 111–124.

Parasuraman, A., Zeithaml, V. A. and Berry, L. (1985). A conceptual model of service quality and its implications for future research. *Journal of Marketing*, **49**, Fall, 41–50.

Payne, A. (1993). *The Essence of Services Marketing*. Prentice Hall.

Pearce, P. L. (1991). Towards the better management of tourist queues. In *Managing Tourism* (S. Medlik, ed.), pp. 215–230, Butterworth-Heinemann.

Peterson, G. L. (1974). Evaluating the quality of the wilderness environment. *Environment and Behaviour*, **6**(2), 169–193.

Rapoport, A. (1975). Toward a redefinition of density. *Environment and Behaviour*, **7**(2), 133–158.

Schreyer, R. and Driver, B. L. (1988). The benefits of outdoor recreation participation. In *Proceedings of the National Outdoor Recreation Forum*, 13–14 January, Florida. (E. Watson, ed.), pp. 472–482.

Schreyer, R. and Roggenbuck, J. W. (1978). The influence of experience expectations on crowding perception and social psychological carrying capacities. *Leisure Sciences*, **1**(4), 373–394.

Shostack, G. L. (1977). Breaking free from product marketing. *Journal of Marketing*, **41**(2), 73–80.

Shostack, G. L. (1985). Planning the service encounter. In *The Service Encounter* (J. A. Czepiel, M. Solomon and C. F. Surprenant, eds), pp. 243–254, Lexington Books.

Surprenant, C. F. and Solomon M. R. (1987). Predictability and personalization in the service encounter. *Journal of Marketing*, **54**, January, 85–101.

Uhl, K. P. and Upah, G. U. (1983). The marketing of services: why and how it is different. *Research in Marketing*, **6**, 231–257.

Wakefield, K. L. and Blodgett, J. G. (1994). The importance of servicescapes in leisure service settings. *Journal of Services Marketing*, **8**(3), 66–76.

Westbrook, R. A. (1987). Product/consumption-based affective responses and post-purchase processes. *Journal of Marketing Research*, **24** (August), 258–270.

Williams, C. (1998). Is the SERVQUAL model an appropriate management tool for measuring service delivery quality in the UK leisure industry? *Managing Leisure*, **3**(2), 98–110.

Wyckham, R. G., Fitzroy P. T. and Mandry, G. D. (1975). Marketing of services. *European Journal of Marketing*, **9**(1), 59–67.

Zeithaml V. A. (1988). Consumer perceptions of price, quality and value: a means-end model and synthesis of evidence. *Journal of Marketing*, **52**(3), 2–22.

Zeithaml V. A., Parasuraman, A. and Berry, L. L. (1985). Problems and strategies in services marketing. *Journal of Marketing*, **49**, Spring, 33–46.

Zeithaml, V. A., Berry, L. L. and Parasuraman, A. (1991). The nature and determinants of customer expectations of service. *Working Paper*, Marketing Science Institute.

10

Measurement of service quality

Isabelle Frochot

Introduction

This chapter lays down the general principles involved in service quality and satisfaction evaluations as it has been portrayed in the services marketing literature. However, one also needs to look at what this implies for heritage service quality evaluations and to reassemble all the concepts into one model.

Quality issues and heritage

Most existing services marketing studies have mainly looked at services which are commercial in nature and have rarely addressed heritage services. In order to understand which commonalties and differences exist between heritage services and other services, the first step is to identify the range of service encounters that characterize heritage services by distinguishing them among the three main categories: physical surroundings, interactions with other customers and employees (this was done in the previous chapter).

Second, one needs to evaluate to what extent the heritage literature can contribute to the development of a quality scale. In fact, if the analysis of service quality in the heritage field has been addressed by several researchers, the information provided by these studies is often limited since they tend to either focus on a single aspect or enumerate the different elements constituting service quality of a specific heritage service but, either way, they do not allow for an overview of its main components and dimensions. For instance, interpretation has been an extensively researched element in the heritage literature with various studies analysing the effectiveness of different interpretation techniques (Herbert et al., 1986; Light, 1995; Prince and Higgins, 1992; Swarbrooke, 1994; Wright, 1989). However, the service encounters characterizing the service provided in heritage sites cover a wider range of components. For instance, other elements of the visitor experience have been less recognized such as the importance of opening and closing times, parking provision, direction signs, staff attitude, catering and retailing facilities, special care towards disabled and children and so forth (Yale, 1991). This range of various elements is usually present in customers' surveys but these serve rather as a checklist with no attempt at understanding the underlying dimensions that might make up service quality.

Consequently, there is a clear need in the heritage field for a tool measuring the quality provided, a tool which would also allow for the identification of various dimensions which make up quality evaluations and which would then help managers to prioritize necessary improvements. If such a scale is not present in the heritage field, the services marketing literature has however identified a scale, named SERVQUAL, which does that precisely. However, this scale has mainly been developed and applied in the context of commercial services and has never been used previously in heritage services evaluations, therefore, its potential application to a heritage context will need to be treated with caution. Consequently, this chapter will first present SERVQUAL and its principles, question its potential application as such to heritage services and then develop an adapted scale, called HISTOQUAL, for the specific context of historic houses. By comparison to museums and galleries, historic houses have been a less researched service but the diversity of the products they offer make them an eclectic and interesting concept. For instance, over the past decades historic houses have extended their product offering by including catering and retailing facilities, organizing exhibitions and various events, providing facilities for children and so forth. The necessity for a scale which would integrate all these components is therefore greatly acknowledged by both practitioners and researchers.

The measurement issue: SERVQUAL

The necessity to develop a standard instrument to measure quality across services was motivated in the late 1980s by American researchers such as Parasuraman and his colleagues who recognized that the research on service quality lacked conceptual foundations. They therefore set out to investigate further the notion of quality and develop an instrument to measure it. Their original research was based on focus group interviews with consumers and in-depth interviews with executives in four service categories: retail banking, credit card, securities brokerage, and product repair and maintenance. They concluded: 'While some perceptions about service quality were specific to the industries selected, commonalties among the industries prevailed. The commonalties are encouraging for they suggest that a general model of service quality can be developed' (Parasuraman, Zeithaml and Berry, 1985: 44).

In other terms, Parasuraman and his colleagues stated that regardless of the type of service considered, consumers used similar criteria to evaluate service quality, hence suggesting the possibility to create a generic model of service quality which could be valid across different service industries. For instance, this implied that banks, education and health services' consumers used similar criteria when evaluating the quality of those services, therefore, a similar scale could be applied to any of them. Their exploratory research identified the various criteria used by consumers to evaluate perceived service quality. These criteria were reorganized in ten dimensions (also designated service quality determinants) which the researchers believed to capture the dimensions upon which customers evaluate service quality. These dimensions were: reliability, responsiveness, competence, access, courtesy, communication, credibility, security, understanding/knowing the customer and tangibles.

The scale was developed from a questionnaire which used specific measurement criteria. To start with, the basic measure used in the scale defined perceived service quality (Q) as the difference between customers perceptions (P) and expectations (E) about the service considered: $Q = P - E$. Perceived service quality was therefore viewed as the degree and the direction of the discrepancy between consumers' perceptions and expectations. According to the model, levels of expectations higher than perceptions $(E > P)$ of performance would suggest lower level of quality. Conversely, expectations which had been met or were lower than perceptions would result in higher quality levels $(E \leq P)$. The degree of this difference was also supposed to influence quality perceptions since modest discrepancies between expectations and perceptions would result in modest levels of perceived service quality. Alternatively, large discrepancies between both measures would result in more extreme perceived service quality evaluations.

The procedure followed by the authors lay in identifying a series of 97 items representing customers' criteria to evaluate perceived service quality. The questionnaire was divided into two series of statements: the first half was designated to measure customers' expectations while the corresponding half measured consumers' perceptions. However, Parasuraman and colleagues did not advocate that the survey should be filled in by respondents before and after the service, but together and once the service had been consumed. Each item was measured on a seven-point Likert scale ranging from 'strongly agree' (7) to 'strongly disagree' (1), with no verbal labels in between. Approximately half the statements were worded positively and half were worded negatively in order to avoid yea-saying and nay-saying.

The expectations statements referred to the level of service customers felt a firm should offer in the service category considered. These statements read: 'Please show the extent to which you think firms offering .... services should possess the features described by each statement.' As regards the perceptions statements, respondents were requested to name a firm they had previously used within the service category and then indicate their perceptions about that firm, the statements read: 'Please show the extent to which you believe XYZ has the feature described by each statement.'

In 1988, the three authors conducted further work on their scale and reduced the number of dimensions from ten to five which were named and described as:

1 *Tangibles*: physical facilities, equipment, and appearance of personnel.
2 *Reliability*: ability to perform the promised service dependably and accurately.
3 *Responsiveness*: willingness to help consumers and provide prompt service.
4 *Assurance*: knowledge and courtesy of employees and their ability to convey trust and confidence.
5 *Empathy*: caring, individualized attention the firm provides to its customers.

Each of the dimensions contained four to six statement sets associated with it. The intent of the statement set was to provide a score for components of the dimension which could also be averaged to provide an overall score of the dimension. Each statement had a corresponding quality score calculated by subtracting the perception score from the expectation score (Appendix 10.1).

Though the authors considered their scale portrayed generic properties, they acknowledged the necessity to adapt the scale to specific services contexts:

> The instrument has been designed to be applicable across a broad spectrum of services. As such, it provides a basic skeleton through its expectations/perceptions format encompassing statements for each of the five dimensions. The skeleton, when necessary, can be adapted or supplemented to fit the characteristics or specific research needs of a particular organisation. (Parasuraman, Zeithaml and Berry, 1988: 30–1)

Parasuraman and his colleagues added that the relative importance of each dimension in influencing customers' quality perceptions could be evaluated by regressing the overall quality score for each dimension. By doing so, the authors identified that reliability appeared to be the most critical dimension, followed by assurance, responsiveness, tangibles and empathy.

Finally, in order to assess the scale validity, customers were requested to rate an overall quality rating of the firm by checking one of the four categories: excellent, good, fair, poor. SERVQUAL's validity was further assessed by establishing other conceptually related variables. These were assessed through two questions relating to (1) whether respondents would recommend the service to a friend and (2) whether they had ever reported a problem with the service consumed. Respondents answering respectively yes and no to the first and second questions were assumed to perceive high levels of service quality.

The potentialities of the instrument, as presented by Parasuraman and his colleagues were various. First, the authors recommended that SERVQUAL would be most valuable when used periodically to track service quality trends. The scores obtained on each of the statements could be averaged for each dimension therefore giving insights into the firm's quality performance on each dimension. Furthermore, an overall measure of service quality could also be produced by averaging the scores across the five dimensions. Parasuraman and his colleagues also recommended use of the scale in multi-unit companies therefore allowing for comparison of the level of service quality provided in each retail outlet. Finally, the instrument could also be used to compare a firm's service performance in relation to its competitors' by asking its customers to indicate their perception scores for competitors. Following the creation of the scale, various criticisms appeared in the literature which led Parasuraman, Zeithaml and Berry to reconsider some aspects of their instrument.

In 1991, the authors published an article in which they refined their scale and introduced some modifications to the original instrument. Following the same methodology, the authors tested again the scale on five companies: one telephone company, two insurance companies and two banks, and the sample ranged from 290 to 487 respondents in each company.

The modifications to the original scale included:

1 *The modification of the statements' wordings*: first, the authors recognized that the 'should' terminology used in the expectations statements led to unrealistically high evaluations. Therefore the statements were reworded to what customers 'would' expect from a firm, and read: 'Excellent telephone companies *will* insist on error-free records.' Negatively worded statements also appeared to create confusion among respondents and were therefore re-worded in a positive fashion.

2 *Substitution of two items*: two original items were changed under the tangible and assurance dimensions. The original item, 'The appearance of the physical facilities of XYZ companies should be in keeping with the type of services provided' was replaced with 'Materials associated with the service will be visually appealing in an excellent XYZ company'. The following item 'XYZ company employees should get adequate support from their companies to do their job well' was changed to 'Employees in excellent XYZ companies will have the knowledge to answer customer questions'.

3 *Estimation of the relative importance of the five dimensions*: Parasuraman, Zeithaml and Berry recognized that the importance of the dimensions should be assessed directly rather than inferring them through regression analysis. They advised the addition of a question to the questionnaire asking respondents to allocate a total of 100 points across the dimensions according to how important they considered each to be.

The lack of transferability of SERVQUAL

If SERVQUAL has been successfully developed and applied by its authors, one has to be careful when applying the scale to other contexts. Indeed, the scale was in fact developed on a small range of specific services which could also be characterized as commercial (banks, insurance companies and so forth). In fact when other researchers have attempted to apply the scale to different contexts, they identified other quality dimensions (Babakus and Boller, 1992; Carman, 1990; Fick and Ritchie, 1991; Leblanc, 1992). Towards the end of the 1990s, barely a decade since the scale was created, it has been commonly acknowledged that when attempting at evaluating quality on a new context, a new scale should be adapted following the SERVQUAL methodology. This was the perspective taken in the present study.

In order to develop a scale which would be applicable to historic houses the SERVQUAL scale methodology was followed and a new scale, named HISTOQUAL, was developed (for details of the study see Frochot and Hughes, 2000). To summarize briefly, the general principle lay in developing a pool of 43 items representing service quality aspects in historic houses. The best way to evaluate a list of service quality items was first to identify the range of service encounters that characterized a service, in other words, identify all the points of interaction between the visitor and the site. One can easily do this by putting him or herself in the place of a customer that consumes the service and take note of all the elements that the consumer comes in contact with. The list identified was then supported by interviews with visitors and managers and an extensive literature review. The list of items was then evaluated by customers and then refined via statistical analysis (factor analysis) in order to reduce the list to the most relevant items (24 in total) and to identify the main underlying dimensions (Table 10.1). In this scale perception statements only (rather than a gap measure) were used for reasons which will not be fully debated in the present chapter. This choice was in fact supported by an extensive literature search which tended to support the superiority of perception based measures rather than the gap score (for a review see Fochot and Hughes, 1999).

The results presented in Table 10.1 indicate the five dimensions identified in HISTOQUAL and the items which constitute each of these dimensions. The right-hand column displays the average scores which were obtained on a sample of 780 visitors spread across three properties. These scores were obtained from visitors' ratings on a 1 to 5 Likert scale, scores close to five indicating a strong level of agreement while scores close to 1 indicate a strong disagreement with the item measured.

Once the five dimensions were identified they were then named according to the range of items they included. The first dimension, Responsiveness, grouped items relating mainly to the staff efficiency and the property recognition of customer needs while the second dimension, Tangibles, included items representing the physical environment of the property and its upkeep. The third, Communications, contained items describing the quality and detail of the historical information provided. This dimension was not present in SERVQUAL but appeared relevant to the present context since because most of the service was indirectly provided by staff, the provision of instruments

Table 10.1   Mean scores of HISTOQUAL across the three properties

Factors	Items	Results
F1		*4.67*
Responsiveness	Staff are always helpful and courteous	4.69
	Staff are willing to take time with visitors	4.73
	Visitors are made to feel welcome	4.64
	Level of crowding is tolerable	4.63
	Staff are well informed to answer customers requests	4.70
	Visitors feel free to explore, there are no restrictions to access	4.52
	The property and grounds are opened at convenient hours	4.72
	Staff are always available when needed	4.78
F2		*4.19*
Tangibles	The property is well kept and restored	4.21
	The general cleanliness and upkeep of the property and grounds is satisfying	4.39
	The grounds are attractive	4.17
	The site has remained authentic	3.98
	Direction signs to show around the property and grounds are clear and helpful	4.18
	The garden and/or park contain a large variety of plants	4.20
	The interior of the house offers a lot of interesting things to look at	4.21
F3		*3.84*
Communication	The written leaflets provide enough information	3.75
	The information on the property and grounds is detailed enough	3.92
	Visitors are well informed of the different facilities and attractions available at the property	4.04
	Foreign language leaflets are helpful	3.63
F4		*3.88*
Consumables	The restaurant offers a wide variety of dishes and refreshments	3.95
	The shop offers a large variety of goods	3.94
	The restaurant' staff provide efficient service	3.64
F5		*2.64*
Empathy	The property considers the needs of less able visitors	2.53
	Facilities for children are provided	2.79

Note: Results in italics indicate the average result per dimension.

to help the guidance and information of visitors therefore became a prominent feature of the service quality. Dimension four, Consumables, contained three items relating to the side services provided by the property such as the restaurant and shop, and the last dimension, Empathy, reflected two items relating to the willingness of the property to take into consideration the needs of children and less able visitors.

The scores shown in Table 10.1 are an indication of the ratings obtained across the three historic houses surveyed. Although there seems to be a fairly good appreciation from consumers of the Responsiveness dimension, and to a lesser extent the Tangibles dimension, one score of concern relates to the Communication dimension which is relatively low. In regard to the recognized importance of interpretation and the managers' concern for interpretation, this score shows that consumers have on average a poorer appreciation of this dimension. Finally, there seems to be scope for improvement on the Consumables dimension and particularly the Empathy dimension, with customers generally disagreeing that the properties are actually considering the specific needs of disabled visitors and/or children.

Importance scores

In order for managers to prioritize the five dimensions it will be useful to obtain importance ratings from visitors. As Parasuraman, Zeithaml and Berry advised in 1991, consumers should be requested to allocate 100 points among the five dimensions in order to indicate their relative importance. In HISTO-QUAL, an importance ranking (from 1 to 5) of the dimensions was preferred in order to keep a similar format to the one used previously in the scale. Results indicated that the ranking of the dimensions by decreasing order was Tangibles, Communications, Responsiveness, Consumables and Empathy. These scores reinforce the analysis of the perception ratings across the five dimensions emphasizing even more that attractions do need to improve their performance on the Communications dimension since this is the second most important one.

The use of the HISTOQUAL scale

The study has presented the HISTOQUAL scale and the usefulness of the results for heritage attraction managers. The scale can bring useful information in order to assess service quality performance across historic house properties and, once developed, HISTOQUAL could be used by property managers in several ways (as suggested by Parasuraman and colleagues). It can be used to evaluate the quality of the service provided in historic houses for each item and dimension and therefore identify potential areas of improvement and consequently evaluate the success of the improvements undertaken. For instance, if a specific interpretation technique has been installed, if staff have been trained with a new customer care programme or if even a new queuing system has been put in place, results on the HISTOQUAL scale can be compared before and after the modifications in order to monitor the efficiency of the changes. Finally, if several properties are managed by a similar organization, the quality evaluations in each of them can be assessed and compared, again using HISTOQUAL.

Additional measures

HISTOQUAL as such evaluates service quality but not satisfaction, in the sense that it assesses the evaluation of the service provided but not the general attitude towards the attraction. In order to evaluate satisfaction several other criteria need in fact to be added to the scale although, as we will see, some of these criteria are not always applicable to the heritage context.

Average quality score

In order to obtain a score measuring the general attitude of consumers towards an attraction, visitors could have been requested to indicate, as in SERVQUAL, their rating of the firm's overall quality by checking categories such as excellent, good, fair and poor. Nevertheless, if one was considering the recent advancements in the services marketing literature, a general measure relating to satisfaction would be preferred to service quality. In fact whether it is attempting to measure service quality or satisfaction, one needs to be cautious about such evaluation. Asking visitors to indicate their degree of satisfaction with the services offered might have the advantage of providing a general evaluation of their satisfaction but there is a possibility that such judgement could be biased. Indeed, visitors tend to consider that heritage sites, even if privately owned, are part of their national patrimony and their identity, and therefore seem to be far more tolerant when evaluating their satisfaction than they would be for private/commercial services. In fact, when conducting surveys and probing visitors on rating the satisfaction with a heritage site visited, it is very common to hear visitors having difficulties making a judgement and making comments such as: 'I suppose they do what they can' or 'I presume it costs a lot of money to look after this property'. This was already observed by Williams (1998) when measuring service

163

delivery quality in the UK leisure industry where it was observed that, in the case of public services, customers were less openly critical when evaluating quality. Here again, in the case of golf services, Williams noticed that customers articulated comments such as 'they do the best they can in the circumstances' even if the public course was actually run by private contractors. Therefore, one should be careful when using this criterion since it might not represent strictly speaking a totally accurate evaluation of satisfaction.

Value for money

Visitors can also be requested to indicate their feeling about the value for money of the attraction visited. This has been recognized as an important factor of satisfaction evaluation and represents a good indicator for managers of the balance between the price paid by visitors and their feelings about the services offered in return.

Repeat purchase

Whether the scale should also include a measure of repeat purchase was a difficult but important question since the services marketing research has indicated that at least two-thirds of unsatisfied customers will not buy from a company again and, therefore, this needs to be assessed in a satisfaction evaluation. For traditional commercial services the fact that a consumer might purchase again from a company is an important business indicator and is often interpreted as a sign of satisfaction. However, in the case of heritage site, a consumer could well indicate that he or she does not wish to visit a property again while this simply means that this person does not enjoy visiting a single property several times. In that case, a consumer indicating that he or she does not wish to visit a property again should not be mistaken for dissatisfaction and, therefore, it might be preferable not to use this indicator.

Word of mouth

Perhaps one of the best ways to check the validity of HISTOQUAL measures is to use other indicators such as word-of-mouth recommendations. For instance, if adding a question simply asking respondents to indicate whether they would or would not recommend a site to friends and family, this could provide as good an evaluation of their degree of satisfaction with the service provided.

Handling problems

It has long been acknowledged that the vast majority of customers who have experienced a problem will become loyal if their problem has been handled quickly and efficiently. It is consequently important to evaluate whether consumers have experienced a potential problem and if it was handled to their convenience.

The final questionnaire incorporating HISTOQUAL and additional evaluation criteria is presented in Appendix 10.2 at the end of this chapter.

What next?

If the application of HISTOQUAL can help managers identify areas of improvements in their service provision, how does it benefit a visitor attraction in the long term?

First, because HISTOQUAL will allow for the identification and correction of potential pitfalls in the long run it will help improve customers perception of the quality provided and, ultimately, their satisfaction with the services offered. This in turn should improve the positive word-of-mouth recommendations and increase in the long run the number of visitors numbers. Furthermore if the attraction also wishes to consider 'promoting' even more its quality, then it can choose to be registered by a quality grading scheme such as the one provided by the Association of Scottish Visitor Attractions (ASVA), which is run by the Scottish Tourist Board, or a similar scheme organized by the West Country Tourist Board. These schemes evaluate the quality of service provided by visitor attractions and allocate different gradings which can then be displayed by an attraction, as a hotel would display a plaque with its number of stars.

Conclusion

In conclusion, although the services marketing field has developed a wide array of concepts and tools to measure service quality and satisfaction, the extent to which all of those can be applicable to a heritage service provision remains questionable. The SERVQUAL scale has been identified as a potential tool to evaluate service quality perceptions but its applicability is limited to the services upon which it was built, or at least upon commercial services, and in the case of historic houses a new adapted scale called HISTO-QUAL was defined. This scale can be used by managers as a 'ready-made' tool to evaluate the quality of the service they are providing and can be combined with more general measures of satisfaction. HISTOQUAL can enable managers to identify potential areas which necessitate improvements, monitor the effect of any training or service provision changes and evaluate the importance of quality dimensions to visitors.

Questions

1 Is the SERVQUAL scale applicable to all types of services?
2 In the HISTOQUAL scale (as in SERVQUAL) five service quality dimensions have been identified. Why should one also evaluate the importance consumers attach to those dimensions?
3 What do the results displayed in Table 10.1 tell us about visitors' perceptions of the quality provided in the three properties surveyed?

References and further reading

Babakus, E. and Boller, G. W. (1992). An empirical assessment of the SERVQUAL scale. *Journal of Business Research,* **24**, 253–268.

Carman, J. M. (1990). Consumer perceptions of service quality: an assessment of the SERVQUAL dimensions. *Journal of Retailing*, **66**(1), 33–55.

Fick, G. R. and Ritchie, J. R. (1991) Measuring service quality in the travel and tourism industry. *Journal of Travel Research*, **29**, Fall, 2–9.

Frochot, I. V. and Hughes, H. (2000). HISTOQUAL: the development of a historic houses assessment scale. *Tourism Management*, **21**(2), 157–167.

Herbert, D. T., Thomas, C., Prentice, R. and Prentice, M. (1986). *Interpretation at Cadw's Sites*. Welsh Historic Monuments.

Leblanc, G. (1992). Factors affecting customer evaluation of service quality in travel agencies: an investigation of customers perceptions. *Journal of Travel Research*, **30**, Spring, 10–16.

Light, D. (1995). Visitor's use of interpretative media at heritage sites. *Leisure Studies*, **14**(5), 132–149.

Parasuraman, A., Zeithaml, V. A. and Berry, L. (1985). A conceptual model of service quality and its implications for future research. *Journal of Marketing*, **49**, Fall, 41–50.

Parasuraman, A., Zeithaml, V. A. and Berry, L. (1988). SERVQUAL: a multiple-item scale for measuring consumer perceptions of service quality. *Journal of Retailing*, **64**(1), 12–37.

Parasuraman, A., Zeithaml, V. A. and Berry, L. (1991). Refinement and reassessment of the SERVQUAL scale. *Journal of Retailing*, **67**(4), 420–449.

Prince, D. R. and Higgins, B. A. (1992). *Leicestershire Museums: The Public View*. Leicestershire Museums, Arts and Records Service.

Swarbrooke, J. (1994). The future of the past: heritage tourism into the 21st century. In *Tourism, the State of the Art* (A. V. Seaton et al., eds) pp. 222–229, Wiley.

Williams, C. (1998). Is the SERVQUAL model an appropriate management tool for measuring service delivery quality in the UK leisure industry? *Managing Leisure*, **3**(2), 98–110.

Wright, P. (1989). The quality of visitors' experiences in art museums. In *The New Museology* (P. Vergo, ed.), Reaktion Books.

Yale, P. (1991). *From Tourist Attractions to Heritage Tourism*. ELM Publications.

Appendix 10.1: The SERVQUAL scale range of expectations and perceptions statements

DIRECTIONS: This survey deals with your opinions of _____ services. Please show the extent to which you think firms offering _____ services should possess the features described by each statement. Do this by picking one of the seven numbers next to each statement. If you strongly agree that these firms should possess a feature, circle the number 7. If you strongly disagree that these firms should possess a feature, circle 1. If your feelings are not strong, circle one of the numbers in the middle. There are no right or wrong answers – all we are interested in is a number that best shows your expectations about firms offering _____ services.

E1 They should have up-to-date equipment.

E2 Their physical facilities should be visually appealing.

E3 Their employees should be well dressed and appear neat.

E4 The appearance of the physical facilities of these firms should be in keeping with the type of services provided.

E5 When these firms promise to do something by a certain time, they should do so.

E6 When customers have problems, these firms should be sympathetic and reassuring.

E7 These firms should be dependable.

E8 They should provide their services at the time they promise to so do.

E9 They should keep their records accurately.

E10 They shouldn't be expected to tell customers exactly when services will be performed. (-)[b]

E11 It is not realistic for customers to expect prompt service from employees of these firms. (-)

E12 Their employees don't always have to be willing to help customers. (-)

E13 It is okay if they are too busy to respond to customer requests promptly. (-)

E14 Customers should be able to trust employees of these firms.

E15 Customers should be able to feel safe in their transactions with these firms' employees.

E16 Their employees should be polite.

E17 Their employees should get adequate support from these firms to do their jobs well.

E18 These firms should not be expected to give customers individual attention. (-)

E19 Employees of these firms cannot be expected to give customers personal attention. (-)

E20 It is unrealistic to expect employees to know what the needs of their customers are. (-)

E21 It is unrealistic to expect these firms to have their customers' best interests at heart. (-)

E22 They should be expected to have operating hours convenient to all their customers. (-)

DIRECTIONS: The following set of statements relate to your feelings about XYZ. For each statement, please show the extent to which you believe XYZ has the feature described by the statement. Once again circling a 7 means you strongly agree that XYZ has that feature and circling a 1 means that you strongly disagree. You may circle any of the numbers in the middle that show how strong your feelings are. There are no right or wrong answers – all we are interested in is a number that best shows your perceptions about XYZ.

P1 XYZ has up-to-date equipment.

P2 XYZ's physical facilities are visually appealing.

P3 YZ's employees are well dressed and appear neat.

P4 The appearance of the physical facilities of XYZ is in keeping with the type of services provided.

P5 When XYZ promises to do something by a certain time, it does so.

P6 When you have problems, XYZ is sympathetic and reassuring.

P7 XYZ is dependable.

P8 XYZ provides its services at the time it promises to do so.

P9 XYZ keeps its records accurately.

P10 XYZ does not tell customers exactly when services will be performed. (-)

P11 You do not receive prompt service from XYZ's employees.

P12 Employees of XYZ are not always willing to help customers.

P13 Employees of XYZ are too busy to respond to customer requests promptly. (-)

P14 You can trust employees of XYZ.

P15 You feel safe in your transactions with XYZ's employees.

P16 Employees of XYZ are polite.

P17 Employees get adequate support from XYZ to do their jobs well.

P18 XYZ does not give you individual attention. (-)

P19 Employees of XYZ do not give you personal attention. (-)

P20 Employees of XYZ do not know what your needs are. (-)

P21 XYZ does not have your best interests at heart. (-)

P22 XYZ does not have operating hours convenient to all their customers. (-)

a) A seven point scale ranging from 'Strongly Agree' (7) to 'Strongly Disagree' (1), with no verbal labels for the intermediate scale points (i.e. 2 through 6), accompanied each statement. Also, statements were in random order in the questionnaire. A complete listing of the 34-item instrument used in the second stage of data collection can be obtained from the first author. b) Ratings on these statements were reverse-scored prior to data analysis.

Source: Parasuraman, Zeithaml, and Berry, L. (1988).

Appendix 10.2: The HISTOQUAL scale

A – DIRECTIONS: The following set of statements relate to your feelings about X historic house. For each statement, please show the extent to which you believe X has the feature described by the statement. Circling a 5 means you strongly agree that X has that feature and circling a 1 means that you strongly disagree. You may circle any of the numbers in the middle that show how strong your feelings are. If you feel that the statement does not apply to your situation or that you do not have an opinion then tick the N/A box.

P01 Staff are always helpful and courteous

P02 Staff are willing to take time with visitors

P03 Visitors are made to feel welcome

P04 Level of crowding is tolerable

P05 Staff are well informed to answer customers' requests

169

P06   Visitors feel free to explore, there are no restrictions to access
P07   The property and grounds are opened at convenient hours
P08   Staff are always available when needed
P09   The property is well kept and restored
P10   The general cleanliness and upkeep of the property and grounds is satisfying
P11   The grounds are attractive
P12   The site has remained authentic
P13   Direction signs to show around the property and grounds are clear and helpful
P14   The garden and/or park contain a large variety of plants
P15   The interior of the house offers a lot of interesting things to look at
P16   The written leaflets provide enough information
P17   The information on the property and grounds is detailed enough
P18   Visitors are well informed of the different facilities and attractions available at the property
P19   Foreign language leaflets are helpful
P20   The restaurant offers a wide variety of dishes and refreshments
P21   The shop offers a large variety of goods
P22   The restaurant' staff provide efficient service
P23   The property considers the needs of less able visitors
P24   Facilities for children are provided

B – The following statements describe the five main dimensions of the service offered in the historic house you have just visited. We would like to know how important each of the following features are to you when you evaluate the quality of the historic house you visited today. Please allocate 5 to the most important dimension down to one for the least important one.

- The knowledge and courtesy of the staff and the property's recognition of visitors' needs such as opening hours and crowding problems.
- The appearance and upkeep of the buildings, grounds and gardens.
- The quality of the historical and general information provided.
- The quality of services offered such as the shop and restaurant.
- The individualized attention the attraction provides its customers, particularly for people with walking difficulties and children.

C – Did you feel that the admission price you paid was:

- Excellent value for money
- Good value for money

- Average value for money
- Poor value for money
- Very poor value for money
- Don't know

D – Would you recommend friends and relatives to visit this property?

- Yes
- No
- Uncertain
- Don't know

E – Your feelings toward the attraction can best be described as:
- Very satisfied
- Quite satisfied
- Satisfied
- Not satisfied
- Very unsatisfied
- Don't know

F – During your visit today, did you report a problem that you experienced?

- Yes (if yes please answer question G)
- No

G – Was this problem resolved to your satisfaction?

- Yes
- No

Part Five

Human Resources

Margaret A. Deery

Introduction

In exploring the theme of how best to manage HVA employees, the first chapter in this part will examine the concepts behind quality service management. It will then detail the ways in which 'best practice' can be achieved in HVAs through human resource management functions such as the recruitment and selection of staff and the training, development and retention of the best HVA employees. The chapter will be interspersed with examples from various HVAs investigated specifically for this text.

In discussing HRM at HVAs, it is crucial that the important role of volunteers is covered. Chapter 12 looks at the role of volunteers in this sector of the tourism industry. Although there are fundamental differences between paid staff and volunteers at HVAs, the two groups must be treated as complementary components of the total human resource package. Both components are essential for the delivery of a quality experience at a HVA and both must, therefore, be planned and integrated into the total package in order to maximize the operational effectiveness of the HVA.

11

Managing human resources

Margaret A. Deery and Leo K. Jago

Introduction

The importance of the quality of the tourism workforce has been noted in a range of studies and over a number of countries (for example, Baum, 1992; Pearce, Morrison and Rutledge, 1998; Swarbrooke, 1995). Summarizing tourism trends to the year 2000 and beyond, the World Tourism Organization (WTO) states:

> The capacity of educational institutions in most countries to train staff at all levels, and for all the wide range of skills required for the travel and tourism sector has rarely been adequate. There is a danger that this problem will worsen during the 1990s at all levels, in all categories and in every type of tourist-receiving country. Human resources could emerge as the single most important issue facing tourism operators in the next century. (WTO, 1992: 40)

The statement above suggests that recruiting and selecting the right people for a tourism job, together with training and developing these employees will become one of the most important tasks for tourism organizations. Nowhere is this concern highlighted more than in the customer-service oriented tourism organization of the HVA. Service quality has now become a focus for these attractions.

In exploring the theme of how best to manage HVA employees, this chapter will first examine the concepts behind quality service management. It will then detail the ways in which 'best practice' can be achieved in HVAs through human resource management functions such as the recruitment and selection of staff and the training, development and retention of the best HVA employees. The chapter also includes examples from various HVAs investigated specifically for this text.

Quality service in heritage visitor attractions

The issue of quality service has been the subject of research for the last two decades, with Albrecht and Zemke's (1985) 'recipe' for quality service providing a useful, accessible approach for service industry practitioners. Academics such as Gronroos, Berry and Bateson were already investigating the issues surrounding quality service; these early studies form the basis of the current debate on how best to achieve quality in the service industry. The issue of quality, however, assumes a number of interpretations. The research into quality service focuses on the differences between the service industry and manufacturing. As a consequence the issues here concern the intangibility of the service, the inseparability of the production and consumption of the service, the heterogeneity and perishability of the service (Zeithaml, Parasuraman and Berry, 1985). Another important distinction to make in discussing quality is that between the quality assurance process and the management philosophy of TQM. The former process is concerned with the adoption of quality standards through the International Standards for quality management systems (ISO 9000 series). The management philosophy of TQM, while ideally associated with the quality assurance process, can operate independently of the accreditation system, but should adhere to the principles espoused by Deming (1982) and Juran (1988). Many of the components of the TQM philosophy are centred on the manufacturing process and are based on the work of Deming and Juran. However, the recommendations of Deming and Juran have been incorporated into the service management literature (see, for example, Fynes, Ennis and Negri, 1995; Schmenner, 1995). In adapting the TQM philosophy to service organizations, East (1993) lists the attitudes and values which should be encouraged if a quality culture is to be implemented:

- total commitment to continuous improvement
- the requirement to do it right first time
- understanding the customer–supplier relationship
- recognition that improvement of systems must be managed
- a commitment to ongoing education and training
- the instigation of teamwork and the improvement of communications
- the development of a systematic approach to the implementation.

The application of the TQM philosophy together with the concepts from the service quality literature, particularly that which deals with improving customer service, to HVAs would seem to be obvious. However, it would appear, in practice, that very few HVAs have adopted neither the TQM philosophy nor the quality assurance process. While Pearce, Morrison and Rutledge (1998) argue that the adoption of quality standards is an industry trend, there is little evidence to support the assertion. Swarbrooke (1995) presents a more realistic view of the industry in suggesting that few heritage attractions have taken advantage of the TQM management style. In particular, Swarbrooke argues that the use of quality circles in heritage attractions would provide a mechanism for increased teamwork. In exploring issues of quality human resource management, the recommendations by Deming, Juran and the researchers of service management will provide a platform for discussion.

Human resource management in heritage visitor attractions

The management of human resources at attractions, could arguably be considered to be the most important aspect of visitor attractions for two reasons. First, as a service industry the attitudes and abilities of the staff will have a crucial impact on the way the service is delivered to the customer and will therefore directly affect their enjoyment of the visit and their perceptions of the attraction. Secondly, for most attractions labour costs are likely to be the largest single item in their revenue budget. (Swarbrooke, 1995: 226)

This quote succinctly explains the importance of HVA staff by highlighting the need for able, motivated staff with strong customer service skills. It also highlights the cost to the organization of those staff. Implicit in Swarbrooke's statement is the cost to the organization if those staff are not the 'right' staff, either through their lack of skills or their lack of motivation. Figures from the Bureau of Tourism Research (BTR) and cited in a recent inquiry into the tourism industry (Industry Commission, 1996: 257) confirm the labour intensiveness of the industry: 'For every $100 paid to labour in the tourism industries about $70 was paid to capital, compared to around $80 paid to capital in the all-industry average.' While this statement refers to all tourism organizations, it is clear that labour costs in the industry are higher than those in the all-industry category. The implication for a customer-service oriented organization is that this figure would be even greater.

Swarbrooke's comment is informative in defining the role of human resource management within a HVA. His statement implies that HVA staff need to possess good customer service skills together with the relevant historical knowledge to pass on to visitors. While human resource management (HRM) has traditionally been concerned with the functions of the recruitment, selection, training and development of staff, today's human resource (HR) manager must also be able to motivate staff, instil them with the organization's culture, and assist in the management of change. The following discussion will address each of these areas and includes information from the interviews with HR managers in HVAs.

Heritage visitor attractions and human resource management

While there is a range of HR models depicting the relationship between the HR functions and the strategic policies of an organization (see, for example, Lengnick-Hall and Lengnick-Hall, 1988), the framework by Collins (1994) (Figure 11.1) of the link between the HR functions and the organizational performance provides a useful tool for the investigation of human resource management in HVAs. It is important that HR managers are aware of these links and are mindful of the difficulties encountered by staff in service industries such as HVA. Lovelock, for example, draws attention to these difficulties:

> Service encounters entail more than just correct technical execution of a task. They also involve such human elements as personal demeanour, courtesy, and empathy. This brings us to the notion of emotional labour, defined by Hochschild (1983) as *the act of expressing socially desired emotions during service transactions.* Hochschild notes that attempting to conform to customer expectations on such dimensions can prove to be a psychological burden for some service workers who perceive themselves as having to act out emotions they do not feel. (Lovelock, 1995: 214)

Hoschild (1983: 33) suggests two main ways in which employees may attempt to induce or suppress feeling within the labour process: surface acting and deep acting. The former involves pretending to 'feel what we do not . . . we

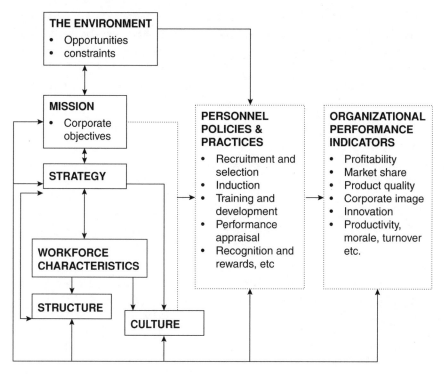

Figure 11.1 A framework integrating the human resource management function
Source: Collins (1994: 42).

deceive others about what we really feel, but we do not deceive ourselves'. 'Deep acting' means 'deceiving oneself as much as deceiving others'. Lovelock's statement above suggests that emotional labour in the service encounter could operate at either level of acting. His statement addresses some of the difficulties in service organizations such as HVAs where staff are often required to take on the persona of a historical character. For example, an HVA which is a re-created medieval castle with staff in period costume, demands of its front-of-house staff, behaviour which may be quite unacceptable for today's employees (e.g. whipping or sexist behaviour) and yet these employees must enter into the spirit of the re-enactment. In order to deal with the strain of emotional labour, HR managers in HVAs need to be aware of the range of influences which could impact on staff who are 'cast' in different roles. For example, frequent breaks and supportive teams of employees may assist in the labour process.

While it is appropriate to use a framework such as in Figure 11.1, it is important to keep in mind the sentiments of Lovelock's statement above. In many ways, the use of emotional labour as an essential component of employment within an HVA, dictates the type of employee the HVA requires. As Lovelock argues, 'performing such labour, day after day, can be stressful for employees as they strive to display towards customers emotions that they do not feel' (Lovelock, 1995: 214). Taking into account, therefore, the uniqueness of the HR requirements of a HVA, the framework in Figure 11.1 provides one way of integrating the HR functions with the strategic functions of the organization as a whole.

As evidenced by Figure 11.1, the HR or personnel policies and practices are influenced by organizational components such as the strategy and mission of the organization, the workforce characteristics and the structure and culture of the organization. The way in which these elements are implemented, impacts the organizational indicators such as profitability, together with workforce behaviour of turnover and absenteeism. In other words, the HR activities are integral to the success of an organization. This is especially true in a labour intensive industry such as the tourism industry, and in particular, sectors such as HVAs. Each of the elements of Collins's model, apart from the organizational performance indicators, will be included in the following discussion.

The environment

Environmental scanning has been an area of research in the hospitality and tourism literature for some time (see, for example, Olsen and Bellas, 1980) and the findings from this body of literature can be applied to HVA organizations. The opportunities, which present themselves for an HVA, are many and varied as are, of course, the constraints. Opportunities for the development of an HVA may depend on external forces such as a change in government and hence a change in funding. Opportunities also arise as a consequence of changes in the labour market. For example, the town in which one HVA was located found that the introduction of a university course in tourism provided the HVA with a qualified and enthusiastic source of employees. Development of the surrounding township may provide not merely a larger pool for recruitment, but may also encourage the development of other attractions and more accommodation which bring further custom to the HVA.

Constraints to an HVA by the environment could present in the form of funding, increased competition, lack of skilled labour and changes in the demographic profile of the labour market which makes the authenticity of the HVA more difficult to maintain. For example, a lack of males as employees for an 1850s re-created mining township would provide an inaccurate historical picture for visitors. A change of government may result in changed funding or a decrease in support for the HVA. Whatever the impact of the environment, organizations such as HVAs, must be constantly aware of protecting themselves from the changes, or exploiting them as appropriate.

The mission and strategy

Mission statements and strategies vary according to the type of HVA, but elements which were in common from the interviews at each HVA were those of authenticity, a quality visitor experience, and a continuing quest for new ways of presenting exhibitions to visitors. Again, the list of quality requirements articulated by East (1993) is relevant here. What is also relevant to this discussion, however, is the relationship between strategy and human resource management. Various models have been proffered to explain the relationship between HRM and the organization's strategy. The Miles and Snow (1978) model (Table 11.1) provides organizational typologies, which are relevant to the discussion of HVA. In particular, it links the structure of the organization to the strategy.

The HVAs investigated for this study, which included historical houses, castles and re-created historical sites, could fall into any one of the above categories. For example the HR manager from one of the research sites argued that, while some of the managers operated in ways which conformed to the 'prospector' category, the director and board of management followed more of a defender strategy. This clash of styles would appear to be quite common in organizations such as HVAs where the difference between departments may be significant. For example, the management philosophy of the historical and research section of a HVA may be quite different from those of the marketing section. Miles and Snow (1978) and various commentators on their work suggest that each typology is appropriate, but only in the right environment.

Table 11.1 Typologies of organizational strategies

Typologies	Objectives	Strategies	Structures
Defender	Protect market share	Fortification	Centralized
Analyser	Protect market share	Market penetration	Tight control
	Locate new opportunities	Market followers	Lose control
Prospector	Locate new opportunities	Growth and development	Decentralized

Source: Adapted from Miles and Snow (1978).

Workforce characteristics

The workforce characteristics of a HVA may vary according to the type of HVA. For example, a historic homestead or a re-created village may require a predominantly male front-of-house workforce for authenticity, with more females in back-of-house responsibilities providing a greater gender balance. There may be a requirement for certain age groups in the 'casting' for particular historical eras; children who were volunteers at some of the historical homesteads assisted in providing a more authentic picture of the era. Similarly, there may be a need for the presence of particular nations. For example, there was a large number of Chinese migrants on the 1850s goldfields as well as Americans, English and Irish prospectors. Servants in castles and wealthy homesteads were often from other nationalities. For example, some of the HVA investigated, made strong efforts to accurately portray the role of indigenous people. In all, the workforce characteristics of a HVA will vary according to the size and complexity of the organization. Not only do the front-of-house staff need to present an authentic portrayal of the era, but the back-of-house staff need to have the skills, such as administrative and organizational skills, to provide support for the front-of-house staff.

Structure

The structure of HVAs will vary, usually according to the size of the organization. From the interviews conducted for this chapter, it would appear that there is no common structure, although several of the larger organizations tended to have complex, tall, hierarchical structures. Smaller organizations were often much 'flatter' with staff being multiskilled and undertaking a range of roles such as HR issues and the marketing of the attraction.

Some HVAs have quite tall structures due to the range of activities involved in running such an organization. These structures were function-based hierarchies, a traditional way of structuring an organization. While the executive director of one of the HVAs in particular, was answerable to the board of the organization, the position of executive director was in fact, quite a powerful one. Although the trend in organizational structures is to a flat organization with fewer middle management positions, some HVAs may have difficulty in implementing this trend due to the many components within such an operation. Swarbrooke (1995) suggests that a more innovative structure for heritage attractions is that of a matrix structure which mixes products with functions.

Culture

The final element of Collins's framework to be discussed before proceeding to the HR functions in HVAs, is that of culture. Culture refers to the underlying values, beliefs and principles of an organization, and provides a basis for management practices and behaviour (Denison, 1990). Culture can be used as an effective management tool, and Mullins (1992) suggests that organizational culture can prove to be a vital component in the standards of delivery of service to customers. There are also many types of organizational cultures. For example, Schneider (1990) argues that there is a number of cultures, which suit service organizations, and a variety of dimensions of culture. These dimensions include managerial behaviour, service rewards, personnel support and, most importantly, for the purpose of this study, a culture which has an enthusiastic orientation to service. Schneider's definition of this dimension of culture includes 'keeping a sense of "family" in the branch' (Schneider, 1990: 396). A service culture is important in providing a quality experience for HVA visitors.

An example of a 'family' culture comes from one of the HVA sites investigated – that of a historic homestead situated outside a large metropolitan city. The culture could best be described as providing a family-like or village environment where everyone knows each other and supports each other. Teamwork is an important component of the culture, as is the ability to be flexible and multiskilled. Staff feel empowered at the operational level. At times, however, they have a sense of powerlessness in the decisions made by the senior executive group. In other words, there are at least two cultures within the paid staff of this HVA. However, the overwhelming sense within the HVA is that of co-operation and support among the staff. Although these two cultures exist, they are both working towards providing a quality experience for visitors which is achieved through constant improvements within both the staff and the HVA itself.

Human resource management policies and practices

Recruitment and selection of staff

The recruitment and selection of HVA staff are perhaps the most important components of HRM at HVAs. Frontline or operational staff, administration and sales staff often need specialized skills to perform their duties. What is important in recruiting staff for a HVA is the ability to be both a teamworker and flexible in the skills offered to the organization. This is often difficult to achieve as many of the positions within an HVA are unique to that organization. For example, a coach wheelwright working in a re-creation of an historical town may only have skills which that particular historical attraction requires. Recruitment of these staff is one of the keys to providing an authentic experience to visitors.

Before addressing the issues of recruitment, it is worth noting that an important part of the recruiting process is the provision and updating of position descriptions. Unfortunately, from the interviews conducted with managers of HVAs for this chapter, none of the attractions was able to provide job descriptions. These position descriptions are important for a range of reasons. First, they provide a benchmark for both the employer and the employee. Such a benchmark is important for understanding whether the employee is actually performing the job. If the employee is not performing the job, the position description provides a document for either improvement in the job or dismissal. The position description also provides a basis for a performance appraisal, which, in turn, may lead to further training, promotion and/or an increase in pay. Interestingly, although the managers interviewed were not able to provide position descriptions, all suggested that this HR function was a high priority for future action.

Recruitment of staff for an HVA can emanate from two sources: internal or external applicants. There are benefits and disadvantages in recruiting from either source.

Internal recruitment

Internal recruitment, particularly for an HVA, has many advantages. For example, the cost of the recruiting process is kept to a minimum, and for HVAs in the private sector, these savings in terms of time and money are often seen to outweigh any disadvantages in the system. For an HVA in the public sector, there are still costs associated with internal recruitment as certain procedures need to be adhered to. However, the key advantage of internal recruitment is that, not only does the employee understand the organization, but also the organization has the opportunity to assess the ability and aptitude of the employee. More importantly, however, the organization can assess the employee's 'fit' with the corporate culture. Many organizations describe themselves as a 'family' and fitting into that family in terms of the values and beliefs of the organization has become crucial in the 1990s. Visiting an HVA may be a 'one off' experience for many visitors. It is therefore important that the experience is a quality one where staff have teamwork and a strong knowledge of the values, beliefs and way in which the attraction functions. In many of the HVAs examined, recruitment was internal, particularly in the larger organizations. Internal recruiting is often an important way of maintaining the culture of the HVA in that the recruits are known to the directors and other staff, and they 'fit' the family culture. More importantly, however, internal recruits know and understand the organization. This is vital to the effective running of any HVA.

Internal recruitment also has some disadvantages. For example, a director of an award-winning re-created gold mining town suggested that when staff are promoted, it is difficult for other staff members to adapt to the staff member in the new position. The attitude of 'but he was only a horseman or miner' is difficult to change. Internal recruitment also means fewer new ideas coming into the attraction. For example, when a member of the administrative staff at a historical homestead was promoted to the position of HR manager, several of the senior staff lamented the fact that the status quo would remain, with few new ways of implementing staff policies being introduced. Baum (1992), however, argues that management should look at their present staff to assess their potential, before turning to outside sources of labour. Implicit in this argument is that companies should undertake training for their employees to ensure that the internal recruits are capable of achieving the new demands on them.

External recruitment

External recruiting perhaps provides greater opportunities for the development of new ideas within an HVA. Baum (1992) suggests that recruitment should be viewed in the light of the longer-term needs of the company, and so the decision to hire from outside the company is one, which requires a great deal of thought. Graduates from hospitality and tourism courses, for example, provide HVAs with a new source of job applicants who have already, by their choice of course, expressed a desire to remain in the industry. The plethora of courses, both at pre-university and university levels, provides a pool of applicants often with some experience of the industry, and with knowledge, albeit theoretical, of the operation and management of hospitality and tourism organizations. However, research by Boles, Ross and Johnson (1995) in their study of the relationship between demographics and employee turnover in the hospitality industry, found that education was positively related to higher turnover intentions. These authors argue that many of the respondents in their study were using the industry as a stepping stone to a better job. It could be argued, however, that career management by the organization would make these industry positions more inviting. These authors also found that work experience was negatively associated with turnover, a finding which again can be used by management to provide a stable work-force.

A key means of encouraging a particular culture is through the recruitment of staff. It is important to hire people who fit the culture and feel comfortable within it. Recruiting staff for many of the HVAs investigated was conducted in both a formal and informal manner. Advertisements are often placed in the local paper as well as word-of-mouth recommendations. In fact, new employees were often found through recommendations from existing staff. One of the HVAs studied is one of the largest employers in the city, and it provides both permanent and temporary employment opportunities for the local population. As a source of employment, therefore, HVAs are strong contributors to the economic well being of the areas in which they are located.

A trend in the HR literature is to promote a better use of what has come to be known as the 'alternative' labour market (see for example, Charles and McCleary, 1997; Kramar, McGraw and Schuler, 1997). This term describes a larger pool of applicants than previously used in the recruitment process, in particular, recruiting women returning to the workforce, retired men and women, disabled people and members of minority groups. In widening the scope of the recruitment market, organizations such as HVAs can attract people with a great deal of knowledge, experience or enthusiasm who have previously been ignored. Take, for example, the type of volunteer to work in HVAs. On the whole, these people are older than the majority of the work-force, but bring with them knowledge and experience which is invaluable to an HVA. There are few reasons why such people could not be employed in the paid workforce.

There are, of course, disadvantages in recruiting externally. These include not fitting the organizational culture and not possessing the right skills. Most importantly, for an HVA, a new recruit whose communication and customer service skills are inadequate can prove to be a cost to the organization. Maresh (1996: 284), in his discussion of effective human resource management in tourism organizations argues that action for recruitment should only be carried out within an 'integrated backdrop, incorporating [the] career development and progression plans'.

Selection

For the selection of staff for a HVA to be effective, various activities need to have taken place first. For example, job descriptions outlining the duties, reporting mechanisms and the skills required to perform these duties well must be completed. However, as stated previously, very few HVAs in the research sample had undertaken the task of writing up the various job descriptions. Another activity, prior to the recruitment process, is to conduct an audit of the staff on site and the staff required for the future. Again, this HR planning as it is known, is practised by few organizations. Stone (1998) reports that a recent survey of organizations in all industries found that only a minority had a formal system of HR planning. The key reasons given for the lack of HR planning are the complexity of the process and the difficulty in predicting environmental influences on issues such as staffing.

In selecting staff for a position within a HVA, it is important that, even if job descriptions are not available, a clear idea of the skills and aptitude are known to the selector(s). In selecting staff from within the organization or from outside, either a panel or a single manager will be involved. Whichever the case, Lovelock (1995) emphasizes the importance of service organizations such as HVA hiring people with different styles and personalities to suit both front-of-house positions and back-of-house ones. Selection criteria, therefore, should reflect the human dimensions of the job as well as the technical requirements. As a consequence, selection techniques could include weighted application forms, personality and employment testing, and behavioural interviews which aim to 'reveal specific choices applicants have made in the past, and the circumstances surrounding those choices' (Janz, cited in Stone, 1998: 227). Other interviewing techniques include group interviews and video interviewing. This last style is useful when a position may require searching overseas for appropriate applicants. In HVAs, there are often specific positions to fill, such as a Cornish boilermaker in a historical attraction, which may require overseas recruitment. Whatever style is used for interviewing, it is important for the interviewers to be trained in interviewing skills.

The selection methods used in the HVAs studied were often *ad hoc* in that there are no job descriptions to provide benchmarks for the positions. Staff were often selected by one of the directors or a middle manager. The HR function in many of the HVAs has been decentralized, so that activities such as hiring and firing are left to either the director of the section or a manager within either the operations, museum or commercial sectors of the HVA. Although interviewing is the main selection tool for managers in the HVA, few of the managers or directors interviewed had received training in interviewing techniques. This was seen as an area in which staff development should occur. The lack of interviewing criteria and expertise, together with the lack of job descriptions, place some doubt on the objectivity involved in recruiting staff to a new position in many of the HVAs. However, the fact that most of the recruits are internal applicants assists in understanding whether the employee is suitable or not. An example of hiring practices of one of the HVAs was the opening of a new centre over which the HVA has control. Although there were many applicants for the positions, which were advertised, in the local paper, and many of these were highly qualified people, staff were recruited from the HVA because 'they knew how things worked'. Because this particular HVA is 'such a complicated place' internal recruiting means that the staff are already familiar with the operations and philosophy of the organization. By recruiting internally, the HVA has the opportunity to encourage the organizational culture, which is most suitable to the organization. However, internal recruiting has the disadvantage of not bringing new ideas into the organization.

Induction

When the appropriate staff have been selected, it is crucial for the organization to conduct induction or orientation programmes. These programmes are especially important for HVAs due to the complexities of historical attractions, which may not function in the same way as current organizations. Stone (1998: 335) argues that induction programmes can achieve cost savings by 'reducing the anxieties of new employees and by fostering positive attitudes, job satisfaction and a sense of commitment'. Research by Deery and Iverson (1996) into the causes of employee turnover in the hospitality industry found that induction programmes can reduce the incidence of turnover.

An induction programme should be comprehensive in its coverage. It should deal with important information about the organization such as the history, philosophy, products and services as well as covering information about specific jobs. Ideally, induction programmes should be held as soon as new employees join the organization. However, this is not always possible and may not be seen as a cost-effective way of dealing with new employees. Some organizations run induction programmes every month; while not the best way of dealing with new employees, this is a more cost-effective way of giving the employee an understanding of the organization. Induction programmes at two of the HVAs studied covered a two-day period. The programme in each HVA gives a full orientation to staff on the layout, workings and key staff of the particular attraction, in this case a re-created castle and an historic homestead.

Training and development

Training is perhaps the most important HR function to be conducted in a HVA and to achieve quality service, training should be an on-going organizational activity. As Swarbrooke (1995) points out, there are many ways of training staff in visitor attractions. These include mentoring and on-the-job training. Both these styles are relevant to training in a HVA where some of the skills are very specific to that attraction and the best people to learn these skills from belong to that organization. Conducting individual research into the characters portrayed in the HVA is also an essential part of training. Short on-site courses such as customer service skills or complaint handling are important forms of training in HVAs. Finally, sending staff on to tertiary studies in, for example museum studies or tourism development courses, can improve not only the knowledge of the employee, but can be a motivating force for employees. Other forms of training can be group problem solving, computer simulation activities, case studies, in-basket exercises and role-plays.

One of the key components of training for a successful HVA is, of course, the effective interpretation of aspects of the attraction. Pearce, Morrison and Rutledge (1998) recommend six principles of designing effective interpretation: vary the interpretive experience; provide personal connections for visitors; practise participation; organize the orientation of the particular part of the attraction; provide clear content; and allow for a range of different audiences. Front-of-house staff therefore not only need to be knowledgeable about their particular segment of the attraction, but they also need to be flexible and sensitive to the needs of the audience. For example, a group of school children would require an interpretation, which is expressed in language they can understand, while a group of international visitors may require a sophisticated interpretation but expressed in clear, unambiguous language. Training staff to communicate both accurately and clearly, together with being sensitive to their audience, is crucial to the success of the attraction.

Training should also cover a range of learning areas, both job and organization specific. As stated previously, customer service skills are important for HVA staff, together with negotiation, assertion and communication skills. It is also important to understand legislative and organizational policies. For example, occupational, health and safety information is particularly important for heritage organizations, which need to balance authenticity with the health requirements of the twenty-first century. Other information on, for example, sexual harassment, needs to be given to staff. Finally, it is important for both staff and the organization to conduct a training audit to determine the needs of staff, together with a mechanism for evaluating the effectiveness of the training programmes.

One of HVA investigated provided training sessions of two-hour duration, covering issues such as customer service, computer training, dealing with international visitors and dealing with difficult customers. Should staff wish to do further study which is related to their work, this particular HVA pays their course fees. As there is a local university nearby, some staff have taken the opportunity to pursue tertiary studies in tourism or management. There is also a trade school in the city, which offers courses. Training is used in the organization to improve staff performance and confidence, as many of the current staff are not well educated. A new system of training, to be used as a model for the rest of this attraction, has just been implemented to improve the confidence of staff. It is an intensive training programme in which the participants must be able to give a ten-minute lecture on their area of the attraction and have a five-minute conversation as the character they portray. Other follow-up training sessions consist of a 'broad brush' approach to provide an understanding of issues such as the etiquette of the era; this takes the form of an elegant dinner where staff must wear their costumes and take on the characteristics of the person they are portraying. This type of training also reinforces the culture of teamwork and support.

Developing staff can take the form of training, but it also refers to career development. A large HVA will be able to provide greater career opportunities than will smaller organizations. In order for the organization to provide career opportunities, it is incumbent on the organization to have a full knowledge of the skills of their employees. This requires a system of recording such skills and developing a career path for the staff based on these skills. There are opportunities for staff to progress through various levels of the organization, particularly if there has been an employment agreement at the particular HVA. Unfortunately, some organizations have found it difficult to accommodate staff needs in terms of promotions due to the 'flattening' of organizational structures. However, development of staff does not need to revolve around promotion. Leibowitz, Kaye and Farren (1990) have recommended various solutions to the problem of career plateaus. These include redesigning jobs, encouraging new ways of doing the task, building strong networks across the organization and providing better opportunities for staff skills to be exposed to a wider audience. All of these suggestions could be implemented in a HVA.

In some of the HVAs investigated, there was a 'ladder' to climb to achieve promotion. In one organization, a public sector attraction, these levels were clearly spelt out. In order to move from one level to the next, certain skills such as research skills need to be acquired. Research skills are important at this particular attraction as each person must come to a thorough understanding of, not only the character they portray, but also of the era. Each employee must conduct their own research into their characters using the archival and library facilities at the park. This particular HVA has a policy of 'growing their own people' which means that promotions occur reasonably regularly; an example from this organization is the co-ordinator of domestic marketing who had previously been a horseman. Another member of staff who had acted as a mine tour guide is now the volunteer co-ordinator, responsible for over 200 volunteers.

Appraisal and performance management

Staff performance appraisals are an integral component in developing staff. Swarbrooke (1995) suggests that there are two attitudes to the appraisals. The first is connected to a negative view of an appraisal as judgemental; the second is associated with the development of staff in a broader sense. Ideally the appraisal should be conducted in the spirit of the second interpretation, and should lead onto further training or perhaps promotion. Again, the importance of job descriptions can be noted here; it is difficult to measure an employee's performance if there is no benchmark to measure the performance against. As stated previously, few of the HVAs studied had job descriptions, making performance appraisals difficult to conduct rigorously. While some of the attractions held informal performance appraisals in at least some divisions, this is certainly an area in which the attractions could improve their HR functions. It was interesting to note, however, that the only attractions which conducted any type of appraisal of performance were those in the public sector.

Performance appraisal may be viewed as an overall measure of organizational effectiveness, while performance management is a broader concept which focuses on strategic planning and development. Performance management measures the progress being made towards the achievement of the organization's strategic business objectives (Stone, 1998). There are, however, difficulties in conducting both performance appraisals and management. For example, the rater must be familiar with the job, and must be objective in measuring the performance of the person. Deming (1982) argues that employees do not differ significantly in their work performance and that any variation in employee performance is predominantly a result of factors outside the individual's control. More importantly, it is impossible for appraisers to distinguish between employee-caused and system-caused variations in performance. However, taking these criticisms into account, organizations such as HVAs need to provide feedback to employees on their performance together with the means and opportunities for improving performance.

Summary

Quality HR practices in HVAs provide the basis for the development of HVA staff. In particular, strategic HR functions can encourage an appropriate culture for the attraction through the selection of the 'right' staff and the continuous training and development of those staff. A commitment to quality and the support of upper management are integral components of a successful quality attraction. While some of the attractions studied in this chapter need to improve their HR practices, others have developed systems to encourage and nurture an appropriate culture to provide a quality experience for HVA visitors.

Questions

1 Why is managing the people in an organization more important in HVAs than in, for example, a manufacturing organization?
2 What recruitment policies work best for HVAs?
3 How can staff development programmes assist HVAs?

References and further reading

Albrecht, K. and Zemke, R. (1985). *Service America! Doing Business in the New Economy*. Dow-Jones-Irwin.

Baum, T. (1992). *Managing Human Resources in the European Tourism and Hospitality Industry: A Strategic Approach*. Chapman-Hall.

Boles, J., Ross, L. and Johnson, J. (1995). Reducing employee turnover through the use of pre-employment application demographics: an exploratory study. *Hospitality Research Journal*, **19**, 19–30.

Charles, R. and McCleary, W. (1997). Recruitment and retention of African-American managers. *Cornell HRA Quarterly*, **38**(1), 24–29.

Collins, R. (1994). The strategic contributions of the personnel function. In *Readings in Strategic Human Resource Management* (A. Nankervis and R. Compton, eds), Thomas Nelson.

Deery, M. and Iverson, R. (1996). Enhancing productivity intervention strategies for employee turnover. In *Productivity Management in Hospitality and Tourism* (N. Johns, ed.), pp. 68–95, Cassell.

Deming, W. (1982). *Quality, Productivity and Competitive Position*. MIT Press.

Denison, D. (1990). *Corporate Culture and Organizational Effectiveness*. Wiley.

East, J. (1993). *Managing Quality in the Catering Industry*. Croner Publications.

Fynes, B., Ennis, S. and Negri, L. (1995). Service quality at the manufacturing-marketing interface: from *Kaizen* to service-driven logistics. In

Understanding Services Management (W. Glynn and J. Barnes, eds), pp. 370–392, Wiley.

Hochschild, A. (1983). *The Managed Heart: Commercialization of Human Feeling*. University of California Press.

Industry Commission (1996). *Tourism Accommodation and Training*. (Report No. 50). Australian Government Publishing Services, Melbourne.

Juran, J. (ed.) (1988). *Quality Control Handbook*. 4th edition. McGraw-Hill.

Kramar, R., McGraw, P. and Schuler, R. (1997). *Human Resource Management in Australia*. 3rd edition. Longman.

Leibowitz, Z., Kaye, B. and Farren, C. (1990). What to do about career gridlock. *Training and Development Journal*, **44**(4), 32–39.

Lengnick-Hall, C. and Lengnick-Hall, M. (1988). Strategic human resource management: a review of the literature and a proposed typology. *Academy of Management Review*, **13**, 454–470.

Lovelock, C. (1995). Managing services: the human factor. In *Understanding Services Management* (W. Glynn and J. Barnes, eds), pp. 203–243, Wiley.

Maresh, V. (1996). Effective human resource management: key to excellence in service organizations. In *Human Resource Management in the Hospitality Industry* (F. Go, M. Monachello and T. Baum, eds), pp. 280–293, Wiley.

Miles, R. and Snow, C. (1978). *Organizational Strategy, Structure and Process*. McGraw-Hill.

Mullins, L. (1992). *Hospitality Management*: A Human Resource Approach. Longman.

Olsen, M. and Bellas, C. (1980). The importance of the environment to the food service and lodging manager. *Cornell HRA Quarterly,* **21**(4), 75–80.

Pearce, P., Morrison, A. and Rutledge, J. (1998). *Tourism. Bridges across Continents*. McGraw-Hill.

Schmenner, R. (1995). *Service Operations Management*. Prentice Hall.

Schneider, B. (1990). The climate for service: an application of the climate construct. In *Organizational Climate and Culture* (B. Schneider, ed.), Jossey-Bass.

Stone, R. (1998). *Human Resource Management*. 3rd edition. Wiley.

Swarbrooke, J. (1995). *The Development and Management of Visitor Attractions*. Butterworth-Heinemann.

World Tourism Organization (1992). *World Tourism Trends to the Year 2000*. WTO.

Zeithaml, V., Parasuraman, A. and Berry, L. (1985). Problems and strategies in services marketing. *Journal of Marketing,* **49**, 33–46.

12

Managing volunteers

Leo K. Jago and Margaret A. Deery

Introduction

Volunteers play an integral role in the tourism industry with two of the more obvious examples being in visitor information centres and in visitor attractions. Volunteers are usually added to the workforce at visitor attractions in order to enhance the visitor experience (Wells, 1996) and, indeed, it is unlikely that many HVAs would be able to survive financially without volunteers. Despite the fact that volunteers produce enormous financial benefits for organizations, they are 'for the most part not managed or badly managed' (Wilson and Pimm, 1996: 24) and the management of volunteers has not yet been recognized as a major focus for theoretical investigation (Deery, Jago and Shaw, 1998).

Swarbrooke (1995) has become a popular text in university programmes focusing on the management of visitor attractions. Although Swarbrooke (1995) stressed the importance of HRM at visitor attractions, his analysis and discussion was based upon the paid workforce and made little more than passing reference to the role of volunteers. With respect to HRM, Swarbrooke (1995) identifies a number of problems at visitor attractions without mentioning the fact that many of these attractions employ both a paid and a voluntary workforce, which substantially complicates the situation.

In discussing HRM at HVAs, it is crucial that the important role of volunteers is covered. Although there are fundamental differences between paid staff and volunteers at HVAs, the two groups must be treated as complementary components of the total human resource package. Both components are essential for the delivery of a quality experience at a HVA and both must, therefore, be planned and integrated into the total package in order to maximize the operational effectiveness of the HVA. Management at a growing number of HVAs now treats seriously the role of HR planning in relation to their paid workforce, but rarely does this seriousness flow through to the volunteer workforce. It can be argued that this factor explains the less than successful volunteer programmes that operate at a number of HVAs. However, 'human resource management planning, especially the action of planning and job definition which precede the attraction, recruitment and hiring of voluntary staff, is finding increasing support' (Tyzack, 1996: 26).

Although it is argued in this chapter that there are strong similarities between the way in which volunteers should be managed and the way in which paid employees are managed, there are some distinct differences. These differences relate to motives and rewards as 'unpaid workers require opportunities for the satisfaction of personal needs which are discernibly different in priority from the satisfactions sought by financially compensated workers' (Pearce, 1980: 443).

This chapter discusses the importance of volunteers and considers the profile of volunteers in the HVA sector. A model is then presented that looks at the relationship between volunteers and HVAs using many of the dimensions that were identified in the previous chapter. This enables the reader to compare and contrast the human resource components of volunteers and paid employees at HVAs. Effort is made to suggest volunteer management strategies that will improve the overall operational effectiveness of HVAs.

The importance of volunteers

A large percentage of the population is involved in some type of voluntary work, many being involved in more than one voluntary organization at any given time. For example, it is estimated in the UK that over 39 per cent of the adult population is involved in a voluntary activity while in the USA the figure is estimated to be over 50 per cent (Wilson and Pimm, 1996). Although it is widely recognized that volunteering adds substantial economic value to the community, it is extremely difficult to estimate the value of volunteering. This difficulty is due to the definitions used to categorize volunteers, problems in the identification of volunteers, and determining an appropriate hourly rate to calculate economic equivalence. In Australia, for example, estimates of the annual economic value of volunteers range from $5.6 billion to $236 billion (Metzer et al., 1997).

The fact that volunteering has 'come of age' and is now regarded as a vital element of today's society is evidenced by the increasing research that is now being conducted into volunteering. For example, there are now academic journals on volunteering, government reports on the roles and impacts of volunteering, and conferences focusing on volunteering. There is also an increasing number of volunteer umbrella organizations that provide advice and co-ordination in relation to volunteer activities.

Volunteers are involved in a diverse range of areas including sport, recreation, tourism, welfare, education and religion. Although some volunteers work in profit-based organizations, it is more common to find volunteers in non-profit organizations. People tend to believe that if something is worthy of them offering their labour without charge, then owners of an organization should not be making a return on capital (Pearce, 1993).

In the interviews with managers of HVAs conducted in order to provide examples for this chapter, there was a unanimous view that volunteers were fundamentally important to the viable operation of the various HVAs. All managers indicated that the visitor experience would be seriously diminished without volunteers, with a number of managers indicating that their particular attraction would not be viable in the absence of volunteers. It should be noted that volunteers operate at two levels in many HVAs, namely, on the board of directors and at the operational level. However, most of the discussion in this chapter refers to volunteers in operational positions.

Volunteer profile

'A volunteer is one who enlists or offers their services to the organisation of their own free will, and without expecting remuneration. The volunteer has personal goals that can be attained through the act of volunteering' (Getz, 1997: 198). Volunteers can perform the same tasks as paid employees with the fundamental difference being that volunteers are not paid for these tasks. However, it should be remembered that 'unpaid work is not free and funding bodies often do not recognise the costs involved in developing and sustaining volunteer programs, including training and infrastructure costs as well as reimbursement for volunteers' out of pocket expenses' (Bursian, 1992: 3).

There has been considerable debate about whether voluntary activity is work or leisure. On balance, however, volunteering appears to be more a leisure activity than a work activity, and volunteers tend not to feel as constrained as paid employees and tend to adopt organizational objectives as they see fit (Pearce, 1993). This poses serious problems for management and means that specific procedures need to be put into place to harness individual volunteer behaviour.

Since volunteering involves so many areas and attracts such a broad cross section of the community, it is not possible to accurately profile the 'typical' volunteer. It is possible, however, to comment upon some broad trends based on statistical data that are now collected on volunteers. The information presented in this section is based upon Australian Bureau of Statistics (ABS) (1995). The most common category of volunteer activity is 'sport/recreation/hobby', which accounts for 42 per cent of all volunteer activity. This is followed by 'welfare/community' 27 per cent, 'education/training/youth' 17 per cent and 'religious' 16 per cent. Volunteer activity at HVAs is not specifically identified but would likely fall into the category of 'sport/recreation/hobby' (SRH), although some HVA volunteer activity would also likely come under the category of 'arts/culture'.

In examining ABS (1995) in the SRH category, the following observations can be made:

1 A greater percentage of females volunteer than do males.
2 Volunteer activity increases with age reaching a peak at around 40 years and then declines steadily with age experiencing a slight increase upon reaching retirement age.
3 There is a very broad spread in the number of hours worked by volunteers over a 12-month period. The median is 75 hours per year but 2 per cent of volunteers work more than 1000 hours per year.

For comparative purposes, a survey was conducted of volunteers at a successful HVA in Victoria and the main demographic observations are listed below:

1 Gender profile is similar to ABS (1995).
2 Age profile of the volunteer was much older than in ABS (1995) with the peak age group being over 65 years old.
3 Volunteers at this HVA worked many more hours than indicated in ABS

(1995), with 90 per cent working more than the median figure in ABS (1995).

Studies have found that a person's propensity to volunteer increases with income, education level, status of occupation and family situation (Pearce, 1993). In contrast to this, some suggest that the less affluent have a higher propensity to volunteer than the wealthy (Getz, 1997). It is difficult, there-fore, to make any categorical statements in this area.

It is important to recognize that there are two types of volunteers, namely, core and peripheral (Pearce 1993). Core volunteers are generally small in number but are passionately involved with the organization; it plays an important role in their lives. Peripheral volunteers are less involved in the organization although some graduate to the core. In considering the number of hours worked by volunteers and the length of service, it can be of value to categorize volunteers using these two groupings. It is also impor-tant not to overload core members despite their propensity to take on more tasks.

Historical visitor attraction volunteer model

Volunteers play an important role at HVAs but it is crucial to recognize that there must be benefits for both the volunteer and the HVA if the relation-ship is to succeed; a balance needs to be achieved. A HVA is often

> staffed by volunteers, making it accessible at an affordable fee and the visitor enjoys being shown around by a knowledgeable and enthusiastic person. The Heritage Trust is able to extend its activities to cover many sites of historic value because of volunteer help. The volunteers are able to enjoy the experience, meet new people, pursue an active interest in an area which fascinates them and increase their knowledge. (Noble, 1991; 9)

This balance is the key to success.

The issue of volunteers at HVAs is a serious business and there is a 'need to adopt a professional approach to the management of volunteers not only to ensure quality of the service delivery but also to provide workplace satis-faction and retention of volunteer staff' (Wells, 1996; 358).

Pearce (1980) developed a volunteer worker placement model for tourism organizations based upon a number of traditional placement models. An attractive element of the Pearce model is that it proposes that success of a volunteer workforce is dependent upon compatibility between the volunteer and the tourism organization. This compatibility relates to the needs and skills of the volunteer compared to the rewards and tasks of the tourism organization. Unless both parties are satisfied with the outcomes on these dimensions, a long-term enduring relationship is unlikely.

The model presented in Figure 12.1 is a modification of Pearce (1980) which has been changed to reflect more specifically volunteers in HVAs and to incorporate the important HRM dimensions identified in the previous chapter. Discussion in the remaining sections of this chapter relate to specific components shown in Figure 12.1.

Volunteer motives

Although volunteering is not a recent phenomenon, with records showing that there were literally thousands of volunteer organizations in nineteenth-century Britain (Wilson and Pimm, 1996), it would appear that the motives for volunteering and the activities now involving volunteers have changed.

It is crucial for management to understand the motives of volunteers and subsequently develop appropriate reward mechanisms for them in order to improve the operation of volunteer systems. The motives for volunteering are now substantially more diverse than they were in the past (Mausner, 1988) which means that the rewards may also have to vary. 'It would be unrealistic and absurd to regard the voluntary workforce as in any way homogeneous. They are extremely disparate because of many factors and indeed the only strong commonality is that they are volunteers but all with different motives, commitments, aspirations, experience and skills' (Wilson and Pimm, 1996: 28).

In the traditional paid workforce, employees work to get paid in order to finance their lifestyle. There are often other motives but this is clearly the primary objective for most and can be used to explain and control behaviour. For a volunteer there are many motives that could prompt behaviour but financial reward is not one of these. In order to have any chance of developing a successful volunteer programme, it is vital that management clearly understand the motives that prompt people to volunteer their services. This forms the basis for developing roles, appraising performance, introducing training programmes and developing reward systems, all of which are necessary for the success of a volunteer programme.

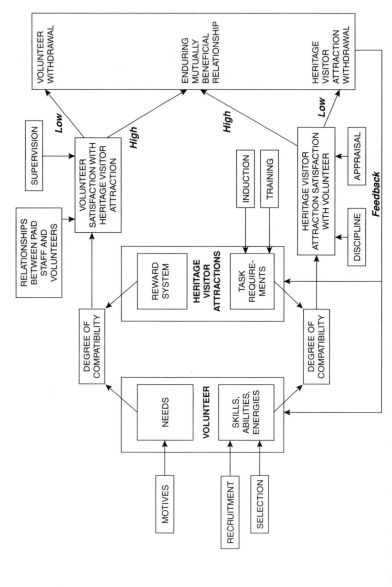

Figure 12.1 Heritage visitor attraction volunteer model

Source: Adapted from the volunteer worker placement model in Pearce (1980)

Some of the early work in the field of volunteers suggested that the prime motive for volunteering was altruistic. Although altruism is still regarded as an important motive, there are now other more 'materialistic' motives for volunteering. Volunteering has come to be

> seen as a means of personal development, increasing skills, elevating status, integrating into a new community, changing pace, meeting requirements of educational institutions and organisations, gaining experience for paid jobs . . . Volunteer programmes now have to be geared to the interests of the volunteer, as well as the needs of the client. (Warren, 1990: 4)

Heritage visitor attractions managers must be careful as volunteers may not be prepared to admit that their motives were for reasons other than altruism; there is a sense of social desirability associated with altruistic motives. In a study conducted at a HVA it was found that only 18 per cent of respondents listed a motive that could be classed as altruistic. The remaining 82 per cent of respondents listed motives that focused on the individual including motives such as 'enhancing job skills', 'needing to fill one's time' and 'interest in history'. This supports work done elsewhere. For example, Pearce (1993) suggested that important motives for volunteers were the 'desire to help others', 'feel useful' and to 'occupy spare time', especially for retirees. Other researchers have listed the key volunteer motives as recognition, power, variety, prestige, job experience and contacts.

According to social exchange theory, volunteers may start out with altruistic motives but their ongoing involvement becomes driven by more specific rewards (Getz, 1997). In contrast to this, however, the data presented in ABS (1995) suggest that more altruistic motives, such as 'doing something worthwhile' or 'helping others' become more important with age. The same report shows that the importance of less altruistic motives, such as 'gaining work experience' and 'learning skills' declined with age. Smith (cited in Getz, 1997: 200) suggested that there are three types of incentives that drive volunteers and these three types interact: 'material rewards (goods or money), interpersonal rewards (prestige or friendship), and purposive incentives (achievement or self-fulfilment)'.

Understanding volunteer motives and building appropriate reward mechanisms can improve volunteer loyalty and volunteer management effectiveness. It should be recognized that there may be a range of motives rather than a single one and that motives change over time. Much of the work on volunteer motivation that has been conducted has focused on what motivated a person to join the organization in the first instance, which although important, is not as important as understanding what motivates volunteers once they belong to the organization (Pearce, 1993). More work is needed in this area. This means that efforts should be made to ensure that management is aware of the key and changing needs of volunteers so that there is an increased likelihood that these needs will be fulfilled. Failure to do so will likely result in high volunteer turnover.

An important reason for some to volunteer their services at a HVA is that they are in a better position to gain full-time employment within the HVA when a position arises. In interviews with managers of HVAs, it was found that some consider favourably volunteer experience when seeking to fill paid staff positions as management has had the opportunity to consider the expertise and commitment of the person as a volunteer. However, management at some HVAs was opposed to volunteers moving into paid positions and has written policies to this effect. This is despite the fact that the same HVAs often had a specific policy of employing friends and family of existing employees. It appears that the policy of restricting volunteers from becoming paid employees was introduced to encourage those who saw volunteering as a useful exercise in its own right, not simply as a stepping stone to a paid position. This seems a strange policy and one possibly counterproductive to obtaining better paid staff and volunteers. It precludes management having the opportunity to evaluate potential staff in the work situation, which would be of great assistance in many organizations.

Relationship between paid staff and volunteers

It is vital that volunteers and paid employees are seen as components of the same programme, not as competitors. If management truly recognizes the complementary nature of the two groups, then there is an excellent chance that each group will regard the other more favourably recognizing their interconnectedness. Often, however, the relationship between the two groups is founded upon suspicion and envy. Indeed, McClam and Spicuzza (1988: 25) suggest that the relationship between the two groups has been 'one of coexistence fraught with ambiguity, resistance, jealousy, and tension'. Unfortunately, research into the relationship between paid staff and volunteers has been 'remarkably sparse' (Wandersman and Alderman, 1993: 68). In the study conducted by Wandersman and Alderman (1993: 75), it was found that the major problem between paid staff and volunteers was due to poor communication and it was concluded that the relationship between the two groups was 'one of negotiation and diplomacy'. Both groups often have opposite views of each other's position in the workplace (Wilson and Pimm,

1996) with volunteers believing that they are doing all the mundane work while the paid employees get all of the powerful and more interesting positions. Paid staff often have the opposite view believing that volunteers only do the tasks that they wish to do and all the unpleasant tasks are left to them.

Paid staff often feel threatened by volunteers, fearing that their positions will be replaced using volunteer labour (Pearce, 1993). It is important for harmonious relations that paid staff do not feel threatened and they should be reassured. At an award-winning HVA in Australia, the initial introduction of volunteers to complement the services provided by paid staff caused substantial angst amongst the paid staff who were concerned that their positions would ultimately be replaced by volunteer staff. As a result, the paid staff actively sought to undermine the role of volunteers. In order to convince paid staff that this was not the case, management of this HVA gave the paid staff an absolute undertaking that volunteers would never be used in any position occupied by paid staff. This commitment, made some ten years ago, has been honoured and paid staff and volunteers work extremely well together. This commitment has meant that at times, management of the HVA has had to temporarily close parts of the facility because of staff absences even though there were volunteers who could have stepped into the position. Management at this particular HVA suggested that in order to alleviate the concerns of paid staff, it was best to structure tasks carried out by the two groups such that they were separate. At this particular facility, the primary role of the volunteer staff is to adopt the persona of characters of the period in order to enhance the visitor experience; volunteers are never used in any position involving cash at this facility.

The silent criticism of each other by volunteers and paid staff can be reduced by continually rotating the positions of both groups in order to blur relationships between the two (Pearce, 1993). The relationship between volunteers and paid staff has an enormous influence on the quality of the overall volunteer experience (Mausner, 1988) and so every effort must be made to ensure that there is real cohesion between the two groups.

The ideal relationship between volunteers and paid staff could be based upon the 'teammate' model whereby the two groups work as equals to achieve the organization's goals (Mausner, 1988). Such a relationship is based upon mutual trust and a balance of power. Fundamental to this is a clear understanding of the organization's specific goals. Sometimes volunteers take a somewhat moralistic attitude believing themselves to be above paid staff since they do not work for financial reward. This view can antagonize paid staff. Effort must be made to demonstrate to volunteers the benefits that paid staff bring, namely, full-time commitment, skills and consistency (Wilson and Pimm, 1996). Paid staff can also become frustrated with the often casual attitude demonstrated by volunteers and the uncertainty about whether they will even turn up. Paid staff often believe that their lives would be so much easier without volunteers. This view is exacerbated by the poor way in which volunteers at many HVAs are managed. Paid staff are sometimes guilty of adopting a 'paternalistic' attitude towards volunteers, an attitude that is often difficult to change (Noble, 1991).

In order to improve the relationships between the two groups, more should be done to explain to each group the roles of the other group. Paid staff should be trained how to handle volunteers and should be involved in planning work for volunteers. Once paid staff understand the important role that volunteers play and what motivates them to offer their services, they are more likely to recognize the need to provide stimulating tasks for the volunteers.

Another factor that seemed to underpin the more successful volunteer programmes at HVAs was that socializing between paid staff and volunteers was encouraged. The authors of this chapter were surprised, however, at the number of HVAs that seemed to discourage such socializing by providing separate volunteer and paid staff facilities and by having quite separate social functions for the two groups. This was often explained by management as being a function of the different demographic characteristics of the two groups which made socializing difficult. In a number of HVAs, for example, the volunteers tended to be retirees and predominantly female whereas the paid staff were quite young and predominantly male. Such demographic differences did not encourage socializing.

Bursian (1992) proposed some principles for volunteer training, which should be seen as underpinning the relationship between volunteers and paid staff. The key principles included:

1 Volunteering is not a substitute for paid work.
2 Volunteers working in positions that should be paid is exploitative.
3 When a job is, or has been, clearly identified as a paid staff position, it is not appropriate for it to be filled by a volunteer.
4 Government funds allocated for vocational training should not be used for the training of volunteers as volunteers.

The adoption of these principles would greatly enhance the relationship between volunteers and paid staff at HVAs. Such adoption, however, must be at all levels of the organization for it to be seen as more than just lip service.

Human resource management functions

Recruitment

Recruitment is generally regarded as a fundamental HRM activity and many organizations expend substantial effort on attracting a suitable pool of candidates from which staff can be selected. With respect to many voluntary organizations, however, there is a view that 'anyone' should be taken as 'we can't afford to be choosy'. This greatly increases the likelihood of taking on volunteers who are totally unsuitable for the organization and the tasks at hand. This approach also adds to the view of many that voluntary programmes do not work. It is critical to the success of voluntary programmes that the recruitment function of volunteers is conducted in the same rigorous manner as occurs in many organizations for the recruitment of candidates for paid positions.

The first step in this process is to have a clear idea of the roles that volunteers are expected to fill and a profile of suitable recruits. Preparing a position description for the volunteer positions will facilitate the recruitment process and will help overcome misunderstandings when a person commences their role within the organization. The position description should include the job title, a list of the tasks included in the job, the name of the person or position to whom the volunteer reports, and the expected time involvement (Warren, 1990). This will narrow the search for recruits.

A common method of recruitment of paid staff is via newspaper advertisements. Due to the expense of this exercise, it is not always possible that HVAs can adopt such an approach in the recruitment of volunteers, nor is this approach necessarily desirable. However, it is often possible to have publicity articles written about the attraction in local newspapers and as part of such articles to have some discussion about the important role that volunteers play and the characteristics of volunteers that are being sought. Articles that demonstrate the success of the facility and the important role that volunteers play in achieving this success help in the attraction of volunteers as people generally like to be associated with 'winners' (Wilson and Pimm, 1996).

It has been suggested that the motives for a person volunteering influence the manner in which such people will join the organization (Pearce, 1993). For example, people who volunteer for social reasons will generally like to be invited by someone that they already know within the organization whereas people interested in the key objectives of the organization are more likely to respond to a newspaper advertisement.

Although a number of HVAs do, in fact, advertise for volunteers, many of these advertisements seem to be doing little more than seeking out people who are prepared to give up their time; they do little to list specific characteristics or skills required of the volunteers. This reflects an attitude of 'we'll take whoever we can get'. Based on a survey of HVAs, there is a growing reluctance to adopt this approach largely because of its indiscriminate results. It is also very difficult to reject someone who is prepared to volunteer their time in response to an advertisement, even though it is clear that the person is totally unsuitable for such a task. It does not do one's ego much good to be rejected for a voluntary position that was advertised in the newspaper. In order to overcome this problem, a growing number of HVAs are relying on referrals from existing volunteers. The advantage of this approach is that existing volunteers understand the culture of the organization and know what is expected of new volunteers. This is more likely to lead to a suitable match between volunteer and the position. Friends and family of existing volunteers are more likely to share the same aspirations and are therefore more likely to 'fit' the organization. According to ABS (1995), nearly 60 per cent of volunteers became involved in voluntary work through word-of-mouth referral; only 4 per cent became volunteers in response to a newspaper advertisement or article. As well as this, managers at many HVAs keep lists of people who approach them to volunteer so that they can be followed up later as appropriate.

In developing recruiting messages, it is important that volunteer recruits understand the benefits that they can get from being associated with the organization as well as the benefits that the organization would expect to get from volunteers. It is important that this two-way relationship which is represented in Figure 12.1, is recognized at the outset. One of the best ways to understand what new recruits could get from the organization is to understand the motives of existing volunteers as was indicated in an earlier section. This can form the basis for recruitment messages. Society tends to expect volunteers to be doing the task as a result of altruistic objectives so the altruistic elements of the task must be included in the message, but so too should be the personal benefits that can be derived from a voluntary role.

If suitable candidates approach the organization seeking to become volunteers, it is important that the organization respond in an appropriately expeditious manner. In a survey that was conducted on volunteers at a number of HVAs, it was found that 43 per cent of respondents also volunteered their services for another organization. Given this propensity to be involved in multiple organizations, it is highly likely that people will seek to offer their services elsewhere if the HVA does not respond in a suitable time frame.

Management at one HVA indicated that it had only two intakes of volunteers per year in order to derive economies of scale in terms of induction and training. However, management found that many of the people who offered their services as volunteers at the wrong time of the year were not available when it came time for the actual intake. This can pose problems in losing suitable volunteers. Responding promptly, even if only to advise a person that they are now on the list for the next intake of volunteers, is an important task and must be done to show the new person that their efforts and interest are appreciated. This is why responsibility for such tasks should be with a paid employee as opposed to a volunteer in order to ensure that it is done in a timely manner.

Selection

For many HVAs, selectivity in relation to volunteers is regarded as a luxury. Interviews with managers of HVAs indicate that the selection of volunteers is conducted in an *ad hoc* way and based on a 'gut feeling' of who would be suitable. However, selection of unsuitable candidates will likely result in high turnover of volunteers and to dissatisfaction among existing volunteers. It is also draining on the organization in that it leads to high resource costs in recruitment, training and morale.

It is important that the organization considers the personality of the applicant in the same way as would occur for a paid employee; will the person fit with the organization and if so, where? Is the person an individual or a team player? In HVAs, volunteers play such an important part in delivering a high-quality visitor experience that the wrong volunteer could have a serious impact on the overall customer evaluation of the visit experience. For this reason it is important to interview applicants for volunteer positions in order to assess their overall suitability and if suitable, to identify appropriate roles. References should also be asked for and checked. In treating such applications seriously, the candidate for the volunteer position will tend to regard the position in a more serious manner.

Clearly, the selection process for a volunteer is unlikely to be as formal as that for a paid member of staff, but this does not mean that there should not be a structured process. A position description, interview process and reference check would greatly improve the value of the volunteer programme and would assist both the volunteer and the organization to ensure that the correct decision is made. It should be possible to not admit people to volunteer positions if they do not seem consistent with the culture of the organization or perhaps to have some volunteer positions that prevent unsuitable candidates from detracting from the overall product offering at the HVA. In other words, it is sometimes useful to have some volunteer positions that keep unsuitable candidates away from core areas, in particular, dealing with the visitors. In areas where volunteers are going to be working closely with paid staff, it can be useful to have these staff members involved in the selection process as would often occur for a paid position.

Induction

Just as induction has become important for paid employees, so too should it be conducted for volunteers. Management at one HVA surveyed as part of this study stated that its turnover of volunteers had reduced substantially since it had been made compulsory for volunteers to complete a two-day induction period before commencing work in the facility. First impressions are very important and the induction programme helps set the scene for a positive first impression. It is very difficult to change the impressions that a new volunteer forms when joining the organization and it is, therefore, imperative that the induction programme sets the scene well.

Prior to the introduction of this compulsory induction programme, new volunteers had been assigned to a more experienced volunteer to 'shadow' them in order to pick up knowledge about the organization. Although this method proved useful in helping the new volunteers to learn specific information, it did not facilitate the transfer of knowledge that was sufficiently broad based. An induction programme is designed to provide the new volunteer with the following:

- the organization's rules and procedures
- the culture of the organization
- the role of the new member
- the structure of the organization
- the members and roles of other staff.

Since most volunteers spend substantially less time 'working' within the organization than do paid employees, it usually takes them much longer to feel a sense of belonging with the HVA. This suggests that an induction period is probably of even greater importance for volunteers than it is for paid staff.

Many volunteers are not overly committed to the organization at the outset and consider their early involvement with the organization as a trial (Pearce, 1993). Their decision regarding whether they stay in the longer term depends on their early impressions which further explains the importance of the induction period for volunteers. Some type of ceremony to mark a volunteer joining the organization has been found to increase volunteer commitment (Pearce, 1993) as it prompts new volunteers to declare publicly their association with the organization. Such a public declaration makes it more difficult for volunteers to not give their roles within the organization a fair chance.

Although much of the work that has been conducted into 'organizational commitment' relates to paid employees, it is also a consideration for volunteers. Cuskelly (1994) suggested that volunteers demonstrating higher organization commitment tended to stay longer with the organization and to put in more voluntary hours. He also proposed that organization commitment can be increased via good induction and training programmes as well as efforts to increase the friendliness and supportive ambience of the organization.

Training and development

It is well recognized that staff require training to perform at their optimum in an organization. Training is an essential element in the provision of a quality product (Swarbrooke, 1995) and should also be regarded as an investment in the future. Since volunteers are often regarded as 'transient workers', it is often not seen as viable to provide them with the necessary training. However, statistics indicate that the average period of employment of volunteers at a HVA is, indeed, often longer than paid staff. At one such HVA, over 60 per cent of volunteers had been active volunteers for over five years, half of whom had been with the HVA for over ten years. Clearly, with this length of service, there is no doubt that the HVA can get a return on the training that is given.

Training provides an opportunity for personal growth and has the potential to enhance a volunteer's sense of purpose. There is every likelihood, therefore, that volunteers will respond well to training and may in fact extend their stay because they are being regarded more seriously within the organization. Certainly training is a real expense for management but the rewards are quite substantial. Since volunteers are so important in the delivery of the product at many HVAs, having skills in the area of customer service, communication and the like would greatly enhance their ability to perform. However, management must be careful to recognize that the training of volunteers can sometimes feed the fears of paid staff that they are more likely to be replaced by volunteer staff (Bursian, 1992).

The cost of training volunteers can be reduced by including them on programmes designed for the paid staff. In this way, the training can be costed on an incremental basis.

Some HVAs have asked volunteers to enter into contracts when they receive training so that the organization has a chance to 'recoup' its investment. However, this seems to be somewhat shortsighted in that the average duration of 'employment' of volunteers is so long at many establishments and basic training should be regarded as an essential element, not as an 'optional extra'.

Although it is argued by some that the popularity of volunteering will be greatly diminished if rules, training and supervision are introduced, there is no evidence to support such a view provided that the systems that are introduced recognize the needs and motives of the volunteers (Tyzack, 1996). However, management must be careful not to make the training of volunteers into an onerous exercise for the volunteers as this may be a disincentive for them staying. Some HVAs have circumvented this problem by having guest speaker programmes and discussion groups coupled with a social evening to make the training side less formal. Many volunteers surveyed within such establishments enjoyed these sessions and did not recognize that they were in fact attending a training session. The problem with this approach is that the benefits of such sessions are not recognized by all volunteers, which can lead to reduced attendance.

With increasing legislation associated with areas such as occupational health and safety, there is now a formal requirement that all staff, including volunteers, are trained in at least these areas. Given that this is the case, there is an opportunity to develop more ongoing training programmes in a variety of areas. As a bonus, it has been found that organizations with more formal induction and training programmes for volunteers have much lower volunteer turnover rates (Pearce, 1993).

Mentoring of volunteers at HVAs has been found to be an important means of providing ongoing training in a less structured manner. This form of 'on the job' training is often the most effective manner of communicating the culture of the organization to new volunteers. This type of training has been found particularly effective in HVAs where volunteers adopt roles relevant to a period in time whereby volunteers seem to find it easier to adapt to a role after having observed others playing similar roles.

Supervision

'There is one common denominator in an amazing number of volunteer programmes experiencing difficulty. It is not the volunteers but the person directing the programme . . . it is haphazardly delegated to any staff person who has some free time' (Wilson, cited in Tyzack, 1996: 25). Generally, there needs to be a single person in the HVA who is responsible for the co-ordination of volunteers and this person should be a full-time member of the paid staff. Heritage visitor attractions that have not adopted this approach seem to have more problems in determining the activities of volunteers. The fact that volunteer work tends to be done in small infrequent blocks of time means that volunteers often do not have a strong social network within the organization (Pearce, 1993) and tend to relate more closely to the volunteer co-ordinator; for many volunteers, the volunteer co-ordinator is their one constant. If this approach is adopted, it needs to be made clear to all paid staff how the tasks required to be carried out by volunteers should be communicated to the volunteers, namely, through the volunteer co-ordinator. Failure to do this often leads to substantial confusion. The person selected to co-ordinate the volunteers needs to be well trained in the handling of volunteers so that they recognize the substantial supervisory differences between the handling of volunteers and paid staff. If this person does not have the necessary skills and is not well trained, the chance of the whole volunteer programme being a success is limited at best. One does not have the same leverage over volunteers that one has over paid staff and therefore a 'lighter' approach needs to be adopted. This person needs to have empathy with the volunteers and thus understand that their roles as volunteers generally form much smaller parts of their lives than does work for a paid employee. People who themselves have been volunteers, often make good volunteer co-ordinators and it is interesting to note that 'the job of volunteer manager is now becoming a career in its own right' (Noble, 1991: 68).

Having a single person being responsible for volunteers enables better control of volunteers and helps identify the volunteers that are more committed who should be groomed for more responsibility. This person is also able to identify the volunteers that would most benefit from additional training.

The person who co-ordinates the volunteers must be able to motivate volunteers and develop a collegiate atmosphere. Lack of motivation usually leads to problems with volunteer retention (McCurley and Lynch, 1989) so this component of the supervisor's role is important to the overall success of the volunteer programme. The supervisor must also be careful not to fall into the trap of overloading the keener volunteers, which happens in far too many voluntary organizations. The result is often 'burnout' whereby the keen volunteer who is overloaded ends up having to leave the organization to escape the problem. Another problem for volunteers that can eventually prompt them to leave is termed 'rustout' (Getz, 1997) whereby volunteers are given such mundane tasks lacking any form of stimulation that they become 'bored to death' and leave the organization. Many HVAs that finding they have high turnover of volunteers would do well to examine the type of work that is being offered to the volunteers. More often than not it will be found that the tasks are boring and lack stimulation or responsibility (Tyzack, 1996). The supervisor must ensure that the tasks allocated to the volunteers are varied to meet their skills and needs, and to ensure that interest levels are maintained among volunteers. It is vital to ensure that the interest of volunteers is maintained during quiet periods (Wilson and Pimm, 1996) and that the volunteer positions as a whole involve sufficient variety to keep volunteers interested and motivated. It has also been found that continuity of leadership of the volunteers greatly increases the effective management of volunteers (Pearce, 1993).

There is a tendency for volunteers to bypass paid supervisors and go directly to more senior staff on the basis that they, the volunteers, do not need to report to a more lowly person in the organization (Pearce, 1993). However, a survey of management at a number of HVAs indicated that this was less likely to happen in organizations where the volunteer co-ordinator was serious about the position and had the respect of the volunteers.

Appraisal

Formal appraisal schemes are now commonplace in industry. However, introducing a formal appraisal scheme for volunteers at an HVA would be 'the nearest thing to a death warrant for ensuring the continuation of the volunteer's support' (Wilson and Pimm, 1996; 36). This does not mean, however, that appraisal should not be conducted but rather, that it should be done on a less formal basis. Volunteers need to be assessed, usually by observation without the volunteers actually knowing that they are being appraised. Such an appraisal can identify elements such as whether the volunteers are working in the best area, or whether they need additional training. It is important that volunteers receive feedback on their performance but done in such a way that they are not aware that they have been specifically appraised. In particular, it is vital that volunteers be given positive feedback and told how much their contribution is being appreciated. This type of feedback will greatly enhance the commitment of the volunteer.

Keeping statistics on how the HVA is performing and providing regular positive feedback on the role that volunteers play in the success of the organization tends to improve the reliability of volunteers. Volunteer reliability tends to fall if they feel that they are not really needed (Pearce, 1993).

Rewards

Although volunteers do not seek financial rewards for their efforts, this does not mean that volunteers do not seek rewards *per se*. The fact that the rewards sought by volunteers are completely different from those sought by paid staff substantially impacts upon the traditional tools of management (Wilson and Pimm, 1996). The traditional financial reward system forms the basis of management's control of paid workers and its obvious non-applicability in relation to volunteers probably goes a long way towards explaining why management has had such a hard time in controlling volunteers and has, therefore, tended to leave volunteers to their own devices.

The reward often sought by volunteers is simply recognition. In the aforementioned survey of HVAs, it was surprising the number of HVAs that did not have any type of recognition system. 'Volunteers, since they are unpaid, are all "paid" equally and relatively cheaply and so there is little economic reason to differentiate among them' (Pearce, 1993: 10). This, however, can cause friction among volunteers. It was of no surprise that this item was the thing that caused the most concern for volunteers themselves, who indicated that they felt that their contribution was not being appreciated.

As indicated earlier, there are now many types of organizations that make use of volunteer services. This means that there is every likelihood that volunteers who do not believe that their services are being adequately recognized or appreciated within one organization, will simply move to another organization where they feel that they will be better appreciated. This can result in a substantial loss of key personnel.

Many of the HVAs with successful volunteer programmes had introduced systems that tracked the contribution of volunteers in terms of the years of service, number of days worked and the like. Performance in these areas was publicly acknowledged via newsletter articles and often via lapel pins for those having reached substantial milestones in terms of the number of years of service or number of visits.

It is important to note that recognition systems can be either formal or informal. McCurley and Lynch (1989: 115) argue that informal recognition systems are more effective than formal systems in that they 'convey a constant sense of appreciation and belonging to the volunteer'. Informal, or day-to-day, recognition systems involve items such as saying 'thank you', involving the volunteers in decisions that affect them, ensuring that volunteers are treated in the same way as staff, and training the volunteers.

Other things that were regarded favourably by volunteers, based on analysis of the survey of HVAs included:

- having their opinions sought on various management issues
- being kept informed about developments, usually via a regular newsletter
- using their skills
- ensuring that they went on familiarizations of other tourist facilities
- having regular social functions
- having their work acknowledged in media releases
- being entitled to discounts and free entries for families
- keeping track of birthdays and anniversaries.

It is vital, therefore, to keep a register of skills of volunteers so that these can be made use of at the HVA. It was surprising how infrequently this was done based on the survey of management at various HVAs.

As stated earlier, if volunteers feel that their services are not being appreciated, there is a growing chance that they will leave the organization. It is, therefore, vital that management constantly inform volunteers about how valuable their services are to the organization. This is a basic human need, not something unique to volunteers.

A growing number of HVAs reward volunteer performance and length of service by having a hierarchical structure among their volunteers such that volunteers can be promoted. Such an approach gives volunteers increased status and responsibility in direct relationship to their performance. This approach has certainly been adopted in the operation of special events, many of which heavily rely upon the services of volunteers (Getz, 1997). However, such an approach may not work at all HVAs, especially in situations where many of the volunteers have strong personal relationships with other volunteers. In such situations a volunteer hierarchy could alienate some of the volunteers.

Discipline

Traditional forms of discipline that are used with paid employees tend to revolve around bonus reduction, failure to promote or ultimately, fear of dismissal. Clearly, these approaches have little relevance for volunteers. The survey of HVAs indicated that the most effective form of discipline for volunteers was peer group pressure further reinforcing the view that volunteers tend to conform to a particular organizational culture. Control of volunteers is greatly strengthened when volunteers have shared values (Pearce, 1993) which is enhanced by recruiting volunteers from family and friends. Leaders then articulate and embody these values (Pearce, 1993). If volunteers have been introduced largely by friends or family, there is quite a high degree of 'loss of face' in non-performance of duties. Also building a strong personal relationship with the volunteer co-ordinator tended to curb the need for discipline.

Although volunteers can be insubordinate, this tends to occur less frequently when the volunteers believe that their tasks are really making a difference to the organization. Therefore, it is important to convince volunteers that specific policies and directions are necessary for the good of the organization in order to extract a higher return.

Conclusion

Overall, it is vital that volunteers and paid staff be seen as complementary components of the HRM function at HVAs. Volunteers are an important human resource that has all too often been ignored and undervalued (Noble, 1991). They must not be regarded as a form of cheap labour, as tends to happen currently at a number of HVAs.

The following list, which is taken from Warren (1990: 46), sums up the needs of volunteers at HVAs in return for their commitment and efforts for the organization:

- I need a sense of belonging.
- I need to have a sense of sharing in planning.
- I need to feel that the goals and objectives arrived at are within reach.
- I need to share in making the rules.
- I need to feel that I will be trained, supervised and supported.
- I need to feel that what I'm doing has real purpose.
- I need to know in detail just what is expected of me.
- I need to have some responsibilities that challenge.
- I need to see that progress is being made.
- I need to be kept informed.
- I need to have confidence in my supervisors and fellow workers.

A successful volunteer programme is essential to the delivery of a quality visitor experience at HVAs. In seeking to build a successful volunteer programme, recognition of the balance between the needs and skills of the volunteers and the rewards and tasks of the HVA, as shown in Figure 12.1, is fundamental.

Questions

1 Who are the volunteers in the HVAs and why are they important to the success of these organizations?
2 What are some of the issues that may cause conflict between paid staff and volunteers?
3 Discuss two key HR functions that would improve the use of volunteers in HVAs.

References and further reading

Australian Bureau of Statistics (ABS) (1995). *Voluntary Work*, Catalogue No. 4441.0, Commonwealth of Australia.

Bursian, O. (1992). *Volunteer Policy Paper*, Community Services and Health Industry Training Board.

Cuskelly, G. (1994). The commitment of volunteer administrators to sporting organisations. *Australian Journal of Leisure and Recreation*, **4**(2), 5–13.

Deery, M., Jago, L. and Shaw, R. (1998). Profiling satisfied volunteers at a tourist attraction. *Journal of Tourism Studies*, **8**(2), 18–25.

Getz, D. (1997). *Event Management and Event Tourism*. Cognizant Communication Corporation.

Mausner, C. (1988). The underlying dynamics of staff–volunteer relationships. *Journal of Volunteer Administration*, Summer, 5–9.

McClam, T. and Spicuzza, F. (1988). An unholy alliance; the professional–volunteer relationship. *Nonprofit World*, **6**(3), 25–27.

McCurley, S. and Lynch, R. (1989). *Essential Volunteer Management*. VMSystems and Heritage Arts Publishing.

Metzer, J., Dollard, M., Rogers, L. and Cordingley, S. (1997). Quality of work life of volunteers. *Australian Journal on Volunteering*, **2**(2), 8–15.

Noble, J. (1991). *Volunteering: A Current Perspective*. Volunteer Centre of South Australia Inc.

Pearce, J. (1980). A volunteer worker placement model for business. *Annals of Tourism Research*, **7**(3), 443–454.

Pearce, J. (1993). *Volunteers: The Organisational Behaviour of Unpaid Workers*. Routledge.

Swarbrooke, J. (1995). *The Development and Management of Visitor Attractions*. Butterworth-Heinemann.

Tyzack, H. (1996). Volunteering: laissez faire or managed? *Australian Journal on Volunteering*, **1**, 23–27.

Wandersman, A. and Alderman, J. (1993). Incentives, costs, and barriers for volunteers: a staff perspective on volunteers in one state. *Review of Public Personnel Administration*, Winter, 67–76.

Warren, N. (1990). *The Volunteer Manual*. Nell Warren Associates Inc.

Wells, J. (1996). Volunteers in the tourism industry: issues, trends and policies. In *Tourism Down Under II: Towards a More Sustainable Tourism* (G. Kearsley, ed.), pp. 357–375, Centre for Tourism.

Wilson, A. and Pimm, G. (1996). The tyranny of the volunteer: the care and feeding of voluntary workforces. *Management Decision*, **34** (4), 24–40.

Part Six

The Future

Nick Johns

These chapters discuss likely future trends in heritage visitor attraction quality, in terms of both visitor demand and the way this can be provided for. In this regard, 'quality' is open to considerable interpretation. It is customary to consider quality as a one-dimensional continuum between 'good/high' and 'poor/low'. However, such an approach is futile for an assessment of the future, since there can be only one trend; customers will demand higher/better quality, and attractions that do not supply it will be forced out of business. Recognizing this, we have sought to treat quality as a multidimensional variable, and to examine not only the way demand may change for existing attributes, but also the likely way the attributes themselves might evolve.

Futurology inevitably takes two forms. *Forecasting* assumes that the future will be more or less like the past, and seeks to extrapolate observations of recent and past demand. This is a conservative approach, and usually only valid for the very near future, since successive small deviations from the forecast exacerbate one another and rapidly become gross deviations. The alternative is to imagine that discontinuous change will occur at some point in the future, and to attempt to predict both what it will be and when it will occur. This approach is also obviously flawed, but not necessarily more so than (assumed) 'scientific' forecasting. The only thing of which one can be certain is that the future cannot be known, and any prediction is at best a gamble. In this spirit the present section of this book seeks to balance assessments of existing demand with 'futuristic' predictions.

Within this balance the reader will find reference to known demographic changes, such as expected age profiles, together with less certain issues of social structure and behaviour. Current trends in travel are considered along-side those in education, leisure and entertainment, all of which seem likely to affect the heritage attractions industry, especially when juxtaposed with demographic factors. However, modes and types of demand are also likely to be affected by modern dreams and myths. Tourism is not just about 'consuming'. It may be 'play' or 'pilgrimage' or an escape from the alien-ation of the modern/postmodern condition. The escape is typically into some mythologized, hyperreal 'history', 'nature' or other fantasy.

Demand, like quality can be viewed as one-dimensional or multidimen-sional. It will become less and less adequate to assess it en masse, or even in terms of increasingly sophisticated market segmentation, since dreams and fantasies are infinite in scope and diversity. In theory heritage attractions supply what their customers want, but in practice they are subject to a number of other influences, including their own, recent historical context. Of course these include the artefacts and exhibits available. They also include the atti-tudes, values and philosophy of the provider, as one can see by considering the following continuum of typical roles:

custodian – conservator – exhibitor – interpreter – educator – entertainer

These are often further influenced by the ownership and funding base of the attraction, which may be public, private or intermediate (e.g. through a community trust, lottery money, etc.). The present section also seeks to offer a global view, broadening out its examples and theory to encompass Asian and American dimensions of heritage issues.

All this amounts to a stimulating challenge, especially in terms of:

■ how to assess and evaluate demand
■ how to match supply to demand

- how to assess and evaluate quality
- how to maintain a broad awareness of the heritage industry and the factors at work in it.

It is intended that the section will stimulate the reader's thought and ideas. It is also hoped that during reading, new questions will constantly present themselves, enriching the reader's understanding and paving the way for further understanding of this fascinating field.

13

Which way for heritage visitor attractions?

Nick Johns and Julian Hoseason

Introduction

The quality of heritage attractions can be viewed as something of a 'push-pull' phenomenon, subject to the exigencies of both supply and demand. Although, on the 'supply' side it might be argued that heritage is a strictly limited resource which cannot be indefinitely renewed, a closer look suggests that this is not so. Heritage as a commodity is constantly being repackaged and reinvented. For example, reconstructed 'native' villages in Sumatra portray lifestyles that in some cases no longer have an independent existence. 'Yesteryear' museums in the English Midlands identify as heritage, artefacts that many of the visitors had in their childhood homes. Heritage is also 'Disneyfied' or caricatured, as at the Epcot Center in Florida, or the Asterix Parc at Paris.

The number, character and quality of heritage attractions are, in part, driven by constant gradual changes in the pattern of visitor demand. For example, increased leisure time is reflected in an increase in heritage attractions worldwide. The well-documented demographic shift towards populations which are generally older in the North and West, but younger in the South and East, has also brought a plethora of 'activity' and 'interest' holidays aimed at the assumedly affluent Western sector, many of which focus upon cultural heritage as their goal. Visitors are also steadily becoming more discerning, sophisticated and hence demanding, in terms of authenticity and service quality. No doubt there will be parallel developments aimed at the younger, more vibrant Pacific rim populations during the early years of the twenty-first century.

This chapter examines the factors likely to affect demand for heritage attraction visits during the early twenty-first century. Its particular concern is the influence that change will have upon the quality of attractions. Most dictionaries offer two main definitions for the word 'quality', which may denote the characteristics of something, or its degree of excellence. Probably the most significant area of change stemming from developments in consumer demand will be in the *characteristics* of heritage attractions. Thus the first and major part of this chapter concentrates upon *qualities*, rather than the quality of heritage attractions and charts their likely evolution, in terms of service design and characteristics. However, changing visitor tastes and interests are also likely to influence the way quality, and particularly service quality are delivered, and this aspect of the subject is also discussed.

The basis of demand for heritage

In the strictest sense, little is known of the motivational structure underlying demand for heritage visits. However, there are two widely accepted views of how demand arises or is formulated. A 'consumer' view, shared by many of those who market holiday packages (and within them, attractions) is that of mass demand, arising within specific segments of the market. These may be defined by their demographic features alone, but are increasingly categorized in more subtle ways, based upon patterns of purchasing or other behaviour, 'lifestyle' or attitudes. Such analyses have given rise to specific segments that have actually entered everyday language, for example 'yuppies' (young urban professionals) and 'dinkys' (double income, no kids yet). This kind of 'consumer view' is subtle and pervasive in its efforts to generalize demand into a relatively few recognizable channels, so that it can be satisfied through simple formulae of design and delivery. However, its appropriateness for heritage attractions should not be accepted without reservation, since demographics and lifestyle arguably form a poor basis for predicting attraction visitor behaviour (Prentice, Witt and Hamer, 1998).

An alternative to this consumer view takes the stance that a visit to an attraction is an essentially unsharable, individual, personal experience. From this it follows that individual visitors are market segments in their own right, selecting their personal choice of aspects to view at a heritage attraction and interpreting the resulting experience in their own individual way. This essentially postmodern view of the attraction experience also has its aficionados, mostly among the academic community, but is growing in importance as a way of understanding visitors' reactions to tourist phenomena (see, for example, Arnould and Price, 1993; Arnould, Price and Tierney, 1997). Ultimately there is a potential collision between the mass-marketing paradigm which has established itself in commercial thinking over the course of the twentieth century, and the postmodern approach, which is growing rapidly at the time of writing, and seems set to increase in importance through the next century. This development appears to parallel a similar shift in consumer demand towards greater freedom of choice, customization and individual service. There is a discernible tension within the marketing profession to reconcile mass segmentation with the needs of individual customers, and the need is nowhere so great as among heritage attractions. One of the objectives of this chapter is to look at ways in which this reconciliation may be achieved, at least as far as it relates to understanding the demand for heritage.

Johns (1999a) proposes that tourism services are unique among the 'service industries' among which they are commonly included by economists. The reason for this is that visitors' 'consumption' of tourism offerings mostly takes the form of out of the ordinary experiences. These are characterized by affective responses and often involve entertainment or sensory stimulation. Thus there is an expectation, even a requirement for such experiences to be 'magical', which makes the consumption of tourist attractions particularly individual in character.

Segmentation issues

Notwithstanding the objections raised above, the demand for tourism 'products' can to some extent be understood in terms of segmentation factors. The following section identifies the main conclusions that may be drawn from such an analysis and pinpoints some of the weaknesses of this approach.

Many commentators have noted that developed nations are experiencing a number of common changes to their demographic profiles and spatial distribution that are likely to have some impact upon the heritage industry. Most Western populations are currently experiencing an 'ageing' process. Bulges in population pyramids, reflecting the so-called post-Second World War 'baby boom' or consumer boom of the 1960s, are now significantly adjacent to the 55–59 and 60–64 age groups. Other age groups, particularly those aged below 16, are steadily declining in proportion to the overall population. Thus annual population growth rates have slowed or stagnated, and forecasts for the period 1995–2020 predict steadily decreasing populations, caused by a continuing fall in the birth rate, together with an increasing death rate as the present, ageing demographic profile reaches average life expectancy. There is also an imbalance between the genders, due to a slightly higher mortality rate among males of all ages. The proportion of women steadily increases with age, since their relative mortality rate falls.

These trends are already impacting significantly upon Western economies, since fewer working people must support an increasing number of economically inactive individuals. In the UK the period 1979–98 saw the mass retirement of older employees at ever younger ages. Changes in union and employment law, have subsequently allowed organizations to make older individuals redundant. In the UK changes are already being made to taxation and pension provision to keep older employees from early access to their retirement spending power. The position has been less drastic in some other Western countries, but the drive appears to be inexorable. The effects upon pensions, insurance and welfare seem inevitably to impact upon consumer habits, lowering levels of disposable income. The easily identifiable 'seniors' market is likely to become ever less lucrative, and there will be a shift in consumer spending patterns or service provision, particularly in discretionary spending sectors such as tourism and heritage. In particular, 'senior travellers' have probably been most taken for granted by the tourism industry, and are probably most in need of reconsideration as a heritage market. This segment has become over-targeted as a consumer group, and former assumptions, that they are at their peak in terms of disposable income, and that they therefore have a high propensity to travel are in need of review. These trends may force custodians of heritage attractions to reappraise service provision (Ananth, DeMicco and Howey, 1992) and shift the focus of interpretation, marketing and service quality by targeting specific market segments in order to optimize the effectiveness of the tourism product.

Besides the demographics of age there is a discernible, steady increase in the divorce rate, and a corresponding rise in one-parent families. Where grandparents are affluent, they may take a supporting role, producing a reagglomeration of social units around a kind of *neo*-extended family. Grandparents are also relatively younger than their counterparts of 20 or 50 years ago, giving them more of an opportunity to enjoy family life. Contemporaneous with this there is a growing number of second marriages in which one of the parents is considerably older than the other, and there is another batch of much younger stepchildren. Thus, directly or indirectly, a significant proportion of the older population may have relatively young families to care for.

As the proportion of individuals of school age within the Western population falls, so will the demand for a curriculum based educational experience of heritage as part of a formal education programme. The role of cultural depository has been an important component of the mission and self-image of many (and particularly of the longer established) heritage attractions. On the other hand, the grouping of old and young visitors may lead to a greater interest in heritage and an increasing demand for attractions, particularly those where circumstances or interpretation make the content accessible to both young and old.

The age structure of a population reflects a historic record. Consumer behaviour not only reflects these demographic changes, but also a variety of external influences rooted in socio-cultural change. These include fashion, taste (Johns, 1995) and lifestyles (Masser, Svidén and Wegner, 1994) which have been used by a number of authors for segmenting markets. Many such segmentations are complex, but few if any are of specific relevance to the tourism sector. However, a simple, operational segmentation used by the travel industry is offered by Elliott and Johns (1993):

- senior travellers
- family travellers
- short stays.

As discussed above, many current senior travellers belong to, or narrowly predate, the baby boom age group. They grew up in the social freedom and technological pessimism of the 1960s and as a result tend to be relatively progressive liberal and even slightly left wing in outlook. This segment is better educated than previous generations and desires something 'more than' and 'different from' what was available to its parents. The individuals making up this demographic group were at the forefront of the consumer boom during the 1960s and have tended to remain so. They therefore have a subtle and discerning eye for quality and are less likely than previous generations to be won over by advertisements or appearances. This age group are noted as 'trailblazers', who prefer relatively independent travel and less regimented holiday experiences. They prefer to be regarded as 'travellers' rather than 'tourists' other things being equal (i.e. as long as the price is right). They value the freedom of choice in where they go, what they do and how they do it. In terms of heritage attractions, this market segment is likely to demand more and better interpretation and the seamless, unobtrusive use of technology and facsimile. The challenge will be to cater for numbers in a way that is sympathetic to the needs of the individual, and especially preserves the perceived historical authenticity of sites and artefacts.

Research by the Economist Intelligence Unit (EIU, 1997) indicates that during the mid to late 1990s, senior travellers dominated the luxury travel, coach tours and cruises and accounted for significant purchases of shoulder and off-season hotel short breaks and foreign holidays. However, this situation is likely to change rapidly as the senior travellers of the 1990s age and are replaced by those on less favourable pensions, perhaps still supporting children. Characteristically, senior travellers have perceived themselves to be younger, fitter, better educated and more widely travelled than their predecessors, and their behaviour has also been much 'younger' in character. These perceptions are likely to persist for this group into the twenty-first century, but their social and economic expression is bound to change. This may for example reflect itself in domestic heritage booms in Europe and the USA, i.e. avoiding the cost of moving extended families over long distances. However, the quality of service provision they demand will probably continue to rise. From the point of view of heritage attractions, these observations imply a demand for educational experiences, but also for 'entertainment' that is progressively deeper and more challenging. The adoption and refinement of interpretation techniques involving 'animateurs', high-technology and facsimile artefacts can thus be expected to blur distinctions between 'educational' and 'entertainment' experiences.

As discussed above, family travellers no longer conform to narrow demographic specifications and cannot be assumed to contain a married couple and '2.4 children'. From a marketing point of view, the family is continuously being reinvented and, as noted above, it contains an increasing proportion of the ubiquitous 'baby boom' group. An extended family tends to have the resources and impetus to travel together, seeking attractions and tourist services that can satisfy the diverse needs of both adults and children (more and more widely spaced in age). Hence sporting holidays are becoming increasingly popular, while family holidays that include lessons and clinics are also on the increase. For heritage visitor attractions there are analogous opportunities for hosting educational presentations and activities, especially the revival of old crafts and the re-enactment of old ways of life.

The short stay traveller segment is also largely determined by lifestyle, economics and other non-demographic factors. They represent a shift in leisure patterns from the traditional two-, three-, or even four-week vacation or trip. Despite the fact that long breaks are strongly culturally embedded, holiday takers are increasingly opting for shorter trips ranging from a long weekend to a maximum of seven days. Those who take short stay breaks tend to fit them around a busy lifestyle which keeps them close to home, office or laptop. However, this pattern also allows them to take more breaks and to sample a much wider variety of experiences and destinations. Recreational resorts have become very popular short stay destinations, both at weekends and during the midweek period (Elliott, 1992). The short break market is also more likely to take an interest in local history and culture, and therefore in heritage attractions. However, this probably also entails 'playing hard' as a balance to working hard, bringing a further emphasis upon hands-on activities and perhaps also on educational experiences.

Demographic and lifestyle analysis also suggests the rise of more demanding and experienced visitors, and as a result service quality may increasingly (Ananth, DeMicco and Howey, 1992) become an issue in cultural heritage. Yet the nature of service quality in this sector is obscure and ill researched at the time of writing. The increasing diversity of emergent market segments implies a comparable diversity both in the attributes by which quality is judged and in the balance of attributes that customers/visitors expect. Johns (1995) identifies the growing importance of nostalgic themes, colours and designs and also notes that politeness and patience will become increasingly important in service quality as visitor populations age. As the 'baby-boomers' re-entered tourism markets, the influences of their generation were widely felt throughout society. As they tire and leave the fray, this will wane, giving way perhaps to the more pragmatic and right-wing outlook of the succeeding generation. However, turning back the clock is not an option. Each successive generation will also have an increasingly critical, exacting attitude to the presentation and interpretation of artefacts and to the service packages in which they are offered. Thus custodians of heritage attractions will have to reshape interpretation and service provision, particularly in areas of secondary purchase where quality must be carefully considered, together with shifts in product perception and its relevance to the heritage attraction.

According to such segmentation analysis, managers of heritage attractions will have to recognize broad changes to consumer behaviour and purchase patterns in order for the industry to remain attractive and competitive to other sectors of the travel and tourism market. Prentice, Witt and Hamer (1998) identify experiential and benefit segmentation as being more applicable to heritage marketing than socio-demographic or lifestyle attributes. In a detailed statistical analysis of visitors at the Rhondda Valley National Park, they identify personal interest (in history or coal mining) or vicarious interest (through the interest of visitors' children) or enjoyment (e.g. of free time outdoors with the family) as the key factors that determine heritage experiences. Thus to an extent they succeed in identifying mass characteristics which predispose visitors to mass consumption. However, their characteristics are determined *post hoc*, on the basis of actual recorded behaviour, and this probably makes such an analysis ineffective for practical market segmentation.

The above discussion follows fashion by concentrating upon Western populations and socio-economic conditions. It is relevant here to say a little about the demographic patterns of the emerging Pacific rim 'tiger economies', which are in general quite different to those of Western nations. An increase in the birth rate of most of these countries from the 1960s onwards has produced demographic profiles with a preponderance of younger people. As in the West, these represent population 'bulges' which in time will age and grow out. In the meantime it is significant that in the late 1990s, despite temporary recession conditions, these countries have great economic potential, but very different demand profiles from those in the West. South East Asian countries contain many important historic sites, and rapid urbanization and environmental exploitation have destroyed both natural and tribal-cultural heritage. Many of these countries are currently concerned to maintain some vestige of the cultural past through stage-managed 'cultural centres' in which, for example, tribesmen from threatened hunter-gatherer communities re-enact their traditional lifestyle before the tourist cameras for a weekly wage. Overall, South East Asian economies are likely to play a growing role in shaping the demand for tourism, by exerting a new-style pressure from differently structured populations. They will also be forced more and more to respond to local cultural pressures that have no counterpart in the contemporary West.

It is legitimate and necessary to question the use of socio-economic profiles for focusing the analysis of tourist motivation. Tourist typologies (Cohen, 1979; Smith, 1978) probably represent different styles of consumption with some degree of accuracy. However, even taken together with segmentation through hierarchical models of experience (Gitelson and Kersetter, 1990) they are inadequate in forming a basis for consumer profiling which managers of heritage experiences can effectively use. An alternative approach, relying upon a subjective interpretation of individual accounts, is discussed in the following section.

Individual demands: the postmodern view

The idea that cultural heritage is an individual experience has been mentioned earlier in this chapter and forms the basis for what may be termed a post-modern view of demand. A considerable body of literature has grown up, emphasizing the phenomenology of tourist experiences (e.g. Cohen, 1979) and their social significance in work, play and other human activities (Cohen, 1992; Moore, 1980; Morinis, 1992). This kind of social/anthropological approach can also be seen in the academic marketing literature, in which various accepted service marketing concepts are held up to postmodern scrutiny. For example, Arnould, Price and Tierney (1997) examine the role of the 'servicescape' and of 'service providers' in visitors' perceptions of white-water rafting holidays. In their assessment, such holidays are about individually determined 'magic' rather than rational construction. Johns and Tyas (1997) pinpoint the difficulties inherent in assessing a restaurant exper-ience through a tick-box questionnaire. They propose that, rather than depending upon conventionally conditioned principles of 'reasoned action', that customers form expectations and perceptions of tourist experiences through the medium of 'mythology'. Myth and magic offer a particularly rich paradigm for heritage experience, through which the otherwise relatively pedestrian notions of 'interest' 'enjoyment' and 'customer satisfaction' can be developed in more productive ways.

It should also be borne in mind that visits to heritage attractions are seldom even experiences in their own right. More usually they are part of a greater individual experience: a trip or a holiday, that plays a component role of greater or lesser importance depending upon the personality and circum-stances of the visitor. The diversity of such experiences has fascinated sociologists and anthropologists for many years, producing a wealth of liter-ature, the central elements of which are individuality and perceptual phenomena. In summary, the individual view is diametrically opposed to the mass-segmental approach of marketers. However, it is possible to generalize to some extent about the nature of the individual experiences making up visits. Hence there is a possibility of reconciling the two approaches, by considering perceptual patterns common to groups of individuals. The next section considers common themes which are currently of cultural relevance.

The cult of the individual

Probably the most important theme underlying and shaping visitor percep-tion is that which brought about the postmodern movement in the first place, namely the cult of the individual. The late twentieth-century Western world is full of icons of individuality, to the point where their direct significance blurs, and they merge into an unquestioned value system. Advertisers frequently use 'being different' a positive value, through which to sell products or services. The tourism industry is in no sense immune from the individuality undercurrent, which manifests itself in various ways in the demand for heritage. Some common themes are choice, novelty, authenticity, journeying, travelling and the environment. An 'anti-individuality' movement can also be discerned within the heritage market, which expresses antithetical attitudes, or weighs up an alternative set of desired characteristics against the culturally favoured ones. These issues are discussed below.

The development of superabundant choice parallels the conspicuous consumption which has been a feature of Western markets for goods and services during the last half of the twentieth century. For example, customers in many bars can express their individuality by choosing one specific beer from 20 other, virtually identical beers. The individuality cult drives this idea further through the concept of customization, where pick and mix subcomponents are assembled into a unique product or service. Heritage experiences, assembled by the visitor (perhaps at the semiconscious level), and with their connotations of myth and magic, have the ultimate potential for such customization. The challenge is to identify and trigger an individual's myths through perceptions which surpass mundanity and become magical.

A demand for novelty is a natural consequence of superabundant choice, but novelty itself is highly subjective, depending for example upon age, education and recent experience. Neither novelty nor choice are necessarily perceived in the same way by everyone. In addition, and partly as a result of this subjective variation, novelty does not have to be 'new'. It must only be perceivable as new within the experience of a particular individual. It is also possible to experience novelty vicariously, for example through the eyes of one's children.

These observations apply to every demand situation. The pressure for novelty can be seen for instance in the constant minor changes to products on supermarket shelves. However, heritage attractions have the potential to approach the demand for novelty in new, creative ways. Heritage experiences are constructed by individual visitors themselves, from personal and cultural constructs of myth and magic. For this reason they have the potential to invent their own novelty. Attractions may take a simplistic view of novelty and employ some basic expedient such as constantly changing the artefacts on display, for example with travelling exhibitions or special displays. The evanescent quality of myth and magic also makes it possible to achieve perceived novelty, by changing the presentation and interpretation of artefacts by devices such as live actors or technology applications. Such 'supermarket' approaches are currently in wide use, but there is also the potential to adapt displays to reflect whole new cultural paradigms. This has for example happened at Sachsenhausen, Berlin's concentration camp, since the opening up of the former East Germany (Lennon, 1998). Indeed the whole 'dark tourism' phenomenon which Lennon and his colleagues address represents something of a new cultural paradigm, hovering on the borders of 'bad taste'. One wonders what new mythologies can be made available, as Western culture evolves and changes. Certainly a potent approach for adapting heritage attractions to the mythological demands of visitors is to continuously update the whole environment to reflect the evolving cultural milieu.

One of the most important myths in cultural heritage is that of authenticity. By definition an artefact is only 'authentic' if it can demonstrate a unique survival, but despite this, authenticity is not an absolute characteristic. Atiyah (1998: 2) puts the case neatly as follows: 'historic connotations never reveal themselves anyway ... people ... go out of their way to visit historical sites ... [which] has nothing to do with being literal and stumbling upon real truths. It is all to do with imagining how things might have been'.

The demand for authenticity springs from a cultural tendency to imbue 'genuine' objects with historic significance, but the authenticity and significance themselves are only a matter of belief. Thus objects whose authenticity comes into question cause feelings of contempt and a sense of being 'cheated'. Yet at the same time, authenticity is as much one's personal property as one's beliefs, so that it is possible to perceive 'authenticity' in almost any situation and context. Atiyah discusses a spurious report that Hitler once dined in a particular seafood restaurant in Barcelona:

> [many] people have written to assure us that Hitler never went anywhere near Spain ... But in another sense, who cares whether or not the story was true. Imagine what a fascinating thing it would have been if Adolf Hitler had dined in that restaurant and raved about the food. (Atiyah, 1998: 2)

Authenticity brings with it connotations of 'seriousness'. Without this almost anything could achieve acceptance as 'authentic' through the medium of the imagination, but there exists a sharp cultural differentiation between perceptions of 'serious' conservation and 'trivial' amusement. For example, the walled town of Carcasonne is clearly 'serious', while the Asterix Parc outside Paris is easily branded 'frivolous'. Yet both strongly reflect the mythology of France, and if anything, Asterix reflects it to a larger audience than Carcasonne. Conservators of cultural heritage are naturally predisposed to prefer 'serious' authenticity, but they do so at their peril. It is easy to dismiss phenomena such as the Asterix Parc (and for that matter Disney World) as 'non-authentic entertainment' but the real issue is the underlying mythological structure upon which visitor perceptions are built. This analysis suggests that there will be an increasing convergence between what are currently regarded as conservation and amusement respectively. Mythology, its perception, realization and satisfaction will be at the centre of this movement, and a key factor will be the evolution of 'authenticity' in the perceptions of the visiting public.

Wider opportunities to travel, superabundant choice, falling prices and a mass-consumption ethos in the package tour industry have together contributed to a mundane view of tourism and an image of the tourist as a figure of fun (Dann, 1997) or distaste (Lodge, 1991). The cult of the individual increasingly prefers the concept of 'traveller' to that of 'tourist', but this becomes harder to support as yesterday's frontiers become the beaten paths of today. Travel writers such as Paul Theroux (1980) increasingly set themselves apart from their countrymen and from other Western travellers abroad, in order to avoid any suggestion of 'tourist' and to reaffirm their status as 'free' individuals.

Travels away from the beaten track may be elevated to the status of 'voyages' fraught with discomfort and perhaps danger. They may recall the mythology of the Odyssey, an epic travail through perilous terrain, in which one meets unpredictable people along the way. They are often strange and may represent danger (turning the travellers into swine) or delight (offering the weary lotus to eat). The scope of travel becomes ever more limited, with those who have 'been everywhere' currently obliged to sign up in the expectation of an as yet unavailable holiday in space. It seems likely that as real journeys become more mundane, their mythology will become more Odysseic. Local cultural heritage may play a large part in supplying and supporting the magic and mythology needed to support such perceptions and maintain the value and appeal of travel against a tide of creeping banality.

Another aspect of the individuality cult is a growing environmental sensitivity among the travelling public. The same impulse which makes mass tourism distasteful renders solitude and the wilderness desirable. As the world becomes more accessible and its population grows there is an increasing demand to 'get back to unspoiled nature'. Both the concept of unspoiled nature and the idea that it is possible to get back to it are mythical ideals, but they sit well with ideas of 'playing hard' by immersing oneself in nature and experiencing nature on a 'hands on' basis; hence the growing popularity of 'exotic' wildlife visits observing whales and swimming with dolphins. Far-flung destinations, such as Antarctica and outer space are also manifestations of this desire to be 'first' and 'alone' in virgin wilderness. The mythological character of the unspoiled environment also makes it susceptible to the increasingly desired interpretation, stage management and active experience. This is evident in the popularity of activity holidays such as wilderness trekking, white-water rafting and balloon safaris. It seems likely that there will be a parallel increase of interest in natural heritage sites of all kinds, and also in related cultural heritage. For example, Arnould and Price (1993) discuss the importance of Native American sites to participants in white-water rafting holidays, and their value in building the mythology of the wilderness experience.

Anti-values

Strong cultural undercurrents generally have associated anti-values, which may be expressed in parallel, or even simultaneously, with their antitheses. The cult of the individual can be identified as having several anti-values, which also shape the demand for heritage experiences. These include desire for companionship, national homogeneity, sojourn, comfort, convenience and safety. Many of these needs conflict with the demand factors associated with the cult of the individual and travellers frequently need to trade off one set of needs with another.

Companionship is the antithesis of the individual traveller's solitude, but social needs and family values mean that most people need or prefer to travel in some kind of social grouping. This means that destinations, including heritage attractions, must often cope with the needs of diverse ages and with small-group social interaction in a variety of situations (for example during meals). At the same time 'quality' will increasingly be equated with solitude and actual or metaphorical personal space. The challenge is to design heritage experiences which accommodate the myth of the lone traveller, representing personal interests, solitude and a perceived degree of danger or discomfort, but do so in a way that caters for the needs of the group and all of its members.

Peculiarities of language and culture mean that individuals often prefer to travel with nationals from their own country. Yet the national homogeneity of travelling groups conflicts vividly with the image of the bold traveller interacting with strange and new peoples at the corners of the globe. Shared culture has a way of altering individuals' perceptions of the world through which they travel, and this filtering effect may jeopardize heritage experiences by trivializing them. The challenge is to present heritage in an 'authentic' way which none the less appeals to different ethnocentric views of the world.

A primary feature of travelling is its continuous quality, passing through locations and ingesting information on the hop. Sojourn is the antithesis of this, as the travel writer Paul Theroux (1980: 360) notes: 'I met another traveller who said he was planning to spend another month in say Barranquilla. "I didn't like Ecuador", an American told me, "Maybe I didn't give it enough time". He had been there two months which seemed like an eternity to me.' Thus, travel destinations are increasingly likely to be judged on their ability to manage movement through time and space by simulating a more lengthy stay. With their potential to create 'customized' mythology, heritage experiences may find themselves in a unique position to offer this impression to a broad band of visitor needs.

Comfort, convenience and safety are the antitheses of Odysseic myths, which typically feature such dangers as Scylla, Charybdis and encounters with the Cyclops. Yet at the same time they are underwritten by Western preoccupations with security, health and longevity. They are prerequisites of stable family life and are also likely to be increasingly in demand for the ageing Western population. Comfort, convenience and safety are also the antitheses of certain forms of 'authenticity'. For example, one would not expect to visit a headhunter chieftain in complete safety. Yet this is precisely where the demand for cultural heritage appears currently to be leading, as exemplified in the heritage 'villages' of Hawaii and some South East Asian countries. Here visitors can view artificial presentations of traditional tribal life that no longer exists in its historic form. They can do this in a relatively controlled environment, from which most of the unpredictability of a real native settlement has been removed. Thus 'authenticity' is traded off against its anti-values, which in this context are equally desirable. In reality heritage attractions are not strangers to artificial authenticity. The most 'serious' museum can only ever offer a picture of the past which has been reconstructed according to someone's myth of how it was. The challenge facing the heritage industry is to admit this and to achieve a satisfactory blend of credible authenticity within the conditions demanded by their visitors.

Service quality: towards the assessment of visitors' true perceptions

An issue touched upon by some authors (e.g. Johns, 1999b) is that of the 'service quality' of heritage attractions. This is an unclear concept, not least depending upon whether one views a heritage attraction as providing a total service offering, or an interpersonal service component within that offering. This aspect of the heritage market is new and it is quite possible that ultimately a new style of interpersonal service may have to evolve to fill the specific needs of attractions. It is clear that the service quality of attractions has no objective existence outside the individual perception of the visitor, and this makes it as difficult to define and measure as the other characteristics discussed in this chapter.

Attempts to measure the quality of heritage attractions commonly centre around questionnaire surveys, in which visitors are asked to rate different characteristics. This is closely related in concept to the assessment of segmented demand described above, although usually specifically focused upon perceived excellence. Questionnaires are frequently prepared on the basis of interview studies, particularly with focus groups. There is then a standard procedure of piloting, testing and purification before the instrument is deemed fit for survey use. This extensive preparation fits uneasily with the wordings of questionnaires, which typically (despite the most rigorous attempts to obtain unbiased information from visitors) reflect the views and assumptions of the attraction provider or researcher. In order to compensate for this, there have been attempts by researchers to produce standardized questionnaires, which conform to some kind of generally accepted academic theory. The most prominent example in the 1990s was the SERVQUAL instrument (Parasuraman, Zeithaml and Berry, 1986) which can broadly be considered to embody the expectancy-disconfirmation theory of Oliver (1981). It assumes that consumers have expectations of services, which are confirmed (or disconfirmed) when they are actually served. However it also assumes the principle of reasoned action, i.e. that people act as the result of a cognitive weighing up of their situation. This is an intuitively acceptable assumption, but exponents of reasoned action tend to assume that the cognitive process is not only reasoned, but reasonable, i.e. to the cognitive scrutiny of others. This is open to dispute.

Survey techniques for measuring service quality share the limitations and objections that have been made earlier to segmentation and mass marketing approaches. The alternative qualitative approaches are satisfactory for identifying myths and magic, but very limited in terms of the sample sizes that can be handled within reasonable cost parameters. However, a few semi-quantitative approaches have been adapted or devised, which offer a way towards reconciling mass and individual approaches, and obtaining a truer picture of the visitor experience. These include 'repertory grid technique' and 'profile accumulation', discussed below.

Repertory grid technique (RGT) aims to identify the personal constructs by which individuals order their perceptions of the world. This is done through interviews, during which subjects identify the important aspects of their experience and rate them using scales of their own devising. Complex statistical procedures enable the researcher to focus the aspects and constructs into a coherent picture. Repertory grid technique makes it potentially possible to study areas such as myth and magic which individuals would be unwilling to discuss in open conversation. However, it is time-consuming and expensive in terms of obtaining a representational sample.

Somewhere between surveys and RGT is profile accumulation technique (PAT), developed by Johns and co-workers (Johns and Lee-Ross, 1996; Johns, Lee-Ross and Ingram, 1998). Visitors indicate the best and worst aspects of their experience directly in text, using free-response questionnaires. Quality can be assessed by counting the numbers of positive and negative aspects and attributes, and moderate sample sizes can be used, i.e. in the hundreds of respondents, rather than thousands. Since respondents are asked for 'the best things' they tend to indicate predominantly tangible aspects or simple issues. However, tangible aspects themselves have a semiotic significance which can form a basis of the analysis for assessing qualitative demand.

Conclusions

This chapter has examined public demand for attractions from several viewpoints. A mass consumption approach based upon demographics provides information about the age, gender and family status profiles within the population. By adding lifestyle parameters it is possible to deduce the possible behaviour of segments of the travelling public. However, segmentation approaches of this kind are at best a vague approximation, because attraction visitors are motivated principally by personal interest, and this tends not to coincide with more observable or convenient characteristics such as age, gender, family status or lifestyle.

It is also possible to use generalizations about individual perceptions to understand the demand for attractions. The basis of this approach is the assumption that myth and magic play a major role in determining the visitor experience and that these are largely culturally determined. This insight can be further strengthened and contextualized by considering it in the light of possible demographic or lifestyle influences. It is acknowledged that a tension currently exists in marketing between paradigms of mass and individual consumption. This chapter has attempted to reconcile these two, which are nowhere more sharply juxtaposed than in the marketing of heritage attractions.

Demographic and lifestyle analysis produces a picture in which the ageing population will continue to grow in the foreseeable future. However, economic pressures mean that these individuals' spending power is likely to be on the wane. In addition, changing family patterns may result in their becoming part of larger neo-extended families or other groups. At the same time, the dwindling income of the older segments means that younger people can be expected to have a comparably greater spending power. All segments of Western populations are likely to become more interested in history, culture, archaeology and the arts, either on their own behalf or for their children or grandchildren. There will also be an increasing demand for learning, i.e. of new skills or knowledge and for 'hands on' activities. All of these lifestyle trends are likely to benefit heritage attractions, but changing income patterns will influence current patterns of consumption and the 'senior traveller' can no longer be taken for granted.

The mythology of travel (as of all modern consumption) centres upon the cult of the individual. This potent ideology reinforces 'being different' as a positive value, and provides a route for understanding many of the features of late twentieth-century consumerism. Issues which particularly concern the heritage industry are:

- superabundant choice
- customization
- novelty
- authenticity, together with related concepts of 'seriousness' versus 'entertainment'
- the environment.

The ideology of individuality renders the 'tourist' a figure of fun, or even distaste, reinforcing as positive values the concepts of 'journeying' and 'travelling', preferably alone among alien peoples. However, since heritage experiences are subjective and individually determined, the cult of the individual also provides heritage attractions with a potent tool for upgrading and customizing their products, and for generating the necessary choice, novelty and authenticity.

The individualist ideology also has its anti-values, many of which are perceivable in the behaviour and values of mass tourism. Those discussed above include companionship, national homogeneity, sojourn, comfort, convenience and safety. Many of them are reinforced by other value systems within Western culture and therefore conflict with individualist-determined values. Both ideologies need to be considered as determinants of demand for heritage attractions.

The overall impact of these pressures is interpreted as follows. Heritage attractions will have to concentrate upon increasing visitor choice and imbuing their offerings with novelty. The pressure is towards greater visitor participation and more subtle and interactive interpretation. Superabundant choice will be developed through themes such as fantasy and nostalgia, repackaged to match the higher aspirations of older, more sophisticated visitors. There will be increased opportunities for retail sales of artefacts that support nostalgia mythologies, and for merchandising these through the semiotics of heritage sites.

All age groups will become increasingly technology-tolerant, offering greater opportunities for technology mediated, personalized interpretation. This will also make it easier to advertise attractions and to predispose customers to specific myths through well designed websites. There will probably be an increasing demand for live interpretation of sites and artefacts, and a corresponding problem of productivity.

Along with increasing concern about the environment, there is increasing interest in natural heritage, which may impinge upon cultural heritage through:

- a need to combine attraction characteristics to include both, in order to appeal to all members of family/visitor groups
- opportunities to harmonize the culture of ancestral peoples, or aborigines with the natural environment, mostly through the 'noble savage' myth.

Some individuals view natural heritage as part of cultural heritage, because it contains important signifiers, which have the power to invoke myths, for example of nationalism.

A growing gap will be experienced between conservatorial 'authenticity', visitors' personal mythologies and the anti-values of the individualist movement. It will be increasingly necessary to support an Odysseic myth of isolation, journeying, discomfort and danger and unspoiled nature or culture. At the same time there will be a greater demand for national group travel, ease of access, safety and security. The challenge facing heritage attractions is how to reconcile and repackage these aspects to satisfy the visitors of the twenty-first century.

Questions

1 This chapter suggests that currently accepted market segments will become progressively less appropriate for marketing heritage visitor attractions. Identify two such market segments and summarize the relevant arguments for each.
2 What are the implications of demographic change in terms of the quality demanded from heritage visitor attractions?
3 To what extent can service quality be measured with customer questionnaires in HVAs?

References and further reading

Ananth, M., DeMicco, F., and Howey, R. (1992). Marketplace lodging needs of mature travelers. *Cornell Hotel and Restaurant Administration Quarterly*, **33**(4), 12–24.

Arnould, E. J. and Price, L. L. (1993). River magic: extraordinary experience and extended service encounter. *Journal of Consumer Research*, **20**, June, 24–45.

Arnould, E. J., Price, L. L. and Tierney, P. (1997). Communicative staging of the wilderness servicescape. Paper presented at the AMA Dublin Conference, 11 June.

Atiyah, J. (1998). The truth about Hitler and that seafood restaurant in Barcelona. *Independent on Sunday*, Travel Section, 3 May, p. 2.

Church, J. (1997). *Social Trends*. The Stationery Office/Office for National Statistics.

Cohen, E. (1992). Pilgrimage and tourism: convergence and divergence. In *Sacred Journeys* (A. Morinis, ed.), pp. 47–61, Greenwood Press.

Cohen, E. (1979). 'A Phenomenology of Tourist Experiences'. *Sociology*, Vol. 13, pp 179-201.

Dann, G. M. S. (1997). Writing out tourists from the periphery. International Tourism Research Conference: Peripheral Area Tourism, Bornholms-forskningscenter, Nexø, Denmark.

Economist Intelligence Unit (EIU) (1997). The seniors' travel market. *Travel and Tourism Analyst*, 5.

Elliott, J. (1992). Trends in international tourism and leisure resort design. Paper presented at the First Regional IJCHM Forum, Anglia Polytechnic University, Chelmsford.

Elliott, J. and Johns, N. (1993). 'Tourism trends and international resort design. *International Journal of Contemporary Hospitality Management*, **5**(2), 6–9.

Gitelson, R. and Kersetter, D. (1990). The relationship between sociodemographic variable, benefits sought and subsequent vacation behaviour. *Journal of Travel Research*, **28**(3), 24–29.

Johns, N. (1995). The developing role of quality in the hospitality industry. In *Service Quality in Hospitality Organizations* (M. Olsen, R. Teare and E. Gummesson, eds), pp. 9–26, Cassell.

Johns, N. (1999a). Quality. In *Heritage Visitor Attractions: An Operations Management Perspective* (I. Yeoman and A. Leask, eds), pp. 127–143, Cassell.

Johns, N. (1999b). What is this thing called service? *European Journal of Marketing*, **33**(9/10), 958–973.

Johns, N. and Lee-Ross, D. (1996). Profile accumulation: a quality assessment technique for hospitality SMEs. In *Services Management: New Directions and Perspectives* (R. Teare and C. Armistead, eds). Cassell.

Johns, N. and Tyas, P. (1997). Customer perceptions of service operations: *Gestalt*, incident or mythology? *Service Industries Journal*, **17**(3), 474–488.

Johns, N., Lee-Ross, D. and Ingram, H. (1998). A study of service quality in small hotels and guesthouses. *Progress in Tourism and Hospitality Research*, **3**(4), 351–363.

Lennon, J. J. (1998). Urban tourism development and dark tourism sites – an examination of Berlin, Germany. *Proceedings of the Seventh Annual CHME Research Conference*, Glasgow Caledonian University.

Lodge, D. (1991). *Paradise News*. Penguin.

Masser, I., Svidén, O. and Wegner, M. (1994). What new heritage for which new Europe? In *Building a New Heritage: Tourism, Culture and Identity in the New Europe* (G. Ashworth and P. Larkham, eds), pp. 31–46, Routledge.

Moore, A. (1980). Walt Disney World: bounded ritual space and the playful pilgrimage center. *Anthropological Quarterly*, **53**(4), 207–218.

Morinis, A. (1992). The territory of the anthropology of pilgrimage. In *Sacred Journeys* (A. Morinis, ed.), pp. 1–28, Greenwood Press.

Oliver, R. (1981). Measurement and evaluation of satisfaction process in retail settings. *Journal of Retailing*, **57**, 25–48.

Parasuraman, A., Zeithaml V. A. and Berry L. L. (1986). SERVQUAL: a multiple-item scale for measuring customer perceptions of service quality. *Marketing Science Institute, Working Paper Report No 86-108*.

Prentice, R., Witt, S. and Hamer, C. (1998). Tourism as experience, the case of heritage parks. *Annals of Tourism Research*, **25**(1), 1–24.

Smith, C. and Jenner, P. (1997). The seniors' travel market. *Travel and Tourism Analyst No. 5*, pp. 43–62, EIU.

Smith, V. L. (ed.) (1978). *Hosts and Guests*. Blackwell.

Theroux, P. (1980). *The Old Patagonian Express*. Penguin.

14

Developing the role of quality

Szilvia Gyimóthy and Nick Johns

Introduction

Heritage attractions and their markets have changed substantially in the recent past and will continue to change in the future. However, as a result of significant social and economic changes, the projected transformation of the heritage industry will probably become even more intensive and conspicuous. This chapter examines the ways in which heritage attractions will need to develop in response to the environmental factors that will likely influence them in the future, as well as the shifting concept of heritage for the coming millennium. The implications of these changes on quality design and development are also illustrated with some examples of successful development cases from Europe.

Conditions and recent trends in the general environment of heritage attractions

Demographic, economic and environmental changes in the Western world have created new and different market potentials for heritage attractions. In spite of lack of precise data on heritage tourism, many observers are convinced that demand is growing (cf. Richards, 1996a). The WTO estimates that cultural tourism currently accounts for 37 per cent of all visitor trips, and that demand is growing by 15 per cent yearly (Bywater, 1993). Increasing demand may imply on the one hand that heritage attractions are not only of interest to declining industrial societies, and on the other that the definition of 'heritage' is broadening and shifting across the world. This section reviews these changes and examines how they may affect attraction quality management operations.

Socio-cultural factors

Most of the developed world is already experiencing a progressive decline in birth rates and ageing population. The proportion of people aged over 65 is expected to exceed 20 per cent in the year 2020, as the 'baby boom' generation nudges into it. Changes in pension arrangements are likely to reduce the importance of the wealthy 'silver generation' who are currently a major target of tourism marketing. At the same time changes in lifestyle have produced the neo-extended family, and this, together with increasing numbers of second marriage families may bring about a resurgence in the importance of family groups. This suggests that physical quality design of attractions must accommodate the needs of older people, for example, by supplying more disabled facilities.

Younger age groups continue to boom in developing countries, and this has led to a new international migration in Europe and North America. Western European countries are becoming multinational melting pots and experiencing growing cultural diversity. Cultural gaps between immigrants and native populations may generate tensions, and heritage may well become a political issue, for example by reinforcing the culture of the host country, and suppressing those of the newcomers. This can be avoided by taking a more liberal approach to the educational function of heritage and accommodating the traditions and values of different cultures (Masser, Svidén and Wegener, 1994).

According to a survey undertaken by the European Association for Tourism and Leisure Education in 1992, the number of heritage visits in Europe rose by 100 per cent between 1970 and 1992. The growth in demand has largely been stimulated by rising levels of income and education. The emergence of a new middle, or 'service class' (Walsh, 1992) is characterized by considerable changes in lifestyle and social fragmentation (i.e. complex changes in the patterns of group and family living), and also in the growing economic independence of women, young people and senior citizens. New manufacturing and service sector technologies have brought further increases in free time, further reinforcing the phenomenon of the 'leisure class'. It is predicted that the leisure industry may account for 40 per cent of all land transport and 60 per cent of air transport in the year 2020 (Masser, Svidén and Wegener, 1994).

Changes in lifestyles are already transforming tourist attitudes and behaviour, and there is a growing demand for active, individualistic and environmentally concerned leisure experiences (Poon, 1993). Also, more people are looking for opportunities to learn something new (preferably actively rather than passively) during their leisure time. (Swarbrooke, 1995). This will lead to the emergence of specialist tourist markets, and further diversity in demand for cultural attractions. Nostalgia and heritage will increasingly feature in tourism development strategies and there is a growing market across Europe for themed heritage attractions.

Economic and technological factors

Since the mid-twentieth century, Western economies have been characterized by a decline in agriculture and manufacturing industries together with an expansion of the service sector. The availability of low-cost labour markets and a reduction of barriers to international trade has led to the globalization of products, technologies and standards. In addition, information and communication technologies continue to bring fundamental changes in a number of areas, including organizational structures, production patterns and labour demand. Yet, in the travel and tourism sector labour demand has grown rather than decreased; and the industry as a whole has benefited from technological advances in distribution and communication. For instance, tourism developers (especially in peripheral destinations) are now able to pull together fragmented tourism components and offer their visitors individualized holiday planning through efficient and cost-effective telecommunications. Technological advances in communication have also triggered an increasing desire for personal interaction rather than merely witnessing historical or other artefacts. The nineteenth-century awe of the museum artefact has largely been replaced by a desire for 'hands-on' interaction concepts.

Western cultural distancing from traditional industries has produced a nostalgic view of recent industrial heritage. Abandoned industrial sites (such as coal and slate mines) and endangered traditional agricultural landscapes (such as hedgerows) have acquired growing heritage value, comparable to historical artefacts, and are increasingly preserved for posterity. To some

245

extent this reflects the replacement of manufacturing values with those associated with services (Masser, Svidén and Wegener, 1994). Thus an essential shift of focus is occurring from the production and sale of physical products towards the presentation of experiences. As a result, heritage attractions can no longer be marketed as static products (such as historic houses and old-style museums), but must be dynamic experiences, e.g. Viking battles or medieval markets. Thus, quality has been displaced from the exhibit to the exhibitor, where the visitor experience is more likely to be generated by high-technology equipment or trained frontline staff.

Sustainability of heritage attractions

A long debated challenge in heritage management is to keep the balance between preserving a site for the future and making it accessible to present visitors. The postwar democratization of education and cultural expansion of the 1960s brought overcrowding to the best known attractions (some examples are Venice, Versailles and the Acropolis), which has, in a matter of few decades, become destructive to these sites. Increased tensions are perceivable between the leisure industry and the conservationists, the latter typically arguing that monuments and their environment fall victim to the vandalism of mass tourist invasion (Abelee, 1990).

Owing to their perceived duty to pass historical sites unspoiled to future generations, the International Council of Monuments and Sites (ICOMOS) and UNESCO put conservation principles above any other considerations. Different strategies have been put forward for achieving this, including restricting, controlling, funnelling or dispersing the flux of visitors, in order to minimize the danger of deterioration. Another means of halting the environmental degradation of heritage sites and artefacts is to market other attractions in the surroundings or to manufacture heritage experiences in the form of replica developments or theme parks. Such is the case of the Caves of Lascaux, next to which a commercial site was built to house an artificial reconstruction of the famous prehistoric paintings. This implies that in the future genuine historical artefacts and collections may be secondary to the heritage theme they feature themselves.

The developing role of heritage attractions in the future

Owing to its role as a carrier of cultural traditions (Nuryanti, 1996), and historical values from the past, heritage assures a special sense of belonging and of continuity for the members of a society (Millar, 1989). The nature of tourism, on the other hand, is dynamic, pursuing activities and out of the ordinary experiences in order to enrich human life (Graburn, 1983). Heritage attractions should thus offer opportunities for visitors to view and experience past manifestations of culture through the 'prism of interpretation' (Nuryanti, 1996). These dual goals present an ambiguous role-set for heritage managers. On one hand, the physical patrimony has to be maintained for future generations, requiring restoration, rehabilitation, renovation and reconstruction. On the other hand, visitors must receive an enriched understanding of the past in the context of the present (Nuryanti, 1996). Heritage management strategies of the nineteenth and most of the twentieth centuries demanded visitors' respect, through scholarly educational displays with dry factual information and through authoritarian protection of the site. Visitor flows were funnelled by cordons, fences and 'do not touch' signs, which intimidated large visitor segments and constrained their appreciation and experience (Schouten, 1995). This created a distance between the average visitor and the site itself, hindering, rather than facilitating understanding.

However, heritage managers are increasingly recognizing that their offering should not only cater for those with a special interest in culture and history, but also for the great number of visitors who wish to experience and understand the past on their own terms. Heritage strategies are slowly changing focus and attempting to integrate sites into a total tourist experience. Appreciation and learning are stimulated by providing visitors with some kind of sensory, or physical experience of the site, rather than by simply exposing them to static data. Thus sites based on heritage themes do not necessarily contain historical collections, as these are only secondary to the main experience (English Tourist Board, 1991). A rapidly growing phenomenon is the use of interpretation, through interactive displays or a staff of interpreters, who enliven history through drama. Prohibitive instructions are rendered unnecessary through the use of reproduction artefacts. In this way, heritage attractions have begun to democratize the dissemination of knowledge, placing the ownership of the heritage experience on the shoulders of the visitor, who becomes an investigator of the past (Crang, 1996).

Parallel to this interpretation revolution, a market-driven 'heritage boom' appeared in Europe during the 1980s, characterized by the emergence of many small commercially oriented attractions (Bianchini and Parkinson, 1993). It is estimated that the number of heritage attractions in Europe grew by 140 per cent between 1970 and 1991 and included not only museums and historical sites, but also events and festivals. The cynical definition 'if in doubt, call it heritage' (Glen, 1991: 73) underlines the popularity of heritage projects in the tourism industry of the late twentieth century. Undoubtedly, as time passes, and as Europe becomes an increasingly multicultural society, the concept of heritage will gain a still broader meaning. Not only the means of presenting a heritage theme are proliferating, but also the themes themselves. There is growing interest in relatively new topics, such as the recent industrial past, the cultural heritage of ethnic communities and the popular heritage of recent decades (the so-called 'retro-culture'). This expansion has been too fast for demand to keep up with supply, and the average visit per attraction actually fell in some parts of Europe during the late 1980s and early 1990s (Richards, 1996b). Hence, young tourism destinations investing in local cultural heritage have to face an increasingly competitive market, where the key to success lies in new ideas, rather than in traditional concepts.

Authenticity and interpretation

Heritage experience concepts are often criticized by the self-appointed guardians of traditional heritage, namely academics and conservationists, who accuse a 'fake heritage business' of devaluating the significance and relevance of 'real' heritage and of draining funds for the wrong cause. According to this camp, marketers of fake attractions are the enemies of cultural heritage, encouraging visitors to '[follow] carelessly the cultural trend without knowing at least something about history'. A scathing example is provided by the following flagellant comment, originating from a 1990 ICOMOS conference (Abelee, 1990):

> Going for 'cultural heritage' has become fashionable . . . and the genuine thing no longer seems sufficient, or adequate to suit the increasing number of tourists. Shrewd heritage managers have discovered a hole in the market and they now increasingly cater for the cultural oriented mass tourism by investing in theme parks and in heritage centres, where in a number of cases some sort of harmless, but mentally polluting entertainment is offered. In their hands, past becomes a pastiche, their money created a fake historic environment, yesterday and today become confused, and the hasty and vaguely bewildered tourist is offered a rose-coloured and grossly falsified version of the past, often brought to life in 'historic' revival scenes. As most of the visitors have no sufficient points of reference and as they want to escape from present, they plunge into a world of unreality, wrongly presented as the way of life and the environment of their ancestors . . . It prostitutes the aspirations for culture

and roots by feeding tourists with a cheap and irrelevant ersatz. The historic centre can fall down the level of an amusement park, with a preponderant presence of cheap souvenir shops sloppy eating places and the predominant smell of hot-dogs and chips as well as paper and waste all over the place . . . The heart and the soul of the place will be destroyed forever.

The protectors of historic heritage often raise their voice in favour of authenticity, i.e. for the unadulterated 'real thing', a concept they believe to be an integral part of all genuine heritage exhibits. Historicity, i.e. the eclectic use of historical artefacts and replicas is criticized for focusing on superficial aesthetic images (Fowler, 1989) that turn heritage into 'tabloid history' (Walsh, 1992). According to these authors, the quality of a heritage site is first measured by its scientific correctness and the authenticity of its interpretation – never mind the visitor's opinion. The pitfalls of this critique lie in its assumptions about the function of heritage preservation, i.e. to represent an *accurate* appearance of 'pastness' (Crang, 1996) which can only be appreciated in one (rational and highbrow) way.

However, just as there is no absolute or true past, heritage production and consumption cannot simply be depicted as a one-way flow of knowledge. The conservation camp overlook the fact that the enjoyment of heritage is also a *self*-reflective activity (Crang, 1996), and that visitors may create emotional and empathetic connections with the era that is represented. This cannot happen if heritage is conceived only as 'genuine' artefacts and sterile information, so that all the visitor experiences is an 'in vitro' image of the departed past. At the same time, visitors see the signs of tourism all over historic sites (souvenir shops and tearooms), which probably complicate their quest for understanding and experiencing the past. Furthermore, it can be argued that authenticity, like quality, exists only in the eye of the customer (Masser, Svidén and Wegener, 1994). Satisfaction therefore depends upon visitors' need for authentic experiences and their perception of 'authenticity' at a particular site (Cohen, 1988). Last, but not least, few visitors attend heritage sites purely for learning. Their motives include enjoyment and fu~ as well as the pursuit of knowledge and of the 'authentic' (as they pe~ it). Indeed, in leisure the pursuit of pleasure is not necessarily ir~ detachable from the quest after knowledge. Thus, the role of the future will increasingly be to assist visitors to make s~ by inviting them to participate in a creative, enjoyable~ process of encountering and interpreting the past.

The developing concept of quality: 'service provided' versus 'service experienced'

Visitor focus will clearly permeate the design and management of heritage attractions in the future. Even in museums, the attitude of 'why care about the visitors: they come anyway' is changing (Schouten, 1995). However, there are major perceptual differences between the way most heritage professionals and customers define their core product and its critical quality features. This paradox of *provided* vs. *experienced* quality (Johns, 1992; Johns and Howard, 1998) is particularly relevant to quality assessment in heritage attractions and points up profound perceptual differences between the service quality thinking of managers, as opposed to visitors. For instance, in order to provide a quality product, managers need to consider diverse aspects of heritage operations, including exhibits, interpretation, staff and various complementary facilities. Thus, they tend to consider quality design and measurement in terms of the elements in the core product, relative to dimensions like scientific correctness, efficiency and accuracy. Customers on the other hand, perceive cultural visits more holistically, not necessarily focusing on distinct elements of the heritage offerings. Their assessment depends upon how effectively the exhibits raise curiosity, appeal to fantasy and challenge the intellect, and little if at all upon scientific authenticity (Schouten, 1995). Furthermore, peripheral quality issues such as toilet cleanliness, ease of parking, shopping and catering choice play an important part in the visitor experience and are likely to contribute disproportionately to the visitor's perception of quality.

Heritage attractions offer the visitor a number of experiences and benefits. They provide opportunities to meet visitor's physical needs. Participation in recreational events may offer physical challenge and exercise, while entertainment-based events offer a chance for relaxation and enjoyment. They offer social and interpersonal benefits, for example the collective experiences of social interaction with family, friends and other visitors. Through attending events, visitors may gain a sense of community and belonging. They also offer experiences of understanding, appreciation and self-fulfilment. They also offer an aesthetic appreciation of art and culture, and the discovery of local culture and traditions. Visitors increasingly identify opportunities for exploration, discovery and learning as the principal benefits of heritage sites (Prentice, 1993).

Experienced quality contains aspects which are not necessarily perceived by managers as part of their offering, and whose contribution to the visitor's experience cannot be stereotyped and standardized. The precise nature of visitors' experiences, and hence of the quality they perceive, depends on the type of the attraction, and on the motivation of individuals. Because the heritage experience only exists as a whole in visitors' minds, they are unlikely to evaluate by simply summing their assessments of separate elements. Consequently, experienced quality cannot be measured solely by quantitative (survey) techniques. However, in order to achieve real quality improvements, managers need to identify critical quality features, and hence, translate and understand individual experiences. Thus, the challenge of quality management at heritage attractions is to arrive at a common denominator between visitor and provider thinking – by using various (both quantitative and qualitative) assessment techniques. This might happen by analysing provided and experienced quality in each other's context and to assess both by asking employees and visitors.

Implications for the design of heritage attractions

As discussed earlier, the central challenge in linking heritage and tourism lies in reconstructing the past through interpretation. The design of heritage sites should make them better places to maintain the enjoyment of the visitor through interpretation. In the future, the cornerstones of any policy of visitor care in heritage management should be, above all, pleasure and personal fulfilment. In contrast to the prevalent curatorial beliefs of some managers (Schouten, 1993), people do not visit heritage attractions primarily to learn, in any traditional sense. Visitors' motivation and their benefits from heritage experiences are best regarded as multidimensional, and include 'extraordinary experiences'. They also provide a vehicle within which individuals may engage in social interaction with their companions (Masberg and Silverman, 1996) and with site personnel (McManus, 1985), as well as absorbing information.

This mosaic of potential experiences requires a conscious selection and planning process from managers, concerning what to interpret and how to present it to visitors. Apart from sensitive and responsible site development, design strategies should contain what Schouten (1995) calls the UNIQUE experience, standing for Uncommon, Novelty, Informative, Quality, Understanding and Emotions. Visitors can only gain such a unique experience if heritage environments minimize the restraint and control that they have often hitherto sought to impose upon their visitors. For instance, an explicit learning environment with conventional communication (i.e. educational displays and prohibitive signs) is controlling and even stressful, as it may make the average visitor feel intimidated and ignorant. In addition, nurturing the popular myths of visitors may be a more durable and successful strategy than other, oversophisticated interpretations of the past.

Thus, information has to be used in an imaginative way to really welcome and orient visitors as well as to communicate the importance and value of a site. By bringing an attraction into life through interpretation not only are unique experiences enhanced, but visitors can also make connections between the site and themselves, and hence learn to respect it. Interpretation is not just about exchanging information or providing descriptions of facts and tangible artefacts but should inspire and even provoke the visitors (Tilden, 1977) to get a deeper meaning and understanding through emotional responses towards what is displayed. This 'meaning' lies with the individual visitor rather than in the displayed object, and it can only be enhanced through representations based on visual and sensory impact. Heritage appreciation in the future will increasingly be connected with entertainment and with personal, emotion-enhancing experiences. Consequently interpretation must increasingly rely upon images, sounds and even olfactory stimuli. Reading will remain a secondary medium for collecting and organizing information.

Thus heritage attractions of the future will be mediators of experience, encouraging postmodern tourists to construct their own sense of history and place, and to create their individual journeys of self-discovery. Creative and communicative interpretation will enable visitors to use their intellect and imagination to travel virtually into an odyssey of heritage reconstruction (Nuryanti, 1996). Revival is a simultaneous creation and transformation, communing with the past through which people not only confirm historical facts, but ascribe history new dimensions (Lowenthal, 1985). However, as different people respond to interpretation differently, interpreters should also aim to stimulate and challenge different market segments (Rumble, 1985). Interpretation can create valuable outcomes for both managers and visitors, and should be seen as an integral part of marketing, management and planning of heritage tourism (Herbert, 1989).

Projected development scenarios

This section features four heritage sites, each of which illustrates a different approach to offering presentation and interpretation. All are comparatively recent developments, born during the 1980s from a perceived need to broaden visitor appeal. Each of the four cases focuses on concrete operational issues, highlighting how the industry is reinventing itself and learning from the commercial world. The case of Llancaiach Fawr Manor discusses human resources and frontline management, the Scotch Whisky Heritage Centre deals with technological advances and interactive exhibits. The Big Pit Museum illustrates issues of funding and competition among similar heritage attractions in an area, while the Chemins de Baroque highlights efforts to meet different cultural needs.

Case study: Llancaiach Fawr Manor, South Wales Valleys, UK

Features

Llancaiach Fawr Living History Museum is a semi-fortified Tudor manor house in the heart of South Wales and operates as a wholly owned independent subsidiary of Caerphilly County Borough Council Valleys. It has been restored to its original seventeenth-century style and is used to celebrate the life and times of Colonel Edward Prichard, a local hero of the English Civil War. Llancaiach Fawr's mission is to enable visitors to understand the life ordinary people lived during 1645, an arbitrarily chosen date from that period. In order to do this, both traditional and live interpretative techniques are used. For example, actor-interpreters in period costume re-enact life at the manor house, taking on the character of historical persons (e.g. a household of servants) and act, speak, and are dressed in seventeenth-century style. In order to make the time journey even more realistic, all visitor facilities are located at a distance from the manor house, and all visitor information (i.e. about the historical background) is provided before guests enter the gardens and manor house. All the furniture and the furnishings in the manor house are reproduction so that visitors can try them out. In effect the site is a hands-on museum, offering plenty of activities for visitors (especially children), including making pomanders and candles, cheese tasting, and seventeenth-century games and dances. The dramatization of documented history in such a relaxed, entertaining environment provides good value for money because visitors can gain out of the ordinary experiences: the tastes, the smells, sounds and speech patterns of Stewart times.

In addition to the manor house there is a shop selling novelty items and artefacts and a small static museum, which aims to prepare visitors for the 'time-warp' experience in the main part of the exhibit. There are teaching rooms and equipment, which are used by visiting school parties, and also for staff training. Over the years Llancaiach Fawr has built up impressive catering facilities. To the original small, informal café-restaurant have been added a conservatory dining area and space for banqueting and functions.

The manor house has operated on a year-round basis since it opened in the early 1990s and received over 150 000 visitors within its first three years of operation (Waycott, 1995). It has gained a number of prestigious, tourist board awards, including best new attraction and best family attraction, as well as education awards. Tudor and Stewart history are a compulsory part of the UK National Curriculum in schools and the Living History Museum is in constant demand for school visits. The Llancaiach Fawr manor house has become a fountainhead of regional rejuvenation, since it effectively acts as a flagship attraction. After almost a decade of operation, it has managed to change people's perceptions of the Welsh valleys, attracting visitors from all over the UK. These, in turn, have discovered the beauty of the countryside and benefit the local tourism industry in increasing numbers (Waycott, 1995).

The essence of Llancaiach Fawr Living History Museum is its atmosphere. Maintaining the impression of a seventeenth-century time-warp is hard work, and actor-interpreters must concentrate upon staying in character. They are trained to 'forget' all that has happened since 1645, and all of the emphasis is upon a light-hearted, but essentially accurate, immersion in the period. The museum's informal mission statement could be 'from hard work to magic'. In the following, human resources issues are discussed.

Employment structure

At the time of writing, Llancaiach Fawr has 32 employees, divided between three notional 'departments': interpretation (12 staff), catering (8 staff) and administration-reception (10 staff). The latter includes staff engaged in the shop and in general maintenance of the site. These numbers do not include extra unemployed persons attached to the operation under the national (UK) 'New Deal Initiative'. In addition to these permanent employees, Llancaiach Fawr employs a number of casual service staff to meet the extra demands of banquets and functions. Volunteers are recruited for the summer months (and for special events) via contacts or newspaper advertisements, asking whether readers would like to 'live as a Tudor'. They have to undergo interviews and training like employees. Volunteers are given extensive notes on the costume and shoes of the period, from which they must make their own costumes. No subsidies are provided for the cost of the costumes. Over the years since it opened the museum has built up a core of expertise among its volunteers and it can now call on teams of specialists. For example, a team of musketeers regularly provides weaponry demonstrations.

Recruitment

All employees and volunteers are recruited from the local catchment area. In principle divisions exist between categories of staff and between the type of work they are expected to do. However, in practice a system of job rotation and an ethos of 'mucking in together' tend to iron out such distinctions. Most applicants are drawn to the museum by an interest in history or theatre. For the first two years of operation, Llancaiach Fawr relied upon the specialist firm 'Past Pleasures' (a leading company in the interpretation field) for assistance with the recruitment of live interpreters. The company acted as a consultant, weeding out unsuitable applicants, sitting in on interviews and participating in the subsequent selection process. However, the museum soon decided to break down all distinctions between the different categories of staff and instituted its own recruitment procedures for all applicants.

Training of interpretation staff

Llancaiach's success depends upon the uniqueness of the product, upon its innovative and positive approach, and also upon the effectiveness of the actor-interpreters. Interpretation staff play a key role in the impact of the site, and therefore have to be highly skilled and knowledgeable. Each new recruit receives the museum's own two week programme of intensive training which provides them with the necessary historical background but also the skills for the job. In order to carry out historic interpretation effectively, it is important to enable visitors temporarily to suspend their disbelief and enter a 'time-warp' in which they achieve a sense of actually being in another time. The goal of training is to make employees confidently convincing in their role, so that the public believes what they say. They must also be able to acquire the skill of deflecting questions to which they do not know the answer or which are intended to challenge authenticity (for example, 'Isn't that an aeroplane up there?') and to avoid stepping out of their allotted role, even for a moment.

Following the two-week intensive course, actor-interpreters receive additional ongoing training, which includes deportment, period knowledge (i.e. costume, speech, manners, social history) and the Welsh language. They are also allowed one day per month for personal research, during which they can develop their character roles and devise new storylines. Rotation between different character roles helps to protect staff from stress and to shield them from actor burnout. In addition, it is Llancaiach Fawr's policy to rotate staff between departments, so that all staff, no matter what their job, spend time working in other areas to understand what the others are doing. Someone who is mainly located in the administrative 'department', for instance, can expect to take an interpretive role for a day, or act as a waitress or a cleaner, if the need arises. This helps to develop a strong cohesiveness and team spirit among all staff at the museum. It also helps develop an understanding of what is operationally practicable. For example, after spending some days in the manor house, a receptionist will not book a group of 50 visitors half an hour before closing on a Friday evening.

All employees, including the actor-interpreters, receive wider training, which includes customer care. Like most Welsh tourism organizations, Llancaiach Fawr has adopted the 'Welcome Host Wales' scheme, managed by the Welsh Tourist Board. This aims to provide consistent standards of customer service, care and hospitality throughout the region. Owing to its success, Llancaiach Fawr now acts as a regional consultant to other aspiring living history centres.

Case study: The Scotch Whisky Heritage Centre, Edinburgh, UK

Features

The Scotch Whisky Heritage Centre, located beside Edinburgh Castle, opened in 1988 is a mixture of a themed museum and industrial tourism attraction. Its mission statement is to 'promote whisky generically in an informative and entertaining way', and hence it tells the story of Scotch whisky. Visitors are informed about the origins of whisky, the secrets of distillation and the ancient traditions that surround the making of whisky. There is, of course, free whisky-tasting for adults before leaving the exhibits. The centre has satellite facilities, including a gift shop selling whisky-related products and conference facilities, and it also offers gifts and activities that can be included in incentive packages. The Whisky Heritage Centre attracted 130 000 visitors in 1993 (mostly groups and families), and this is projected to grow steadily to the year 2000 (Swarbrooke, 1995). It has also won several awards, especially for its services for foreign-speaking and disabled visitors.

Technology

The Scotch Whisky Heritage Centre was developed by Heritage Projects of York (who also developed the Jorvik Centre in York). Features include theatrical sets and audiovisual programmes as well as museum-style displays and aim to provide the equivalent of a distillery tour in the heart of Edinburgh's Old Town. A ghostly presentation of the art of the masters blender precedes a journey through time in a 'whisky barrel'. Visitors can listen to a commentary in a choice of seven languages while they are transported around the site in special, whisky-barrel shaped electric vehicles (similarly to the Jorvik Centre's time cars). An average ride lasts for about one hour, during which guides are also available to explain the whisky production process to the visitor – in several different languages, if required.

In contrast to Llancaiach Fawr, the key of the Whisky Centre's success lies in evoking visitor interest by the use of high-technology, interactive displays, and providing entertainment through novel features, such as the electric car rides. It provides a voyage of discovery through the centuries that brings the history, mystery and magic of the spirit of Scotland into life. This new generation of innovative museums that allow interaction with their exhibits prompts visitors to participate actively in the exploration. The sights, sounds and smells of the whisky trail evoke a vivid and memorable picture of Scotch Whisky, and visitors are provided with a concentrated, intense experience during the relatively short duration of the ride. This also has the advantage of controlling visitor flow through the attraction, and hence of achieving higher operating margins.

Because of the relatively high proportion of interactive technology, attractions like the Whisky Heritage Centre are relatively expensive to build, and therefore need to serve large populations or holidaymaker catchments. It is estimated that museums of this kind need to bring in a minimum of 250 000 visits per year (ETB, 1991). In order to keep the quality of the discovery experience up to a high standard, the exhibits have to be of durable materials and considerable labour is required for daily maintenance. The site also needs continuous improvements and modifications or special events if it is to attract repeat visitors.

Case study: Big Pit Mining Museum, Blaenafon, South Wales

Features

The Big Pit is one of the oldest deep-shaft coal mines in Wales, reopened in 1983 as a 'working heritage museum' to celebrate the heyday of Welsh coal industry. Its mission is to conserve and document the landscape, society and culture of Welsh mines for the future. There are 12 listed buildings on the surface and, among others, visitors can explore the winding-engine house, the blacksmith's shop, the pit-head baths and stables for the pit ponies. The former miners' canteen is now the cafeteria and the souvenir shop is located in the former engineering works. There are exhibitions and simulated mining galleries throughout, where visitors can learn about coal mining from the commentary of ex-miner guides. The unique part of the visit is a genuine pit-cage ride in the 90-metre shaft. The underground experience takes about an hour and leaves a great impression on visitors when they feel the sensation of total darkness and hear about coalface working conditions from ex-miners. (Wanhill, 2000)

Funding and operation

The development of the Big Pit offers a number of lessons for industrial heritage attractions. Prior to its closure in 1980, a development plan and a feasibility study was made to turn the mine into a working museum and a year-round tourist attraction. The unspoken objective was to revitalize the area and help the population to adjust to a lower standard of living in terms of employment opportunities. The Joint Steering Group gave way to the Big Pit Trust Limited, a charitable company limited by guarantee, emphasizing the *public good* aspect of the venture. Because the museum undertakes commercial activities that are not in accordance with its charitable status, the shop and catering activities are let out as concessions.

The economic success of a heritage attraction depends on the creativity of the concept in combining authenticity with interpretation, accessibility and realistic vision (Wanhill, 2000). Industrial sites face particular threats in terms of the cost of restoring and operating large physical installations. The development study of the Big Pit Mining Museum identified that a minimum annual throughput of 250 000 visitors would be needed. The threshold feasibility to cover operating costs was estimated at 100 000 visitors per year, thus giving a sufficient margin of safety. The site is located in close geographical proximity to urban centres and main road links, offering a catchment population of 5.2 million within two hours' and 32.5 million within four hours' travelling. These optimistic estimates were based on the Big Pit's similarities with the already successful Llechwedd Slate Caverns in North Wales, which at that time had 220 000 visitors per year.

However, during the first years of operations, even after extensive investment into facilities, visitor numbers were well below feasibility study target, averaging only 110 000 annually. Since 1995 the Big Pit has experienced a steady decline in attendance figures (dropping to 85 000 in 1998), which was not enough to cover operating expenses. This, together with dwindling grant aid, forced the trust to consider closing the attraction in 1998. At this time the Big Pit Mining Museum was taken over by National Galleries and Museums of Wales (NGMW), guaranteeing permanent access to state funding. This was consistent with the NGMW's objective: to maintain its long-term educational mission about the history of special industries in Wales, such as coal mining.

Two issues may account for what went wrong financially with the Big Pit Museum. First, in contrast to other attractions, fixed operating costs were relatively high, due to the necessary safety requirements of a working mine and the authentic pit-cage ride.

259

If mines are presented as working attractions, safety dictates the need to shore-up roofs, pump out water, ventilate tunnels and make emergency exits. This made the project vulnerable to cost miscalculations and left the mine operating without a margin of safety to reinvest in facilities or site conservation. Another problem lies in the way the museum was organized. Its feasibility was complicated by conflicting objectives, since it was conceived in terms of the public good, yet expected to operate as a commercial attraction. Furthermore, other mining projects in the area also used public funds to generate competing attractions and diverted some of the Big Pit's market share.

Competition

In South Wales many local authorities saw the possibility of creating heritage attractions from the declining coal industry. This 'me too' reaction inevitably resulted in visitor displacement in a market where few wanted to see more than one mining heritage museum. The Big Pit has now three direct competitors in the area, the Cefn Coed Colliery Museum, the Afan Argoed Miners' Museum and the Rhondda Heritage Park. In addition there is a new hands-on science attraction, Techniquest, at Cardiff Bay, which may also draw market share away from the Big Pit (e.g. school groups visiting the area).

The largest direct competitor is the Rhondda Heritage Park which features the theme 'Black Gold: the Story of Coal' through interactive multimedia presentations, a simulated pit-cage ride and an activity park for children. Like the Big Pit Museum, the Rhondda Heritage Park uses ex-miners as tour guides, telling their first-hand experiences. Substantial investment in audiovisual presentation and simulated pit cage rides (an authentic ride like that of the Big Pit is impossible for safety reasons) brought great increases in visitor numbers, because this technology enables the park to link education, entertainment and involvement in a manner that surpasses the experience provided at the Big Pit. In this respect, the Big Pit is showing its age in its lack of modern interpretive facilities that are expected by visitors, particularly by younger age groups. However, the recent listing of the whole Blaenafon area as a potential World Heritage Site, may turn the entire locality into a prestigious heritage destination, attracting larger number of visitors, and ultimately benefiting the Big Pit.

Case study: Les Chemins du Baroque, Savoie, France

Features

In 1992, as a part of the European Cultural Routes programme, the French region of Haute-Savoie launched its Baroque Route Project (Les Chemins du Baroque), aimed at promoting local culture and re-profiling the region's image. The project included the construction of an ethnographic route, linking together religious and vernacular attractions as well as village communities, and emphasizing heritage as a living entity. The Chemins du Baroque offer a series of cultural activities every year, such as guided weekend tours, excursions and concerts. The different elements of the cultural tourism product, such as churches, chapels and visitor centres are selected to provide easy access for the independent tourist. Apart from signposting and guidebooks about the route, commercial guides and local 'heritage volunteers' are trained to provide what the locals call *animation*. These people not only provide third-person interpretation of the built heritage, but also tell visitors about mountain culture and the daily life of the villages. For instance, in the summer months, visitors to local tourist centres are welcomed by *animateurs* in Savoyard costumes, who tell them about the legends and history of the valley. Thus the baroque heritage of Savoie is open to a variety of different personal interpretations, depending on the visitor's origin, culture and interests (Bauer, 1996).

Chemins du Baroque differs from the other three case study attractions presented in this chapter, in the sense that it is not one single commercial attraction but a themed, mostly free, self-guided tour. It tells a story of the Maurienne and Tarantaise valleys, primarily for the benefit of walking or touring visitors to the region. Visitors can choose whatever elements of the route they wish and let the native guides enliven the 'real Savoie' for them. The route and its *animateurs* bring out aspects of mountain culture that would be difficult to reproduce by any other means. Rather than just seeing a building that has been preserved and restored, Chemins du Baroque creates the possibility of building effective links with the people of the past, and the people who live there now. Visitors gain a sense of the difficulties of living in the region in historic times and the present dependence upon agriculture and the tourist season. This privileged view of the backstage of 'authentic' Savoie shows not just a collection of buildings and aesthetic facades, but the whole past and present vernacular culture of the valleys.

Different interpretations

Heritage interpretations depend on the cultural origin of the visitor and the way of tourism is promoted, both within and outside the region. This may lead to conflict between their educational and other roles. In a review of media coverage about Chemins du Baroque, Bauer (1996) demonstrates that the Baroque heritage of Savoie is used not only as a means of education, but also as confirmation of prejudices. For example, visitors of different religious background can interpret the pompous fresco scenes in the churches either as demonstrating the vitality of the inhabitants or as exploitation of the locals by the church. Such differences may be significant even among visitors from similar European cultural backgrounds. Guides and *animateurs* must take these different interpretative possibilities into account and structure their performance accordingly.

Conclusions

The success of heritage attractions depends upon their ability to provide a unique and renewable experience for visitors. The cases presented here show typical scenarios through which this can be achieved, using both high-technology and 'high-touch' interpretative approaches. Both categories will undoubtedly evolve to become still more sophisticated in the future, with further, at present undreamed of, dimensions. Distinctions between 'educational' heritage sites and entertainment type of heritage experiences will become increasingly blurred as the market becomes more discerning and competition intensifies. At the time of writing, it seems unlikely that local heritage sites will develop strong brand identities, comparable to that of Disney, because a good concept seems enough in itself to differentiate a site from its competitors. However, if copied too often or not developed through the years, even the most enticing interpretative strategy may become boring for the visitor, and this may conceivably give way to other marketing approaches, such as branding.

This chapter has argued for a more visitor-oriented approach to quality management in heritage attractions. In the authors' opinion, a greater shift of focus is needed from physical environments and architectural heritage towards a more holistic, transcendent provision of culture or history, catering for postmodern tourists whose focus is an individualized experience. Heritage is a living tool with the power to give us a picture of ourselves. In order to do this, it needs to take into account (and re-enact) festivities, games and traditions and to reflect the spirit, myths and symbolism built up over the years by our cultural forefathers (Moulin, 1991). Only through this strategy can it maintain the impetus of cultural tourism development into the twenty-first century.

Questions

1 This chapter identifies a tension in the heritage attractions industry between 'authenticity' and 'entertainment'. Discuss how these issues are tackled by two of the cases: Llancaiach Fawr Manor and South Wales coal-mining exhibits.
2 What practical challenges may heritage attraction managers face in satisfying both historical authenticity and customer entertainment?
3 Discuss the development of customer quality in heritage attractions and its impact on HRM in such operations.

References and further reading

Abelee, A. van den (1990). Tourism and heritage: enemies or allies. ICOMOS European Conference on Heritage and Tourism, Canterbury, Kent.

Bauer, M. (1996). Cultural tourism in France. In *Cultural Tourism in Europe*. (G. Richards, ed.) CAB International.

Bianchini, F. and Parkinson, M. (eds) (1993). *Cultural Policy and Urban Regeneration: The West European Experience*. Manchester University Press.

Bywater, M. (1993). The market for cultural tourism in Europe. *Travel and Tourism Analyst*, **6**, 30–46.

Cohen, E. (1988). Authenticity and commoditization in tourism. *Annals of Tourism Research*, **15**(1), 371–386.

Crang, M. (1996). Magic kingdom or a quixotic quest for authenticity? *Annals of Tourism Research*, **23**(2), 415–431.

English Tourist Board (ETB) (1991). Heritage experience attractions. *Insights*, **C3**, 1–14.

Fowler, P. (1989). Heritage: a post-modernist perspective. In *Heritage Interpretation: The Natural and Built Environment (Vol. 1)* (D. Uzzel, ed.), pp. 57–64, Belhaven.

Glen, M. H. (1991). If in doubt, call it heritage? In *Tourism Resources, Issues, Planning and Development* (D. McDowell and D. Leslie, eds), pp. 73–85, University of Ulster.

Graburn, N. H. (1983). The anthropology of tourism. *Annals of Tourism Research*, **10**(1), 9–33.

Herbert, D. T. (1989). Leisure trends and the heritage market. In *Heritage Sites: Strategies for Marketing and Development* (D. T. Herbert, R. C. Prentice and C. Thomas, eds), pp. 1–15, Avebury Press.

Johns, N. (1992). Quality management in the hospitality industry: definition and specification. *International Journal of Contemporary Hospitality Management*, **4**(3), 14–20.

Johns, N. and Howard, A. (1998). Customer expectations vs perceptions of service performance in the foodservice industry. *International Journal of Service Industry Management*, **9**(3), 248–265.

Lowenthal, D. (1985). *The Past Is a Foreign Country*. Cambridge University Press.

Masberg, B. A. and Silverman, L. H. (1996). Visitor experiences at heritage sites: a phenomenological approach. *Journal of Travel Research*, **35**(2). 20–25.

Masser, I., Svidén, O. and Wegener, M. (1994). What new heritage for which Europe? In *Building a New Heritage: Tourism, Culture and Identity in the New Europe* (G. J. Ashworth and P. J. Larkham, eds), Routledge.

McManus, P. (1985). Worksheet-induced behaviour in the British Museum. *Journal of Biological Education*, **19**, 237–242.

Millar, S. (1989) Heritage management for heritage tourism. *Tourism Management*, March, 9–14.

Moulin, C. M. (1991). Cultural heritage and tourism development in Canada. *Tourism Recreation Research*, **16**(1), 50–55.

Nuryanti, W. (1996). Heritage and post-modern tourism. *Annals of Tourism Research*, **23**(2), 249–260.

Poon, A. (1993). *Tourism, Technology and Competitive Strategies*. CAB International.

Prentice, R. C. (1993). *Tourism and the Heritage Attraction*. Routledge.

Richards, G. (ed.) (1996a). *Cultural Tourism in Europe*. CAB International.

Richards, G. (1996b). Production and consumption of European cultural tourism. *Annals of Tourism Research*, **23**(2), 261–283.

Rumble, P. (1985). Interpreting the built and historic environment. In *Heritage Interpretation: The Natural and Built Environment (Vol. 1)* (D. Uzzel, ed.), pp. 24–33, Belhaven.

Schouten, F. (1993). The future of museums. *Museum Management and Curatorship*, **12**, 381–386.

Schouten, F. (1995). Improving visitor care in heritage attractions. *Tourism Management*, **16**(4), 259–261.

Swarbrooke, J. (1995). *The Development and Management of Visitor Attractions*. Butterworth-Heinemann.

Tilden, F. (1977). *Interpreting our Heritage*. 3rd edition. University of North Carolina Press.

Walsh, K. (1992). *The Representation of the Past: Museums and Heritage in a Post-Modern World*. Routledge.

Wanhill, S. (2000). Mines: a tourist attraction. *Journal of Travel Research* (in press).

Waycott, R. (1995). Llancaiach Fawr living history museum. *Insights*, January, 25–33.

Index

THE
BUSINESS CASES
WEB SITE

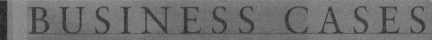

Quality case study materials from quality authors

Instant access to cases & tutor support material

'Quick view' summaries & author profiles

Download PDFs and 'copy' for use on specified courses

No registration fee

Pay on-line or open an account

Check out this excellent site today
www.businesscases.org

BUTTERWORTH
HEINEMANN

LIMELIGHT PUBLISHING

COMPANY LTD

Library and Information Services
University of Wales Institute, Cardiff
Colchester Avenue
Cardiff
CF23